Also by Elisabeth Rozin

Ethnic Cuisine: The Flavor Principle Cookbook (1983)
The Flavor Principle Cookbook (1973)

Blue Corn and Chocolate

Blue Corn and Chocolate

by Elisabeth Rozin

Paper cut-out illustrations by Barbara Balch

ALFRED A. KNOPF NEW YORK 1992

THIS IS A BORZOI BOOK
PUBLISHED BY ALFRED A. KNOPF, INC.

Copyright © 1992 by Elisabeth Rozin
Paper cut-out illustrations copyright © 1992 by Barbara Balch

Library of Congress Cataloging-in-Publication Data

Rozin, Elisabeth.
Blue corn and chocolate / by Elisabeth Rozin.—1st ed.
p.   cm.—(The Knopf cooks American series)
Includes bibliographical references and index.
ISBN 0-394-58308-6
1. Cookery, International.   2. Food.   3. Gastronomy.
I. Title.   II. Series: Knopf cooks American.
TX725.A1R688   1992
641.59—dc20   91-57915
                                                       CIP

Manufactured in the United States of America

Published March 25, 1992
Second Printing, June 1992

This book
is for my children
Lillian, Seth, Lex, and Phuc
with love

Contents

Acknowledgments   ix

Introduction: A New World of Food   xi

A Word about the Recipes   xv

Corn   3

The Potato   41

Capsicum Peppers   73

Tomatoes   107

Beans, Pumpkins, and Squashes   139

Turkey   169

Chocolate and Vanilla   195

Peanuts   227

Odds and Ends   251

    Pineapple 255, Achiote 258, Avocado 259, Cashew 261,
    Sunflower 263, Jerusalem Artichoke 264, Wild Rice 265,
    Maple 266, Allspice 267, Pecan 269, Brazil Nut 272

Selected Bibliography   275

Index   279

Photographic Acknowledgments   297

Acknowledgments

To Judith Jones, who defines the art of editorship: her guidance, her support, her enormous skill and intelligence contributed immeasurably to this book.

To Kathy Zuckerman, who was always cheerful, helpful, and extremely competent.

To Barbara Balch, a designer of great talent and commitment, who was a pleasure to work with.

To Lillian Rozin, who provided invaluable assistance and support in the preparation of the manuscript.

To Seth Rozin, for his fine photography and creative input into the visual part of the project.

To my recipe testers, whose enthusiasm, hard work, and constructive criticism were valuable beyond measure: Melinda Beuf, Marion Briefer, Alyne Freed, Sandra Norman, Marcia Pelchat, Patricia Pliner, Lex Rozin, Lillian Rozin, Marci Stricker, Kirsten Wasson, and my friends and colleagues of the Philadelphia Women's Culinary Guild.

And to Hermie and Woofie, who tasted everything and cleaned up the kitchen floor behind me.

Introduction: A New World of Food

Every year on October 12 schoolchildren throughout America celebrate in song and story the discovery of their country by Christopher Columbus. It is an appealing and inspiring tale: the three small ships braving an unknown ocean; the visionary Italian explorer setting foot at last upon land and claiming it for King Ferdinand and Queen Isabella of Spain.

No matter that Columbus landed not on the mainland of America but on a small island in the Bahamas; no matter that he continued to believe, after three more voyages and indeed for the rest of his life, that he had discovered the coveted lands of the Orient. No matter that the motive for the discovery was greed for wealth and lust for power, or that in opening the door to a whole new culture he set in motion the forces that would destroy an ancient one. No matter. To Columbus must belong the credit of doing what no one had done before, to breach this unknown New World and to dissolve forever the invisible barriers that separated it from the Old.

Despite the enormity of his discovery, Columbus came back to Spain a frustrated and bitter man, for he never found the source of the pepper, the spices, and the gold that his patrons so avidly desired. It is ironic that he was never to know that this New World was itself a storehouse of culinary gold, as exotic and ultimately as valuable as that of the fabled East. That knowledge would come later, after his death, when a host of new and unknown foods would make their way to the Old World and be taken into traditional cuisines with the same enthusiasm as nutmeg and cloves, changing forever what the world ate.

How many of us still believe that the potato originated in Ireland? That the Mediterranean, and particularly Italy, is the ancestral hearth of the tomato and its tradition of savory sauces? That the fiery chile pepper is an ancient and enduring part of the cuisines of India and Southeast Asia? That the pineapple is as native to Hawaii as chocolate is to Vienna?

We believe such things for the good reason that these foods have become very heavily identified with certain cuisines and certain areas of the world. But before that fateful day in 1492, these foods, and many more, were not known and could not have been known to any but the inhabitants of the New World, for it was here that they originated and here that they were used exclusively. They include corn, tomatoes, potatoes, the capsicum peppers, many kinds of beans, squashes, and pumpkins, turkey, pineapple, chocolate and vanilla, peanuts and pecans. As European explorers returned, they took these new and exotic products with them to every corner of the Old World, and it was not long before New World foods were changed and adapted to fit into traditional cuisines, adding original and valuable dimensions to the nutritional and gastronomic experience.

But that was only the beginning of the story, for these new foods, venturing forth to unknown lands, were transformed and refashioned along the way. Then they came back to their native shores, brought by the many immigrants who settled America, dressed up in new seasonings, prepared with a variety of new techniques, remodeled and reworked through the traditions of their adopted cuisines. And once they had returned to their original homeland, they were transformed yet again, to fit into the shifting patterns of an emergent American cuisine.

Each of these foods has its own unique and particular history, for each traveled in a different direction and was changed in different ways, reflected through a multitude of ethnic prisms. But all those separate histories, like the people who generated them, came together on these shores, creating the multifaceted and ever-changing whole that is our palate and our cuisine. For what we eat is who we are—and we are Asia, we are Africa, we are Europe and the Mediterranean and the Middle East; indeed, our food, like us, is the world.

If the American table became what it is through this wealth of New World foods, we must acknowledge not only what was brought to it, but what was given. For these wonderful foods were the result of many long centuries of careful refinement and cultivation. They represented the accumulated horticultural and culinary traditions, knowledge, and labor of the original inhabitants of this brave New World—the Old Ones—who had studied the land and knew its ways and cherished the abundant fruits of its harvest. We repaid them by wiping them out, in an excess of religious fanaticism, racism, and greed. But they are a fundamental part of us, those ancient farmers and hunters and naturalists and cooks, and their food too is our food.

Our table is unique in all the history of the world, for it combines everything that ever was: the old and the new; the traditional and the trendy; what has been, what is, and what is becoming. It is not a melting pot, but rather a vast kaleidoscopic smorgasbord that even the visionary Columbus could not have foreseen. To understand how that smorgasbord came about is in large measure to understand what happened to the whole New World of food that Columbus opened up. A day in October some five hundred years ago set in motion the culinary events that led to everything we hold to be uniquely and profoundly American, from French fries and ketchup to cornflakes and Baby Ruth bars, from chili and gumbo to pizza and turkey sandwiches. In eating, if nowhere else, we celebrate the unity that comes from diversity.

A Word about the Recipes

This book is about the foods that were indigenous to the New World before the Columbian discovery of 1492, foods that in large part became the backbone of American cuisine. To understand the evolution of these foods is to understand a great deal about the evolution of our national character and our changing palate. Cuisine is a dynamic enterprise, always growing, sometimes in great steps, at other times in small subtle ones, but always shifting and altering its patterns to reflect a changing social and ethnic scene. It was not my aim to show what our forefathers ate at the beginning, or at any particular time in our history, but rather to illustrate through the recipes how our perceptions of food have changed through the centuries. Our palate has undergone some stunning alterations, starting with its initial English and northern European profile, and enlarging with the subsequent influx of Latino, African, Mediterranean, and Asian cultures. Where hot peppers and spicy sauces would once have been unthinkable exotica, they are now an accepted and loved part of the mainstream; where less than 200 years ago tomatoes were shunned as poison, they have now become entrenched as a fundamental ingredient in our daily diet. The recipes were developed to show the dynamic ongoing process that is our cuisine, to illuminate how that cuisine developed in terms of the special foods that were native to the New World.

The recipes are necessarily, then, a very mixed bag, from some very old traditional preparations to the most novel and contemporary. Wherever possible I have tried to provide a recipe that offers something a little bit different; if you don't yet know how to roast the Thanksgiving turkey, there are plenty of other books that will tell you how to do it. I felt it would be more interesting to illustrate other perhaps less familiar or less accessible aspects of the turkey tradition in America.

Without doing damage to the tradition or the food, I have attempted to update the recipes to fit more comfortably into our current notions about health and nutrition. If we no longer deem it wise to consume gobs of butter and jugs of heavy cream, then we must find a way to reconcile our preferences with our beliefs. Moderation is always the guiding line; there are no "bad" ingredients or "good" ingredients, and we all need to be aware that there should be balance in all things. Sugar, salt, and fat are substances our bodies require; it is only when the need is overindulged that we find ourselves in trouble.

Similarly, it would be foolish of me to ignore the fact that most of us do not have the time for long arduous hours in the kitchen. The recipes are as streamlined and efficient as possible, and processed foods are frequently taken advantage of. For many of us, a good quality canned tomato is preferable to the out-of-season gassed waxen globes sitting lifelessly in their cardboard tombs.

Finally, a word about my personal style. I have always believed that in the experience of food, taste is the bottom line, that flavor is all-important, and that if it doesn't work in the mouth it won't work at all. Obviously there are many variables involved in flavor—the freshness and quality of the ingredients, the care with which they are handled, the selection and balancing of the seasoning. I am not a particularly subtle cook, but a fairly open-handed seasoner; indeed, my children have accused me of forever spoiling their palates, for most of the food they eat out in the world is just not "tasty" enough. I am mildly wary of pinches of this and sprigs of that, since pinches and sprigs rarely seem to work for me. When I use a clove of garlic, I use a nice fat clove, not a wimpy little sliver, and when I use a handful, I mean a handful. So you are hereby fore-warned. Whatever the seasoning, whatever the dish, whatever the occasion, do it generously and with love, for that in the end is what the shared experience of cooking and eating is all about.

Blue Corn and Chocolate

Chicken Corn Chowder

Chinese Crab and Corn Soup

New Mexican Posole

Vegetable Posole

Tortilla Bread

Roast Chicken with Tortilla Stuffing

Grits Milanese

Cornmeal Mush

I. with peanut sauce and greens

II. Balkan style, with feta cheese and dill

III. polenta-stuffed beef rolls

IV. vegetable scrapple

Pecan Polenta Rounds

Chili-Cheese Spoon Bread

Confetti Corn Custard

Corn and Shrimp Fritters Thai Style

Dried Corn and Smoked Salmon Casserole

Super Succotash

Marinated Baby Corn and Peppers with
Black Bean–Garlic Vinaigrette

Blue Corn and Pepper Frittata

Navajo Triple Corn Muffins

Grilled Chicken in Bourbon Barbecue Sauce

Bourbon Eggnog

Christmas Bourbon Balls

Maple-Corn Coffee Cake

CORN

And those who came were resolved to be Englishmen,
Gone to the world's end, but English every one.
And they ate the white corn kernels, parched in the sun,
And they knew it not, but they'd not be English again.

So wrote the poet Stephen Vincent Benét, and it is as accurate an account as any of what corn meant in the formation of this country. For corn is the ultimate, the essential American food, the one that began here, the one that stayed here, the one that nourished all who came here. Unlike many other New World foods that crossed the oceans to find new homes in a host of Old World cuisines, corn was accepted outside its ancestral home only in a few areas characterized by extreme poverty and deprivation—regions of rural Italy, Spain, and France, the Balkans, and much of sub-Saharan Africa.

The primary reason for the failure of corn to find acceptance in most of the Old World is not difficult to understand. Corn is a cereal, belonging to the family of grain foods that includes wheat, rice, barley, oats, and rye. People become very attached to their traditional, basic foods and are reluctant to give them up or to accept substitutes for them. Corn, though it might be easier to grow and more generous in its yield, is significantly different from traditional grains. It does not produce the kinds of products—breads, pastas, pilafs, porridges—to which the Old World was accustomed; its flavor, aroma, and texture are unique and different. It was almost universally rejected as proper food for humans and was utilized primarily as animal fodder.

But for those Old World emigrants who sought a new life in the New World, corn was not so easy to reject. For here there was no substitute; on these shores corn was King, a beloved and worshipped grain that had nourished and nurtured the aboriginal populations for many thousands of years. Here corn, or maize as it is more correctly termed, had long been hybridized into dozens of varieties, each with its own special function; and here had developed a traditional and complex technology for realizing the full nutritional and aesthetic potential of this valuable food.

So for the first European settlers, particularly those farming the rocky soil of New England, it was corn or nothing, and even a strange and initially distasteful food was preferable to starvation. Traditional grains, particularly wheat, required more acreage and time than corn to produce satisfactory yields. By the time enough land had been cleared so that the old European grains were yielding a sufficient harvest, many years had passed and corn had become established as a staple of the pioneer diet, by this time a familiar, reliable, and well-liked food. It was corn that transformed the settler into the settled, the foreigner into the American, and it remains today the single food most closely identified with the American character and the American myth.

At first, everything we knew about corn came from the native inhabitants. From them we learned about the different varieties, how to cook and eat corn as a fresh vegetable, and, most important, the techniques for drying, storing, and processing corn for use in breads and cereal dishes. These early recipes form the basis of the American repertoire, including such preparations as cornmeal mush, simple breads like hoecakes and corn pone, and stewed dishes like hominy and succotash, the traditional mixture of corn and lima beans.

It was not long, however, before the new Americans began to experiment with corn, using techniques and ingredients imported from their Old World homes. Primary among these was the attempt to obtain products from corn that more closely resembled the leavened breads of Europe. Wheat, the most favored bread grain, is different from other grains because it contains significant amounts of gluten, a protein that enables the dough to expand and rise when a fermentive agent like yeast is added. Corn contains no gluten and cannot therefore be leavened in traditional ways to produce the light, spongy breads to which Europeans were accustomed. To compensate for this, American cooks mixed cornmeal with wheat flour, and added ingredients that provided aeration to the dough and thus produced a more desired texture. These ingredients—eggs, acids such as those that occur in sour milk, and later chemical leaveners like baking powder and soda—lightened the heavy cornmeal batters and produced the many baked goods that are still so much a part of our tradition.

The second great innovation came with the use of fat—fat for frying, fat for shortening, fat for flavoring. In this regard, one cannot but marvel at the intense, intimate, and ongoing relationship between corn and pigs. For as corn was the grain of necessity, the pig, imported from Europe, was the domesticated animal of choice. Its meat, fresh, but, more important, in a variety of preserved forms such as ham, bacon, and sausage, was the preferred meat of the American farmstead, and its rendered fat—lard—the primary cooking fat. Corn fed the pig, of course, just as the pig nourished its owner, and from that culinary alliance of corn and pork came such American classics as cracklin' bread and scrapple, fritters and hush puppies.

The third great transformation of corn came with the introduction of dairy products, previously unknown to the New World with its lack of domesticated dairy animals. Milk, cream, and butter all enhanced and enriched the flavor and texture of corn, both as a fresh vegetable and as a dried, ground meal, producing our creamy chowders, our moist buttery muffins and breads, our buttered cobs.

These early innovations shaped the basic character of American corn cookery as it exists today. Later immigrant groups would add their own unique touches, but these were primarily the introduction of new seasoning ingredients, rather than novel cooking techniques. Impressive indeed is the incredible longevity and conservatism of the New World corn tradition. Not only is our contemporary repertoire based solidly on that of our earliest immigrant forebearers; theirs was based solidly on a tradition that began some five or six thousand years ago when corn was first domesticated in the highlands of central Mexico. Those ancient Amerindians ate corn fresh—on the cob, in soups and in stews; dried whole and then cooked into hominy or grits; dried and ground into meal for breads and beverages; dried and popped for a light tasty snack that even today is a vital part of our Saturday night movie.

Of course, modern technology has developed products that those ancient corn eaters could not have dreamed of—corn oil, corn syrup, cornstarch, and, thanks to Mr. Kellogg, that most American of breakfast foods, cornflakes. Nonetheless, most of the corn we eat today is in much the same form as it was those many centuries ago, with only here and there a new twist.

Popcorn balls, those sticky delights, are an amalgam of an aboriginal food with a modern derivative, Karo syrup; tortilla chips and nacho chips are a fried and seasoned update of the oldest Mexican flat corn bread. The dishes we enjoy so much today have their beginnings in a long distant past, a past to which we as Americans are connected. For if our ancestors did not all originate in this New World, they became a part of it by eating its most treasured food.

You can eat tomatoes in Italy, peppers in Hungary, potatoes in France. But, with few exceptions, you can only eat corn, in its wealth of forms, here on its native shores. The golden ear, freshly picked and dripping with butter, is the unique culinary symbol of the bounty of the American homeland.

Chicken Corn Chowder

Once at a harvest food festival, I passed out small samples of this soup; a portly gentleman ate his and promptly offered a proposal of marriage. Now I think that was something of an overreaction, but it *is* a very good soup, a genuine American classic. It uses both grated and whole fresh sweet corn kernels, and although canned or frozen can be substituted, the flavor will not be as good. To cut corn kernels off the cob, hold the cob upright on a plate or shallow dish; with a sharp knife in the other hand, slice down hard against the cob. Rotate the cob until all the kernels have been sliced off. Keep and use any of the white liquid, or milk, that comes from the cut corn kernels; it contains both starch and sugar that contribute to the flavor and texture of the dish.

Serves 6–8

2 Tb. butter
2 large leeks, mostly white parts, finely chopped
1 carrot, diced
2 stalks celery, with leaves, diced
1 medium potato, peeled and diced
2 cups (about 3 ears) fresh sweet corn kernels
4 cups chicken stock
Several good grinds black pepper
½ tsp. sugar
½ tsp. dried marjoram
½ cup cooked diced chicken
½ cup light cream

1. In a medium saucepan heat the butter over low to moderate heat. Add the leeks and carrot and sauté slowly, stirring occasionally, until the leeks are wilted, about 10 minutes.

2. Stir in the celery and the potato and continue to sauté, stirring occasionally, for another 5 minutes.

3. Process 1 cup of the corn kernels in the food processor into a coarse paste (no need to puree completely).

4. To the sautéed vegetables add the processed corn, the stock, the pepper, sugar, and marjoram. Bring to a simmer, then lower heat and cook for about 20 minutes until the potatoes and carrots are tender.

5. Stir in the reserved cup of whole corn kernels and the diced chicken. Bring to a simmer, then cook over low heat for about 10 minutes.

6. Stir in the cream and heat until very hot.

Chinese Crab and Corn Soup

Creamed corn was once a staple of the summer farmhouse kitchen, a simple and delicious combination of fresh sweet corn, butter, and cream. When the food industry redid creamed corn as a canned product, they sweetened it more heavily and left out the dairy ingredients entirely, thickening it with starch. This "cream-style corn" is, curiously, one of the few forms in which corn has found its way into Oriental cuisine, turning up frequently as a component of delicate flavorful soups.

Serves 4–6

4 scallions, white parts only, finely minced
2 tsp. finely minced fresh gingerroot
1 Tb. peanut oil
1 15–16-oz. can cream-style corn
2 cups chicken stock
2 Tb. rice wine
1 Tb. soy sauce
Several good grinds white pepper
½ cup flaked crabmeat (diced cooked chicken or shrimp may be substituted)
1 tsp. sesame oil
1 egg, lightly beaten
Reserved green tops of scallions for garnish, chopped

1. In a medium heavy saucepan sauté the minced scallions and gingerroot in the peanut oil for a few minutes until aromatic.

2. Add the corn, stock, wine, soy sauce, and pepper. Simmer over low heat for about 10 minutes.

3. Stir in the crabmeat and sesame oil and bring just to a simmer.

4. Pour the egg slowly into the hot soup in a thin stream, stirring lightly with a fork to form strands.

5. Garnish the soup with the chopped green tops of the scallions. Serve immediately.

New Mexican Posole

Posole is an ancient dish of Mexican origin, a stew of the whole limed corn that Americans call hominy. In Mexico it seems to have been a festive preparation that frequently involved the whole head of a pig; the New Mexican version has simplified that tradition by using various cuts of pork. Posole is a simple, earthy, tasty dish that will fill your kitchen with the savory aroma of the Southwest.

Serves 4–6

1¼–1½ lb. lean boneless pork, cut in very small cubes
1 cup dried hominy, or 2 cups cooked or canned hominy, drained
1 large onion, coarsely chopped
2 large dried New Mexico chiles, seeded
3 cloves garlic, crushed
1 tsp. oregano
½ tsp. ground cumin
3–4 cups cold water
½ tsp. salt, or more to taste
Finely chopped fresh hot chiles for garnish

1. In a large heavy skillet or pot combine all the ingredients except the salt. (If you are using cooked or canned hominy, do not add it at this point, but reserve for the last ½ hour of cooking.)

2. Simmer the stew over low to moderate heat, uncovered, for 2–3 hours until the meat is very tender and the hominy is swelled and tender. If the mixture becomes too dry while cooking, add more water.

3. When the posole is done, add salt to taste. The mixture should be a sort of soupy stew, best served, like chili, in bowls. Pass the chopped fresh hot chiles to add as desired.

Vegetable Posole

Although posole traditionally meant a stew of limed corn and pork, it has come to mean any soup or stew of Mexican or Southwest style that uses hominy. This soup, with its mix of New World vegetables and hominy, is bright and flavorful. It can be served quite simply as is, garnished with a bit of fresh coriander leaf, or dressed up with a spoonful of Pumpkin Seed Pesto (see p. 161).

Serves 6–8

1 small onion, chopped

1 carrot, diced

1 small sweet green or red pepper, seeded and diced

2 cloves garlic, crushed

2 Tb. oil

2–3 plum tomatoes, chopped

6 cups chicken or turkey stock

Good pinch crushed dried hot peppers

½ tsp. oregano

2 Tb. fresh lime juice

1 1-lb. can hominy (2 cups), drained

1 small zucchini, diced

Small handful chopped fresh coriander leaf (cilantro)

Additional chopped coriander leaf for garnish or Pumpkin Seed Pesto
    (see p. 161)

1. In a medium saucepan sauté the onion, carrot, green pepper, and garlic in the oil until the onion just begins to turn gold.

2. Add all the other ingredients except the garnish and simmer uncovered over low heat for 20–30 minutes.

3. Serve the soup very hot with the additional chopped coriander leaf for garnish, or stir a spoonful of pumpkin seed pesto into each bowl.

Culinary Ashes

One of the least known aspects of the corn tradition is the ancient and pervasive use of what are known as "culinary ashes." From long distant times throughout the New World many different substances— juniper branches, chamisa (salt bush), mussel shells—were burned to produce ashes used for the processing of corn. The ashes were mixed with water and then strained out, resulting in an alkaline solution in which dried corn was soaked. This alkaline processing of corn had many desirable effects. First, it facilitated the removal of the tough outer hull of the dried corn kernel; the hulled corn could then be cooked whole in liquid, a product called hominy. Coarsely grated, the corn was known as hominy grits. The processed corn could also be ground into a meal or flour that produced a finer, more even textured bread than untreated corn. In addition, the alkaline processing liberated some of the nutrient content of the dried corn, making it more valuable for human consumption. For centuries Mexicans have used lime, another alkaline substance, in the production of *masa*, the corn flour from which tortillas are made, and in the American Southwest solutions of culinary ashes are used to change blue corn flour, which is actually a darkish gray, into the true blue color that is of ritual significance. In all these cases, the desired culinary goals of better color or improved texture went hand in hand with the goal of enhanced nutritional value from the most basic staple food. The elaborate age-old technology for processing corn with alkaline solutions made from culinary ashes and other substances never traveled beyond the New World; it surely developed here as a sophisticated and essential response to a primary food that would otherwise have been less valuable nutritionally.

Tortilla Bread

The Mexican tortilla is made from lime-soaked dried corn (*nixtamal* in the Aztec tongue, *hominy* in North American dialects) that is wet-ground into a dough called *masa*. Rolled or patted into a flat pancake and baked on a hot griddle (the *comal*), the tortilla, like other traditional New World corn breads, is unleavened. European settlers introduced wheat flour and the tradition of yeast-raised breads. In this recipe the unique flavor of the corn tortilla is captured in a leavened bread. It is a dense, crusty loaf, perfect for dunking in a bowl of chili or a thick bean soup.

Makes 1 loaf

1¼ cups warm water
1 Tb. sugar
1 Tb. active dry yeast
2–2½ cups all-purpose flour
1 tsp. salt
1 cup masa harina (corn tortilla flour)*

1. Pour the warm water in a mixing bowl; stir in the sugar. Sprinkle the yeast over the water and let it proof for a few minutes.

2. Add 1 cup of flour and the salt and beat until well blended.

3. Add the masa harina and beat again until well blended.

4. Add the additional flour if necessary, and knead thoroughly, to make a firm, elastic, non-sticky dough.

5. Place the dough in a lightly greased bowl, cover with a clean towel, and let it rise in a warm place for 1½–2 hours or until fully doubled in bulk.

6. Punch the dough down, knead for a little bit, then shape it into a round or oval loaf. Place the loaf in a 9-inch baking pan, cover, and let it rise again until doubled in bulk. Preheat the oven to 400°F.

7. Slash the top of the loaf with a sharp knife. Bake for 30–35 minutes until it is nicely browned and crusty. Turn out and let cool on a rack.

*Available in Latin American or Mexican groceries, as well as some supermarkets.

Roast Chicken with Tortilla Stuffing

Whenever there's stale bread, there's bound to be stuffing. This one, made of Mexican corn tortillas, is a nice change of pace from the usual herbed bread stuffing, and turns an ordinary roast chicken into a delicious *pollo Mexicano*.

Serves 6–8

1 6–7-lb. roasting chicken, or 2 3–3½-lb. small roasters

1 large onion, chopped

1 large sweet green pepper, seeded and chopped

2 Tb. vegetable oil

2 cloves garlic, crushed

1–2 small fresh hot green chiles (serrano or jalapeño), seeded and minced

12 small stale corn tortillas, coarsely torn or shredded*

1 Tb. ground chile ancho, plus additional ground chile ancho

1 tsp. oregano

1½ cups chicken stock

Good handful chopped fresh coriander leaf (cilantro)

1 cup shredded Monterrey Jack cheese

1 Tb. olive oil

1 clove garlic, crushed

Salt

1. Wash the chicken inside and out with cold water; pat it dry and set aside.

2. In a small skillet sauté the onion and the green pepper in the oil until the onion just begins to wilt. Add the 2 cloves garlic and the fresh chile and sauté a few minutes longer.

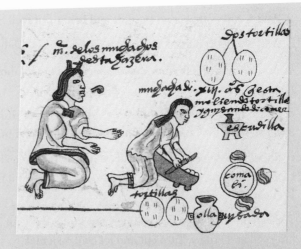

From a sixteenth-century Aztec manuscript, this drawing shows a mother teaching her daughter how to make tortillas. The girl rolls the dough on the metate (grinding stone), then cooks the tortillas on the *comal* (griddle). On the bottom right are some tortillas, and the pot (*olla*) containing the lime water in which the dried corn is soaked.

3. In a large bowl combine the tortilla pieces with the sautéed onion mixture, the 1 Tb. ground chile ancho, the oregano, and the stock. Mix lightly with a fork until the tortilla pieces are evenly moistened. Stir in the chopped coriander and the cheese.

4. Stuff the chicken lightly with the stuffing; do not pack the stuffing too tightly. (Any remaining stuffing can be placed in a buttered casserole and heated while the chicken roasts.)

5. In a small cup combine the olive oil and the remaining garlic. Brush the chicken thoroughly all over with the oil, then sprinkle it with salt and the additional ancho chile. Preheat oven to 350°F.

6. Roast the chicken for about 2–2½ hours for a large one; 1½ hours for smaller chickens. Baste occasionally with the pan juices. Let the chicken stand 5–10 minutes before carving.

If stale tortillas are not a part of your kitchen inventory, buy a 10-oz. package of corn tortillas. Place the tortillas in a single layer in a 300°F. oven for about 10–15 minutes. Cool, then proceed with the recipe as directed.

A Mexican woman making tortillas. Note the similarity of her equipment to that depicted in the Aztec drawing on the facing page.

Grits Milanese

Grits, like the whole hominy from which it is made, is a uniquely American food that never traveled beyond its land of origin and, indeed, is not heavily used outside the American South. There it is a traditional old-fashioned dish, customarily served as a breakfast cereal like oatmeal or porridge, or as a main course side dish like rice or potatoes. It is usually boiled in water, salted, and served with a little butter or bacon drippings. Experimental chefs are now using grits in more inventive and interesting forms. The following recipe adapts grits to an Italian risotto preparation, and it is very nice with poultry, though I have a friend from Alabama who ate a panful of it cold for breakfast and said it was wonderful!

Serves 4–5

1 Tb. butter
1 Tb. olive oil
1 medium onion, finely chopped
2 cups chicken stock
Several grinds black pepper
½ tsp. dried sage
½ tsp. dried rosemary
½ cup grits
⅓ cup fresh or frozen peas
2–3 Tb. finely chopped flat-leaf Italian parsley
½ cup chopped sautéed mushrooms (optional)
1 Tb. freshly grated Parmesan cheese

1. In a medium saucepan melt the butter with the oil over moderate heat. Add the onion and sauté until it begins to turn golden.

2. Add the stock, the pepper, the sage, and the rosemary and bring to the boil.

3. Gradually sprinkle in the grits, stirring. When all the grits have been added, turn the heat down and cook covered, stirring occasionally, for 15–20 minutes. Add the peas for the last 5 minutes of cooking.

4. Remove the grits from the heat and stir in the parsley, the mushrooms, if desired, and the cheese. Cover and let stand for 10 minutes.

Note: This mixture is very good stuffed into large buttered mushroom caps, topped with grated Swiss or Cheddar cheese, and baked in a moderate oven for 15–20 minutes.

Cornmeal Mush

How telling are the politics of cuisine! If faced with a choice between *mush* or *polenta*, which do you think most diners would choose? Let's face it—mush is not a pretty word. It conjures up long repressed memories of nasty hot breakfast gruel, ladled down constricted little throats. But polenta—ah, polenta!—now that's Italian, isn't it? And if it's Italian, it must be good. So much for sophisticated ethnogastronomy, for, of course, mush and polenta are exactly the same thing: cornmeal cooked in hot water to form a thick porridge or paste. In Romania it is called *mamaliga*; in Africa, depending on the language, *nshima*, *putu*, *ugali*, or *corn foo foo*. In southern Louisiana it is called *coush coush* and in the West Indies *cou-cou*, both names recalling a sister grain dish, the couscous of North Africa. No matter where you come from or what you call it, it is the same thing—cornmeal mush—the food that nourished our forefathers and that has come to nourish a large part of the world. In America mush was traditionally eaten as a thick porridge, sometimes with milk and sweetened with sugar or maple syrup, or salted and enriched with butter or meat drippings. The cooked mush, if allowed to stand and cool, "sets up" or hardens into a firm mass that can be sliced and fried. The technique for making mush, one that originated with the ancient corn eaters of the New World, remains the same today; it is only the seasoning and the saucing that have changed, to suit a national palate that is growing ever more worldly.

Cornmeal Mush I
(WITH PEANUT SAUCE AND GREENS)

The most important variable in the final texture of any cornmeal mush is the amount of liquid: the less the liquid the firmer the mush. Second is the coarseness or fineness of the cornmeal grind; coarser grinds produce a grittier, more textured mush. Cooking time is also critical; the longer the cooking the firmer the finished mush will be. As to the variety of cornmeal, that is a matter of personal taste and experimentation. In general, a high-quality stone-ground meal is to be preferred to the cheaper supermarket varieties; many cooks swear by imported Italian polentas that have a somewhat different flavor from American brands. Instant-cooking polentas have recently been introduced and are a useful time-saver. If you want to keep only one variety on hand, a medium-grind stone-ground yellow or white meal is your best bet. Whatever the texture or seasoning, the technique for making the mush is the same. The liquid should be at full boil. Add the cornmeal in a slow stream with one hand, while whisking or stirring briskly with the other. As soon as all the meal is whisked into the liquid, turn the heat to low and continue to cook, stirring, for 10–15 minutes for coarse meal, less for fine meals, which cook very quickly. The following recipe is for a mush that is to be served directly from the pot, without any chilling or setting up.

Serves 4–6

2½ cups water
1 tsp. salt
1 cup cornmeal
1 recipe Peanut Sauce with Greens (see p. 233)

1. Bring the water to a boil in a heavy saucepan; add the salt.

2. Keeping the water at the boil, add the cornmeal in a slow steady stream with one hand, while whisking or stirring briskly with the other hand. When all the cornmeal has been added, lower the heat, and continue to cook the mush, stirring occasionally, for about 5–10 minutes, or until thickened.

3. Spoon the hot mush into individual serving bowls. Top with the hot peanut sauce.

Cornmeal Mush II
(BALKAN STYLE, WITH FETA CHEESE AND DILL)

Cornmeal mush is a staple food of much of eastern Europe, where it is frequently enriched with dairy products—butter, sour cream, and a variety of cheeses. This is a light-textured mush with a delicate and unusual flavor, best served with a light tomato sauce.

Serves 4

3 cups water
½ tsp. salt
1 cup stone-ground cornmeal
4 oz. feta cheese, mashed or finely crumbled
3–4 Tb. finely snipped fresh dillweed
1 cup tomato sauce
½ lemon
Good grind black pepper

1. In heavy saucepan bring the water to a boil; add the salt.

2. Keeping the water at a boil, add the cornmeal in a slow steady stream with one hand, while whisking or stirring briskly with the other. When all the cornmeal has been added, lower the heat and continue to cook the mush, stirring occasionally, for about 15 minutes.

3. Add the feta cheese and dill to the hot mush and mix thoroughly.

4. Spoon the mush into a 9-inch pie pan, cake pan, or 1-quart casserole.

5. In a small saucepan heat the tomato sauce. Season with a good squeeze of lemon juice and some black pepper. Heat to a simmer, then serve over the mush.

Cornmeal Mush III
(POLENTA-STUFFED BEEF ROLLS)

The Italians have dozens of delectable ways of preparing their beloved polenta. It can be served with tomato sauce, meat sauce, sausages and peppers, or layered with mushroom sauce and cheese. In this recipe the polenta should be fairly firm so that it retains its texture as it cooks inside rolls of thinly sliced beef in a savory tomato sauce. The word *polenta* probably comes from the Latin *puls,* meaning a stew or porridge of grains or legumes.

Serves 4

2 cups chicken stock
1 tsp. crumbled dried sage
1 cup yellow cornmeal
1 lb. thinly sliced beef for stuffing (braciole)*
Flour for dredging
2 Tb. olive oil
1 medium onion, coarsely chopped
Salt and pepper
2 cups canned crushed tomatoes
½ tsp. dried basil
½ tsp. oregano
4–5 mushrooms, sliced

1. Add the sage to the stock and bring the stock to a boil.

2. Keeping the stock at a boil, add the cornmeal in a slow steady stream with one hand, while whisking or stirring briskly with the other. When all the cornmeal has been added, lower the heat and continue to cook the polenta, stirring occasionally, for about 10 minutes. Remove from the heat and let cool slightly.

3. Spread each beef slice with the mush, to within ½-inch of the edges. Carefully roll up the beef slice from the long end, tucking in the short ends as you roll. Fasten the rolls with wooden toothpicks. Continue until all the beef slices have been stuffed and rolled. (Any remaining polenta can be cubed and added to the sauce just before serving.)

4. Dredge the beef rolls lightly with flour.

5. In a large heavy skillet heat the oil over moderately high heat. Add the beef rolls and brown, turning the rolls to brown evenly. While the rolls are browning, add the chopped onion to the pan.

6. When the rolls are browned and the onions lightly sautéed, salt and pepper the rolls generously. Add the tomatoes, basil, oregano, and mushrooms.

7. Bring to a simmer, then cover and cook over low heat for about 45–55 minutes until the beef is tender. Turn the rolls in the sauce occasionally as they cook. Add additional cubed polenta to the sauce for the last 10 minutes of cooking, if desired.

8. Remind diners to remove toothpicks before eating.

*Braciole *is very thinly sliced boneless beef round; the slices are usually 3–4 inches by 2 inches, and come about 4 to 6 slices per pound.*

In early times, corn was shelled by hand and the cobs were turned into a variety of useful items—corncob pipes, dolls and other playthings.

Cornmeal Mush IV
(VEGETABLE SCRAPPLE)

Another union of corn and pork, scrapple was the unique invention of the Pennsylvania Dutch (a corruption of *Deutsch*), who settled the rich farmlands of central Pennsylvania. Waste was anathema to these thrifty German farmers and they utilized every edible scrap from the pig butchering in late autumn. Bits and pieces from all parts of the animal were boiled, mixed with cornmeal mush, and heavily seasoned with herbs and pepper. The mixture was chilled, then sliced and fried. Scrapple is a genuine regional specialty and is generally not available in most other parts of the country. In this recipe bits of vegetable substitute for the pork; the firm chilled mush can be sliced and fried in oil or butter, or reheated and served with a light tomato sauce.

Serves 6

2 Tb. butter

1 medium onion, finely chopped

1 stalk celery, with leaves, finely chopped

1 carrot, finely chopped

1 small sweet red pepper, seeded and finely chopped

1 cup fresh mushrooms, finely chopped

½ cup fresh peas or green beans, finely diced

3 cups chicken stock

⅛ tsp. black pepper

½ tsp. marjoram

½ tsp. crumbled dried sage

¼ tsp. dried rosemary

1½ cups cornmeal

Flour for dredging

¼ cup vegetable oil

1. In a heavy saucepan melt the butter over moderately high heat. Add all the vegetables and sauté, stirring, for a few minutes.

2. Pour in the stock, add the seasonings, and bring the mixture to a full boil.

3. Keeping the liquid at a boil, add the cornmeal in a slow steady stream with one hand, while whisking or stirring briskly with the other. When all the cornmeal has been blended in, turn the heat low and continue to cook the mush, stirring occasionally, for about 20–30 minutes or until it is very thick. Taste for salt.

4. Rinse a 9 x 5 x 3-inch loaf pan out with cold water. Turn the mush into the pan, spreading it evenly and smoothing it down. Chill the loaf for several hours or overnight.

5. Run a sharp knife around the edges of the pan, then unmold the loaf. Cut the loaf in ½-inch slices. Dredge the slices lightly with flour, handling them carefully.

6. In a heavy skillet heat 2 Tb. of the oil over moderately high heat. Fry the scrapple on both sides until nicely browned and crisp. Continue frying the slices, adding more oil as needed.

Note: To make the more traditional pork scrapple, cook 1 lb. lean boneless pork in 4 cups water, with a chopped onion, a bay leaf, and salt and pepper for a couple of hours until it is very tender. Drain the meat, reserving the liquid. Shred or finely chop the meat. Use the strained cooking liquid to make the mush. Omit the chopped vegetables and add the chopped meat and the seasonings to the mush after it has cooked. Taste for salt and pepper (it should be very well seasoned), and proceed as directed above.

A unique tourist attraction in the heart of American corn country, the Corn Palace in Mitchell, South Dakota. The entire structure is made of corn cobs.

Pecan Polenta Rounds

Here is a nice update on old-fashioned corn cakes or cornmeal mush—flavored corn-meal studded with sautéed pecans, then cut into rounds and lightly sautéed. They can be eaten just as is, a nice change of pace from rice or potatoes, or used as a base for creamed chicken or turkey, beans, or chili. They are especially good with Turkey in Double Mushroom Sauce (see p. 188).

Double Mushroom Sauce (see p. 188).

Makes 12–14 rounds

2 Tb. butter
⅔ cup coarsely chopped pecans
2½ cups chicken stock
¼ tsp. nutmeg
Several good grinds black pepper
1 cup coarse-ground yellow cornmeal
Butter or vegetable oil for sautéing

1. In a small skillet heat 1 Tb. of the butter over moderate heat. Add the chopped pecans and sauté, stirring, until the nuts are just lightly browned. Remove from the heat and set aside.

2. In a medium saucepan combine the stock, the remaining 1 Tb. of butter, the nutmeg, and black pepper. Bring the mixture to a full boil.

3. With one hand, slowly pour the cornmeal into the boiling stock, while whisking or stirring briskly with the other hand. When all cornmeal has been added, turn the heat to low and cook the polenta, stirring occasionally, for 10–15 minutes until it is quite thick. Remove the polenta from the heat and stir in the sautéed pecans.

4. Spread the hot polenta evenly in a 12-inch round or rectangular baking pan, smoothing it into an even layer. Let it cool completely.

5. With a cookie, biscuit, or doughnut cutter, cut the cooled polenta into 2 to 2½-inch rounds. Remove the rounds carefully with a spatula and sauté them in butter or oil until just lightly browned on both sides.

Chili-Cheese Spoon Bread

Spoon bread was a colonial American invention, simply a cornmeal mush enriched with butter and milk, lightened with eggs, and baked in a casserole. It is really more a custard or a soufflé than a real bread, spooned rather than sliced or cut with a knife. Like mush, spoon bread can be made with any kind of cornmeal—yellow, white, or blue. The South has always preferred the white variety for its many cornmeal dishes: Some authorities claim that this preference reflects an attitude that equates lightness or whiteness with superiority. The more richly colored yellow corn was given to the more richly colored slaves. This spoon bread, layered with chili and cheese, is a hearty and economical one-dish meal. It is also a good way to use up a cup or so of leftover chili.

Serves 4–6

2 cups milk
2 Tb. butter
1 tsp. salt
1 Tb. sugar
Good dash cayenne pepper
1 cup cornmeal
3 eggs, well beaten
1–1½ cups leftover chili (meat, bean, or whatever—your choice—but it should be fairly thick). See for example Chocolate Chili (p. 199)
1 cup shredded mild Cheddar or Monterrey Jack cheese

1. In a medium heavy saucepan combine the milk, butter, salt, sugar, and cayenne. Heat over moderate heat until small bubbles appear around the edge.

2. Slowly stir the cornmeal into the milk, whisking as you pour to avoid lumps. Continue to cook, stirring, until the mixture is smooth and thickened. Remove from heat and let cool slightly.

3. Stir the beaten eggs into the cornmeal mixture, whisking thoroughly. Preheat the oven to 350°F.

4. Pour half of the cornmeal mixture into a buttered 2-quart casserole. Spoon the chili in small spoonfulls all over the batter. Sprinkle the cheese evenly over the chili. Pour the remaining batter over all.

5. Bake the spoon bread for 35–45 minutes, until the top is puffed, firm, and lightly browned. Let stand for a few minutes before serving.

Pellagra

It is ironic that corn, the grain that nourished the people of the New World for so long, now has a deficiency disease associated with its consumption. Pellagra is a malady that results from a dietary deficiency of niacin. The problem with corn is twofold: first, corn is very low in tryptophan, an amino acid that potentiates the body's manufacture and absorption of niacin; and second, the niacin content of corn itself is largely unavailable for human nutrition unless released by certain kinds of processing. Pellagra occurs when the most of the diet is unprocessed cornmeal with no sufficient supplement of other protein- or niacin-rich foods. Pellagra made its appearance after 1492 when corn gained acceptance as a food of only the desperately poor, in parts of Europe and Africa, eaten primarily in the form of cornmeal mush, with few additional foods. Pellagra, known also as the Plague of the Polenta eaters, spread with corn, a disease of severe poverty and malnutrition. The indigenous inhabitants of the New World avoided pellagra by developing from ancient times the alkaline processing of corn to release the niacin content, and by combining corn with beans, a food rich in both niacin and tryptophan. The tradition of combining plant proteins, usually a cereal grain and a legume, in order to obtain a proper dietary balance of amino acids, can be found in cultures throughout the world—as in the constant combination of rice and soybeans in China, and of wheat and pulses in India.

Native Americans ate corn and beans together at almost every meal and planted them together in the same hill of earth, emphasizing the intimate culinary and nutritional relationship they have always shared. This ancient traditional wisdom did not travel with corn when it left its native shores, and pellagra was the unfortunate result.

Confetti Corn Custard

This old-fashioned dish is claimed by the South, but it is one that, in fact, developed in a variety of forms throughout corn-eating America. It belongs to a whole family of puddings and custards that used "green" corn, the old term for fresh, sweet corn. The dish can be made with canned or frozen corn, but then the incomparable flavor of freshly picked corn will be missing. Confetti Corn Custard is an effective way to introduce foreign guests to the delights of fresh corn.

Serves 6–8

2 Tb. butter

1 medium onion, minced

1 medium sweet red or green pepper, seeded and diced (or a mixture of both)

1 stalk celery, with leaves, diced

1 carrot, diced

4 cups fresh corn kernels (about 5 ears' worth)

2 cups light cream

½ tsp. salt

½ tsp. sugar

Several good grinds black pepper

Good dash cayenne pepper

¼ tsp. mace

2 eggs

1 Tb. flour

1. In a medium saucepan heat the butter over moderate heat; add the onion, diced pepper, celery, and carrot and sauté, stirring occasionally, until the onion is wilted.

2. Add the corn, cream, and seasonings; bring to the simmer and cook, stirring occasionally, over moderate heat, for about 10 minutes. Remove from the heat and cool slightly.

3. Whisk the eggs, then stir in the flour and whisk to blend thoroughly. Stir the eggs into the corn mixture and blend well. Preheat the oven to 350°F.

4. Turn the mixture into a buttered 2-quart casserole or baking dish. Bake for about 30 minutes until the custard is set and the top is lightly browned. Let stand for a few minutes before serving.

Corn and Shrimp Fritters
Thai Style

From the moment that European emigrants met up with corn in the New World, they designed ways to fry it, both as a fresh vegetable and as a dried ground meal. Hush puppies, fritters, and corn "oysters" were all well-loved fried products that added taste and texture to the corn repertoire. Asian cuisines, with their long history of savory fried crispy foods, have enlarged this tradition, adding delightful new flavors to the ever-growing American corn experience.

Makes about 30 small fritters

1 cup peeled and deveined raw shrimp (about ½ lb. with shells)
1 cup (8½-oz. can) cream-style corn
1 small onion, coarsely chopped
1 egg white
½ tsp. sugar
¼ tsp. salt
¼ tsp. powdered lemongrass
Good dash cayenne pepper
⅓ cup yellow cornmeal
3–4 Tb. peanut oil

1. Cut up the raw shrimp coarsely and combine in a food processor with the corn, onion, and egg white. Process the mixture briefly until it is well blended but not completely pureed. There should be bits of corn and shrimp in the mix.

2. Transfer the mixture to a bowl; stir in the seasonings and cornmeal and mix until well blended. Let stand for 20–30 minutes.

3. Heat the oil in a heavy skillet over moderately high heat. Drop the batter by scant tablespoons into the oil; do not crowd the pan. Fry, turning once with a spatula, until well browned on both sides.

4. Drain on paper towels; serve hot with dipping sauce, if desired.

DIPPING SAUCE

2 Tb. rice vinegar
1 tsp. sugar
1 tsp. fish sauce (Vietnamese nuoc mam *or Thai* nam pla*)*
⅛ tsp. crushed dried hot peppers
1½ Tb. finely chopped salted dry-roasted peanuts
2 Tb. finely chopped fresh coriander leaf (cilantro)

Combine all the ingredients in a small bowl and mix well.

Modern products processed from corn—breakfast cereal, corn starch, and corn oil

Dried Corn and Smoked Salmon Casserole

Dried corn was an essential part of the early corn kitchen; ground, it provided meal for bread, and soaked in liquid and cooked, it functioned as a vegetable during the long lean winter months. Dried corn is very different from its fresh equivalent, having a more intense corn flavor and a much chewier texture. There are many varieties; the chicos of the Southwest are larger and less sweet than the more delicate dried sweet corn of the Pennsylvania Dutch. The recipe for this casserole is inspired by the traditional foods of the northwest coast of America, where smoked fish, and particularly the abundant salmon of the Columbia River, were, along with corn, the focus of the diet. It is an interesting illustration of how the traditional foods and techniques of necessity become hooked into our aesthetics; we may no longer need to dry corn or smoke salmon in order to preserve or store them, but we value them, and indeed, pay heavily for the gustatory pleasures they provide.

Serves 4–6

1 cup dried sweet corn
1 cup milk
4–5 juniper berries, crushed
2 eggs
1 cup light cream
1 Tb. sugar
1 tsp. salt
Several good grinds black pepper
1 Tb. prepared horseradish
3–4 Tb. finely snipped fresh chives
1 cup coarsely flaked smoked salmon

1. In a small bowl combine the dried corn, the milk, and the juniper berries. Mix well and let stand for 2–3 hours.

2. In a large bowl whisk the eggs thoroughly, then blend in the cream, sugar, salt, pepper, and horseradish. Mix well. Preheat the oven to 350°F.

3. Add the soaked corn mixture to the egg mixture, then stir in the chives and the salmon. Mix thoroughly. Turn the mixture into a buttered shallow 1½- to 2-quart casserole.

4. Bake the casserole for 30–35 minutes until it is slightly puffed, firm, and lightly browned.

Super Succotash

Succotash is the early colonists' rendering of an unpronounceable Narragansett word, *Msickquatasch*, which meant a dish of whole corn and beans cooked together. It is only one example of the pervasive New World tradition of combining corn and beans to provide a nutritionally balanced meal. Many different mixtures of corn and beans, both fresh and dried, were used, but the North American version most quickly adopted by European emigrants was fresh green lima beans and fresh sweet corn stewed together and lightly sweetened. The colonists enriched this mixture with butter and cream. Succotash can be a very simple dish or, like this one, rather more elaborate; the Parmesan cheese is unorthodox but good.

Serves 4–6

2 cups shelled small fresh green lima beans,
*   or 1 10-oz. package frozen baby limas*
2 cups fresh or frozen corn kernels
1 medium onion, finely chopped
1 Tb. butter
1 large ripe tomato, coarsely chopped
¼ tsp. salt
Several good grinds black pepper
⅛ tsp. nutmeg
¼ cup light cream
1–2 Tb. freshly grated Parmesan cheese

1. Cook the beans in boiling salted water for about 5 minutes or until just tender. Add the corn, bring just to a simmer, then remove from heat, drain, and set aside.

2. Sauté the onion in the butter until wilted. Add the tomato and cook over moderate heat, stirring occasionally, until the tomato is soft and the liquid is somewhat reduced.

3. Stir in the salt, pepper, nutmeg, and cream. Add the beans and corn and cook over low heat until the mixture comes to a simmer.

4. Remove from heat and stir in the Parmesan. Taste for salt. Serve hot.

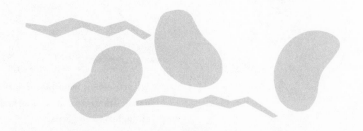

Marinated Baby Corn and Peppers with Black Bean–Garlic Vinaigrette

One of the few ways that corn went away and returned to its ancient home in a new form was as baby corn, in its sweetest and most immature state. Of course, corn growers in America knew and appreciated this tender little vegetable but could not afford to sacrifice a significant part of the harvest for such a gastronomic luxury. In recent years baby corn has been used in many of the cuisines of Southeast Asia, where it is valued for its sweet flavor and crunchy texture. In this recipe it appears as a salad vegetable with a dressing of Oriental influence.

Serves 4

1 1-lb. can baby corn, packed in brine
1 sweet red pepper, seeded and cut in strips
1 sweet green pepper, seeded and cut in strips
2 tsp. Chinese fermented black beans
1 large clove garlic, crushed
⅓ cup peanut oil
2 Tb. rice vinegar
2 Tb. chopped fresh coriander leaf (cilantro) for garnish

1. Rinse the corn in cold water and drain thoroughly. In a serving bowl combine the corn with the pepper strips.

2. Mash the black beans thoroughly, then combine them with the crushed garlic.

3. Combine the oil and the vinegar, then add the black beans and the garlic. Whisk to blend thoroughly.

4. Pour the dressing over the vegetables and mix well. Let stand 1–2 hours. Mix again, then sprinkle with the fresh coriander. Serve at room temperature.

Advertisement from 1885 depicting native American corn as king and queen of the farm and garden

Blue Corn and Pepper Frittata

The frittata, an omelet that is either cooked in a skillet or baked in the oven, is the way eggs are often prepared in Mediterranean cooking. A variety of vegetables and/or cheeses are frequently added to the basic egg mixture; Italians favor artichokes, mushrooms, and spinach, while the Spanish lean toward tomatoes and potatoes. In this frittata both sweet and hot peppers add zing, while blue cornmeal provides subtle, earthy flavor. It is a nice dish for brunch or a light lunch, served with a tomato and avocado salad.

Serves 3–4

3 Tb. olive oil
1 medium onion, chopped
1 large sweet green pepper, seeded and chopped
1 large sweet red pepper, seeded and chopped
1 fresh jalapeño pepper, seeded and minced
6 eggs
½ tsp. salt
Good dash cayenne pepper
¼ cup (4 Tb.) blue cornmeal
8 oz. shredded mild Cheddar or Monterrey Jack cheese

1. In a heavy cast-iron skillet or heavy shallow range-to-oven casserole heat the olive oil over low to moderate heat. Tilt the pan and swirl the oil so that it lightly films the sides of the pan.

2. Add the onion and the chopped and minced peppers and cook slowly, stirring occasionally, until the vegetables are soft and the onion is lightly browned.

3. In a medium bowl whisk the eggs with the salt and the cayenne until they are just frothy. Whisk in the cornmeal, 1 Tb. at a time, until it is smoothly incorporated and there are no lumps. Preheat the oven to 350°F.

4. Pour the egg mixture over the vegetables in the skillet. Sprinkle the grated cheese evenly over the top.

5. Place the skillet or casserole in the oven and bake for 12–15 minutes until the omelet is set and the cheese is melted.

6. Let the frittata stand for a few minutes, then cut into wedges to serve.

Blue Corn

When Columbus first set foot in the New World, there were many varieties of corn in cultivation, types for popping, for parching, for eating fresh, for grinding into meal. And there were many colors— yellow, white, red, blue, black, and speckled. Blue corn found a special niche in the American Southwest, where it is valued by the Hopi, the Zuñi, and the Pueblo people for its distinctive color and unique earthy flavor, more intense than the more familiar yellow and white varieties. Blue corn is usually dried whole or ground into a meal for breads, gruels, and dumplings. The meal is also toasted to make *atole*, a thick, sweetened porridge-like drink. The lavender-blue color that is so specially regarded by the people of the Southwest is achieved by treating the grain with an alkaline substance; native traditions use saltbush or juniper ashes, but much the same effect can be obtained with ordinary baking soda or calcium carbonate (the common component of calcium dietary supplement pills). So important was corn, of all varieties and colors, that it became a fundamental part of native mythology, and a sacred offering to the gods:

> My gods I give you
> this cornmeal
> and thank you.

Navajo Triple Corn Muffins

This recipe is an adaptation of a Navajo cake that is made with a combination of blue and yellow cornmeals. Canned cream-style corn provides the liquid and produces a muffin that is moist and slightly sweet, with an intense corn flavor. These are nothing at all like the sweet cake-like store-bought muffins of the commercial bakery; here is a real, earthy, down-home corn muffin.

Makes 12–16 muffins

½ cup yellow cornmeal
½ cup blue cornmeal
1 cup all-purpose flour
2 tsp. baking soda
½ tsp. salt
½ cup firmly packed dark brown sugar
1 egg
2 Tb. oil
1 15–16-oz. can cream-style corn
½ cup light or dark raisins

1. In a large mixing bowl combine all the dry ingredients and mix thoroughly.

2. In a smaller bowl beat the egg lightly, then add the oil and creamed corn and blend thoroughly.

3. Add the wet ingredients to the dry ingredients and mix just until completely blended. Stir in the raisins. Preheat the oven to 350°F.

4. Grease muffin tins (12–16) or line them with paper liners. Fill the tins about two-thirds full with batter.

5. Bake for 15–20 minutes or until lightly browned and firm.

New World corn gods and corn symbols.
Left to right: Aztec, Hopi, Maya, Pueblo.

On the Cob

Our ancestors learned to eat corn on the cob from native Americans, who taught them everything there was to know about the New World's staff of life. These tribes boiled their corn in water or, more commonly, roasted the ears in their husks in the hot ashes of the hearth fire. This slow, enclosed roasting, which can be duplicated in the hot coals of the backyard barbecue, carmelizes the sugars in the corn, producing a sweet, browned ear. In many cultures, where corn on the cob is eaten as a street or snack food, the husked ears are roasted or grilled over hot charcoal; in Mexico, India, and Southeast Asia, the roasted ears are then sprinkled with salt, chile pepper, and an occasional squeeze of lemon or lime juice. Only in America is corn on the cob boiled and then slathered with butter, a tradition begun by early settlers from the dairy cultures of northern Europe. Convention has it that the water in the pot should be boiling before the corn is picked because the natural sugars in the corn quickly change to starch after the corn is picked. For the optimal sweet corn experience, on or off the cob, corn should be as fresh as possible and should be cooked for only three or four minutes. And yes, fresh sweet corn is significantly better than its canned or frozen counterparts.

Grilled Chicken in Bourbon Barbecue Sauce

America's own corn whiskey, bourbon, isn't just for sipping—it's fine for cooking, too. Like other distinctive spirits, it gives a unique flavor to sauces and marinades. This chicken is unusual and very good, and is equally successful grilled over hot coals or baked in the oven.

Serves 4–6

$\frac{1}{4}$ cup Kentucky bourbon
2 Tb. soy sauce
2 Tb. vegetable oil
1 medium onion, coarsely chopped
3 cloves garlic
$\frac{1}{2}$ tsp. paprika
$\frac{1}{8}$ tsp. cayenne pepper
3 lb. chicken breasts on the bone

1. In a blender or food processor combine all the ingredients except the chicken. Puree until smooth.

2. Cut the chicken breasts in half and remove the skin.

3. Pour the marinade over the chicken breasts and rub it in well. Cover and refrigerate for 3–4 hours, turning the chicken once or twice in the marinade.

4. Grill the chicken over hot coals, turning once, about 10 minutes on each side. Or broil in the oven. Baste with the marinade while grilling. Or, bake the chicken with the marinade in a casserole in a preheated 350°F. oven for about 40 minutes, turning once or twice during the cooking and basting with the pan juices. When the chicken is done, remove it from the pan; cook down the liquid until it is a thick, dark coating sauce.

The Spirited Grain

The Scots and Irish who emigrated to the northeast part of America brought with them a taste for whiskey and the know-how to make it. Substituting for barley and rye, the traditional grains of northern Europe, was the American grain corn: cheap, easy to grow, and readily available. Fresh corn kernels were sprouted in warm water, then drained and mashed. After fermentation and distillation the resultant brew was a raw, powerful beverage, variously known as corn "likker," white lightning, mountain dew, or, if produced illegally (as most of it was), moonshine. It was later discovered that this potent corn whiskey could be mellowed and tempered by aging in charred oak barrels, for at least four years. So was born America's unique whiskey, bourbon, named for the county in Kentucky in which it was created.

Bourbon Eggnog

Bourbon, made from fermented corn, is smoother and lighter than the malted Scotch and rye whiskeys of Europe, and its mellow flavor is esteemed by Americans on its own or in any number of mixed drinks, including that traditional Southern favorite, the mint julep. It also makes a superb eggnog.

Makes about 30 4-ounce servings

12 eggs
3 cups sugar
1 fifth bourbon whiskey
1 quart milk
1 quart heavy cream, whipped
Freshly grated nutmeg

1. In a large bowl (or punch bowl) beat the eggs until light and frothy.

2. Slowly beat in the sugar and continue beating until the mixture is pale and thick.

3. Slowly stir in the bourbon, then the milk.

4. Gently fold in the whipped cream.

5. Garnish each serving with freshly grated nutmeg.

Note: I realize that cooking with raw eggs has recently become questionable because of the possibility of salmonella contamination. It seems a sorry thing that we should have to forego some of the delectable dishes that use raw eggs—mousses, mayonnaise, Caesar salad—and so I offer this recipe in the hope that things will change or that there are enough of us with access to untainted eggs.

The corn harvest and husking were social and festive events in rural communities; corn "likker" frequently contributed to the merriment.

Christmas Bourbon Balls

Here we have the old-fashioned English sugarplum, redone with a chocolate coating and the special flavor of America's unique whiskey, Kentucky corn-mash bourbon. These little confections are very rich, so make them small.

Makes about 3 dozen

1 cup firmly packed dried apricots
1 cup firmly packed golden raisins
1 cup walnut meats
2 Tb. bourbon whiskey
6–8 oz. semisweet or bittersweet chocolate

1. Grind the apricots, raisins, and walnuts together, or process finely in the food processor.

2. Add the bourbon, then knead the mixture with your hands until it is thoroughly blended.

3. Form the mixture into small balls, about the size of a large grape, place in a waxed paper–lined container, cover tightly, and let sit for a week or two.

4. Melt the chocolate in the top of a double boiler.

5. Using a toothpick, dip balls in the melted chocolate, swirling to coat completely. Let the excess drip off, then place the coated balls on a tray lined with waxed paper. Let the chocolate coating harden thoroughly, then place the candies in little fluted papers.

Maple-Corn Coffee Cake

Corn, as the traditional American grain, was used not only for the many breads, muffins, fritters, and mushes that were the basis of the daily diet, but for a variety of sweet dishes as well. Sweetened spoon breads were baked with stewed fruits, while cornmeal was enriched with eggs and molasses and milk and baked into that rib-sticking classic, Indian pudding. This corn cake is reminiscent of *karidopita*, the traditional Greek cake rich with cinnamon and walnuts and moistened with honey or sugar syrup. But the flavor here is wholly American; the cake is very good cut into small squares and served with freshly brewed hot coffee.

Serves 10–12

½ cup (1 stick) butter, softened
1 cup sugar
3 eggs
1 tsp. vanilla
½ cup yellow cornmeal
1½ cups flour
2 tsp. baking soda
½ tsp. salt
⅔ cup buttermilk
1 cup finely chopped walnuts or pecans
¾ cup maple syrup

1. With an electric mixer cream the butter and sugar together until pale and fluffy.

2. Add the eggs one at a time, beating well after each addition. Stir in the vanilla.

3. Combine the cornmeal, flour, baking soda, and salt and mix well.

4. Add the flour mixture to the butter mixture in thirds alternately with the buttermilk, mixing well after each addition. Preheat the oven to 350°F.

5. Stir in the chopped nuts and mix well.

6. Spread the batter evenly in a buttered 13 x 9 x 2-inch baking pan. Bake for 30 minutes until firm and lightly browned.

7. Remove from the oven and pour the maple syrup evenly over the top of the cake. Return the pan to the oven for 5 minutes. Remove from oven and let cool completely before serving.

Potato Leek Soup

Thai-Style Vichyssoise

Potato Chowder with Roasted Garlic and Pepper Puree

Bloody Mary's Consommé

Colcannon

Potato Filling

Potatoes with Tomatoes and Chile

Patate Tricolore

Potato Moussaka

Potatoes with Clams and Tomatoes

Oven-Fried or Roasted Potatoes

Deluxe Scalloped Potatoes

Gratin of Potato and Root Vegetables

Saffron Potato Rolls

Potato Latkes

Potatoes Vinaigrette

1. with leeks

2. with mussels and dill

3. with purple and yellow potatoes

All-American Potato Salad

Caribbean Seafood Pie in Sweet Potato Crust

Sweet Potato Pone

Sweet Potato Cake with Toffee–Cream Cheese Frosting

THE POTATO

Mashed, baked, or French fried, in hash, chips, or chowder, the potato is one of our national culinary treasures. Despite its unglamorous appearance, it turns up as a fashionable component of the most elegant meals, while at the same time appearing in humbler forms on the daily tables of most American families. It is no mean tribute to this homely vegetable that it is at one and the same time the most popular fast food in the country and the pampered darling of three-star chefs.

The reasons for this widespread acceptance are clear: The potato is cheap, easy to produce, always available, and amenable to almost any culinary treatment. It can be boiled, steamed, baked, roasted, fried, sautéed, or braised; it can be prepared whole, sliced, shredded, mashed, or pureed. It allows itself to be dressed with dozens of sauces and seasonings, providing an almost unlimited variety of texture and flavor experiences.

But this tuberous marvel did not always have the popularity it enjoys today. It required a number of voyages far from its ancestral home in the New World before it returned triumphant to these shores, the prodigal culinary son. Discovered by the Spanish conquistadores in the Peruvian highlands, the potato had served the people of that ancestral hearth as a food staple for many thousands of years. The natives of Peru utilized the potato primarily in the form of *chuño,* a product resulting from a process of alternate freezing, pounding, and dehydrating. The most refined *chuño* was milled into a fine flourlike substance that was used to make bread. So important was the potato in the diet of the ancient Andean people that it was worshipped as a god.

The Spanish quickly saw the value of this tuber as a good source of nourishment for the poor. The potato is adaptable to a wide variety of climatic conditions, tolerant of cold, dampness, and aridity; it is easily propagated vegetatively, by simply hoeing tubers or pieces of tubers into the earth. Even in poor soils and with little cultivation it can produce relatively high yields. It was, therefore, as a cheap, easy, hardy, and productive food for the poor and for livestock that the potato was introduced into Europe.

Small wonder, then, that the potato was not immediately and enthusiastically taken into the kitchens of Europe. The moment people are told that a new food is as good for them as it is for their animals, you are likely to meet with some resistance. The potato quickly earned the reputation for causing leprosy—perhaps because of its bumpy and sometimes scabrous appearance; it would not be for another two hundred years or so that that belief would die out, only to be replaced by the notion that the potato was a potent aphrodisiac.

There was, however, one corner of Europe where the potato was taken into the hearts and hearths of the common people with an enthusiasm that has never been matched. Within eighty or so years of its discovery in Peru the potato was already firmly established in Ireland, possibly introduced by Sir Walter Raleigh. The reasons for its instant acceptance have to do with a host of social and economic factors unique to Ireland in the sixteenth century: a difficult climate and geography; a system of penniless tenant farmers with limited acreage and little time for labor; and a land constantly under the ravages of war. To all these problems the potato seemed a miraculous solution; it grew well under adverse conditions, required a minimum of care and cultivation, and repaid its grower with an adequate source of calories. Furthermore, the potato fitted into the already existing culinary pattern of the Irish poor, who were accustomed to bland food cooked in a single large kettle suspended over a peat fire. Whatever was available—a leek, a turnip, a few leaves of cabbage—was tossed into the pot with the potatoes, supplemented only by occasional milk from the family cow. The unremitting diet of potatoes—an adult was said to consume between ten and fourteen pounds a day—was apparently so satisfying that the Irish poor quickly became completely dependent on it and planted no other crops; consequently, when the potato blight struck in 1845, widespread famine, disease, and death resulted. Thus ended the ancient tenant farming system, and so began the mass emigration of the Irish to America.

Elsewhere in Europe, between the seventeenth and nineteenth centuries, the potato was gradually accepted as a basic food, particularly in areas where growing conditions for other crops were not ideal. In England, Scotland, Germany, Scandinavia, Poland, and Russia, the potato became an important and well-loved staple of the diet, especially of the poor, though never with the unfortunate exclusivity that it achieved in Ireland.

In France the story was a little different. In the middle of the eighteenth century, Parmentier, a pharmacist who, as a prisoner of war in Germany, had lived for several years almost exclusively on potatoes, understood the value of this plant as a food crop for the masses. He made the mistake initially of attempting to introduce the potato in the form of a processed flour to make bread, a product the conservative French rejected out of hand. With the backing of King Louis XVI and Marie-Antoinette, however, Parmentier redirected his efforts; he prepared the potato as a vegetable in ways consistent with French culinary tradition—with butter, cream, cheese, and herbs. So successful was he that the potato has become entrenched as a national favorite, and the adjective "Parmentier" honors his contribution by designating a dish made of potatoes. Nowhere else has the humble potato so fully realized its gastronomic potential as in the cuisine of France; the great chef Escoffier described in his *Guide Culinaire* almost fifty recipes that have become standard in the French repertoire. The modest tuber, which was intended to fill the stomachs of the poor folk of Europe (as well as their pigs and cows), became worthy of art as well as nourishment.

And this is perhaps what it comes down to—that the potato is a food of enormous versatility, capable of satisfying on the simplest, most basic rib-sticking level, while at the same time accessible to the most elaborate and refined culinary techniques. Its light color, bland flavor, and unique starchy, absorbent composition provide a large variety of distinctive eating experiences.

The potato is still cheap and still easy, but it cannot be taken for granted. There follows a collection of recipes that testifies to its adaptability and indicates the many ways it has fitted itself into the individual culinary patterns of cultures throughout the Old World. And we shall see how the potato, returned again to its ancient home through a host of immigrant groups from the Old World, was transformed once more into our very own—the great American spud.

Potato Leek Soup

When the potato traveled to Europe, it formed an instant alliance with the leek, that delicate yet distinctive member of the onion family, and the two cooked together were the basis of many tasty, filling soups. Potato leek soup can be prepared with butter and herbs, as in the French version, or, as it is commonly done in American cooking, with the familiar and well-loved flavor of bacon.

Serves 6–8

3–4 slices bacon, chopped
3–4 leeks, mostly white parts, coarsely chopped
4 medium all-purpose potatoes, peeled and cubed
6 cups chicken stock
⅛ tsp. freshly ground black pepper
½ cup half-and-half
Salt and pepper to taste

1. In a medium saucepan brown the chopped bacon until crisp and brown. Remove the bacon with a slotted spoon, drain on paper towels, and reserve.

2. Discard all but about 1 Tb. of the bacon fat from the pan. Add the chopped leeks and sauté over moderate heat until soft.

3. Add the potatoes, then the stock, then the pepper. Bring to a simmer and cook, uncovered, over moderate heat until the potatoes are very soft.

4. Puree the soup in a blender or food processor. Put in the pan and bring to a simmer.

5. Stir in the half-and-half and heat until hot; do not boil. Taste for salt and pepper.

6. Sprinkle the reserved bacon bits over the hot soup just before serving.

In the eighteenth century, the cuisine of France was about to undergo a major change. Parmentier shows his first crop of potatoes to Louis XVI.

Thai-Style Vichyssoise

Vichyssoise, the chilled leek and potato puree that is so elegant a preamble to summer meals, does not come, despite its name, from France. It appears to have been developed at the beginning of the century by a French chef, Louis Diat, working in the Roof Garden Restaurant of the Ritz Carlton in New York City. My recipe for vichyssoise takes its character not from the herbs and cream of European tradition, but from the distinctive flavorings of Southeast Asia, which have begun to have a significant impact on American cooking. Coconut milk supplies the creaminess, while the leek, lemongrass, fish sauce, and coriander combine to provide a delicate and intriguing flavor.

Serves 6–8

3 large leeks, mostly white parts, coarsely chopped
2 Tb. vegetable oil
3 medium all-purpose potatoes, peeled and cubed
4 cups chicken stock
1/8 tsp. white pepper
2 Tb. fish sauce (Vietnamese nuoc mam *or Thai* nam pla*)*
1/2 tsp. powdered lemongrass
2 cups unsweetened coconut milk (or 1 14-oz. can) (see p. 239)
1 Tb. fresh lime juice
Good handful chopped fresh coriander leaf (cilantro)

1. In a medium saucepan sauté the leeks in the oil over moderate heat until soft.

2. Add the potatoes, then the stock, pepper, fish sauce, and lemongrass. Simmer, uncovered, over moderate heat until the potatoes are very soft.

3. Cool slightly, then puree the leek and potato mixture with the coconut milk in a food processor or blender.

4. Transfer the puree to the pan or bowl, add the lime juice and coriander, and blend thoroughly.

5. Chill the soup thoroughly, then taste for salt and lime. Garnish individual servings with a little of the chopped coriander.

Names and Nicknames

From the very beginning there has been confusion about the potato's name. The sweet potato that Columbus found in the West Indies was called *batata* by the natives, and it was that name that subsequently became attached in English to the white potato. When the Spanish found the white potato in Peru, they adopted its Peruvian name *papa*, and called the sweet potato *camote*, another West Indian name for the sweet tuber. The French coined the term *pomme de terre*—apple of the earth—and this designation was adopted by many European languages—*Kartoffel* in German, *erdappel* in Dutch, *tartuffe* in Italian—all variations on earth apple or earth truffle. If that were not confusing enough, the potato became known in America as the "Irish" potato, for it was thought to have originated there. Indeed, many of our nicknames for the potato come from its Irish association: A "mickey" was a potato roasted in the hot coals (presumably by an Irishman or "mick"); a "hot potato" became a euphemism for an issue or problem that was too difficult to handle. The term "spud" came from the name of the 3-pronged fork that was used to dig up potatoes in the old country. The Irish so loved the potato that they even ate it raw; in *A Tree Grows in Brooklyn*, the poignant novel about immigrant Irish life in the early part of the century, Betty Smith describes the children snacking on raw potatoes, just as good as apples, they thought, and much cheaper! From the apple of the earth in Europe, the potato became the apple of the poor in America.

Potato Chowder with Roasted Garlic and Pepper Puree

Chowder gets its name from the French *chaudière*, a large iron pot used to cook flavorful soups and stews. Although there are no hard and fast rules, a chowder generally implies a hearty, chunky soup. Chowders were originally thickened with stale bread or crackers, but in America they almost always have potatoes as the primary ingredient. This is a simple and robust soup; the roasted garlic is a wonderful foil for the potatoes, providing a smoother and mellower flavor than sautéed garlic.

Serves 4–6

1 medium onion, coarsely chopped
2 Tb. olive oil
1 large red ripe tomato, coarsely chopped
2 medium all-purpose potatoes, peeled and diced
4 cups chicken stock
Several good grinds black pepper
5–6 cloves roasted garlic*
1 large roasted red pepper (homemade, see p. 95, or jarred roasted pepper)
½ cup light cream or half-and-half

1. In a medium saucepan, sauté the onion in the olive oil over moderate heat until the onion is just beginning to turn golden.

2. Add the chopped tomato and sauté 5 minutes or so until the tomato is soft.

3. Add the diced potatoes, mix well, and sauté another few minutes.

4. Stir in the chicken stock and pepper, then simmer, uncovered, over low heat for about 30–40 minutes until the potatoes are very soft.

5. In a blender or food processor combine the roasted garlic, the roasted pepper, and the cream. Blend until smooth, but there is no need to puree completely.

6. Stir the garlic-pepper puree into the hot soup and mix well. Bring just to a simmer, then remove from the heat.

*To roast garlic: Choose a head of garlic with largish cloves, which will make the subsequent peeling easier. Wrap the whole unpeeled head lightly in foil, then place in a 300°F. oven for 50–60 minutes. Remove from the oven, unwrap, and let cool. With your fingers, peel the outer skin from each garlic clove. The inside will be soft, lightly brown, and fragrant.

Bloody Mary's Consommé

Surely the most thorough transformation of the potato after it left its Andean homeland took place half a world away, in Russia, where the versatile tuber was fermented, distilled, and filtered through charcoal to produce that powerful spirit, vodka. Vodka did not return to America until well into the twentieth century, when it became a popular component of mixed drinks. The most famous of these is the Bloody Mary, named for Mary Tudor, the fanatically religious queen who ruled England for five years before Elizabeth I. It is amusing that the way we chose to Americanize vodka was to mix it with two other uniquely New World foods—tomatoes and hot peppers. Here is the Bloody Mary translated into a spicy, heart-warming soup: a nice pick-up for a cold winter day.

Serves 4

1 small onion, minced
1 clove garlic, crushed
1 stalk celery, finely chopped
1 Tb. olive oil
4 cups clear beef stock
3 Tb. tomato paste
½ tsp. celery seed
Good handful fresh celery leaves, chopped
2 Tb. finely chopped flat-leaf Italian parsley
¼–½ tsp. Tabasco sauce
Several good grinds black pepper
½ fresh lime
¼ cup vodka

1. In a medium saucepan sauté the onion, garlic, and celery in the olive oil over moderate heat until the onion is just wilted.

2. Add the stock, tomato paste, celery seeds and leaves, parsley, Tabasco, and black pepper. Bring to the simmer and cook uncovered over low heat for about 20 minutes.

3. Stir in a good squeeze of lime juice, then add the vodka. Bring just to the simmer. Serve hot and pass additional Tabasco sauce to taste.

Colcannon

Wherever the potato has traveled it has combined easily with other vegetables, and the Irish were surely among the very first to discover this. Colcannon is a national dish of Ireland, traditionally eaten on All Hallows' Eve, with tokens of good fortune sometimes hidden in the mixture. This combination of potato, cabbage, and leek makes a wonderful mashed potato dish.

Serves 4–6

3 large leeks, mostly white parts, finely chopped
3 Tb. butter
1 small head green cabbage, coarsely chopped (about 4 cups)
1 cup chicken stock
6 medium all-purpose potatoes
½ cup hot milk
½ tsp. salt
⅛ tsp. freshly ground pepper
2 Tb. snipped fresh chives

1. In a large skillet sauté the leeks in the butter over moderate heat for about 5 minutes, or until the leeks are just tender.

2. Add the cabbage and chicken stock and simmer over low heat for about 10–15 minutes, or until the cabbage is tender.

3. While the cabbage is cooking, boil the potatoes in water to cover until they are soft. Drain and peel quickly.

4. Mash the potatoes with the milk, salt, and pepper. Add the cabbage mixture to the mashed potatoes, and mix well. Stir in the chives.

Potatoes fed the poor of America as well as those of Europe. In this photograph from the late 1800s, potatoes are sold on the lower east side of New York.

Potato Filling

You've heard the ad: "Tired of potatoes? Try stuffing instead!" Well, the Pennsylvania Dutch thought of that long ago by concocting a combination of potatoes and stuffing in the same dish. It's a wonderfully tasty, old-fashioned recipe; it can be served just as is, or as a stuffing for poultry, or baked in a buttered casserole until lightly browned. In the unlikely event you have any left over, form the chilled mixture into small patties, dredge lightly in flour, then sauté until lightly browned in butter or oil. Filling, fattening, and delicious!

Serves 4

2 large all-purpose potatoes, cut in quarters
½ cup milk
1 large onion, finely chopped
2–3 stalks celery, with leaves, finely chopped
2 Tb. butter
1 cup herb-seasoned dry stuffing mix, homemade or store-bought
½ tsp. dried marjoram
½ tsp. dried sage
½ tsp. salt
Several good grinds black pepper

1. Cook the potatoes in their skins in boiling water until quite soft. Drain them, quickly peel off the skins, then mash with the milk.

2. In a medium skillet sauté the onion and the celery in the butter until just wilted.

3. Combine the mashed potatoes, onion mixture, stuffing, and seasonings. Mix thoroughly. If the mixture seems a little thick, add a tablespoon or two more milk.

Digging and transporting potatoes in the Andes— from a seventeenth-century Peruvian codex

Potatoes with Tomatoes and Chile

You like tomato and I like tomahto,
You like potato and I like potahto

So go the lyrics of that old Gershwin classic "Let's Call the Whole Thing Off." However you pronounce them, potatoes and tomatoes go well together and always have. The ancient people of the Peruvian highlands, where the potato was hybridized in a variety of forms never duplicated anywhere else, cooked potatoes with tomatoes and chile peppers in a dish that may well have been very similar to this one. It is easy and extremely good. Use a firm waxy potato like the Red Bliss that will retain its texture after cooking.

Serves 4

1 medium onion, coarsely chopped
3 cloves garlic, crushed
1 small fresh hot red chile, seeded and minced
2 Tb. olive oil
4–5 medium firm waxy potatoes, cut in ½-inch cubes
1 cup canned crushed tomatoes or tomato sauce
½ tsp. salt
½ tsp. oregano
Good handful chopped fresh coriander leaf (cilantro)

1. In a heavy skillet sauté the onion, garlic, and chile pepper in the olive oil over moderate heat, stirring, until the onion begins to brown.

2. Stir in the potato cubes and sauté, stirring, a few minutes more.

3. Add the tomatoes, salt, and oregano, and mix well. Cover the skillet and cook over low heat for about 30–40 minutes until the potatoes are just tender. Uncover the skillet and continue to cook over moderate heat until most of the liquid has cooked away and the potatoes are uniformly coated with the sauce.

4. Stir in the chopped coriander and mix well. Serve hot, but note that this dish is also very good cold or at room temperature.

Patate Tricolore

A bunch of spuds get together to pay homage to Italy, in a tricolored puree that forms the Italian flag. This dish is a bit of a nuisance, as there are three separate purees to be made, but it can be done in advance. It makes an impressive presentation and tastes wonderful, especially for those who love mashed potatoes—and who doesn't?

Serves 6–8

1 10-oz. pkg. frozen chopped spinach, defrosted
6 medium all-purpose white-fleshed potatoes (about 2½ lbs.), peeled
½ cup milk
⅓ cup light cream or milk
4 Tb. butter
2 Tb. freshly grated Parmesan cheese
¼ tsp. nutmeg
Good dash white pepper
1½ tsp. salt
4 Tb. tomato paste
2 Tb. olive oil
¼ tsp. oregano
¼ tsp. dried basil
1 clove garlic, crushed
Several good grinds black pepper

1. Drain the defrosted spinach and squeeze as much liquid from it as possible; set aside.

2. Cook the potatoes in boiling water until they are very tender. Drain thoroughly.

3. To make the green puree: combine ⅓ of the potatoes, the spinach, ¼ cup of the milk, 2 Tb. of the butter, the Parmesan, the nutmeg, ½ tsp. of the salt, and several grinds of black pepper. Puree until smooth.

4. To make the white puree: combine ⅓ of the potatoes, the ⅓ cup light cream or milk, the remaining 2 Tb. butter, ½ tsp. of the salt, and the white pepper. Puree until smooth.

5. To make the red puree: combine the remaining potatoes, the remaining ¼ cup milk, the tomato paste, the remaining ½ tsp. salt, several grinds of black pepper, and the garlic. Puree until smooth. Stir in the olive oil, the oregano, and the basil, and mix well. Preheat the oven to 350°F.

6. Generously butter a rectangular glass or ceramic baking dish (a 9 x 12-inch Pyrex dish is fine). Spoon the green puree into one end of the dish, the white puree in the middle, and the red puree at the other end.

7. Cover the baking dish lightly with foil. Bake for 20–30 minutes until the purees are bubbly. Remove the dish from the oven, uncover, and let stand for 5 minutes or so before serving.

A scarcity of potatoes in England early in the 1900s and during World War I was commemorated in humorous and nostalgic postcards. An American GI in World War II, however, bemoans an overabundance of spuds in KP.

Potato Moussaka

Wherever the potato was accepted it took on the characteristic seasonings of its new home—bacon and vinegar in Germany, curry spices in India, sour cream and dill in Scandinavia. In Greece and Turkey the potato was appropriated for any number of dishes that traditionally used other vegetables or grains, like rice and eggplant. Moussaka is a dish of layered eggplant and meat sauce, topped with a *béchamel*-type sauce. With sliced potatoes substituting for the eggplant it is a recipe that is particularly appealing to Americans, who love ground beef in tomato sauce on just about anything; the cinnamon and allspice provide a flavor that is familiar and well liked.

Serves 4–6

4 medium potatoes, sliced about ¼-inch thick
1–2 Tb. vegetable oil
1 lb. lean ground beef (ground chicken or turkey may be substituted)
2 Tb. olive oil
1 medium onion, chopped
2 cups tomato sauce
1¼ tsp. salt
⅛ tsp. black pepper
1½ tsp. cinnamon
¼ tsp. ground allspice
1 lb. small-curd cottage cheese
2 eggs
3 Tb. freshly grated Parmesan cheese
¼ tsp. nutmeg
Several good grinds black pepper
Paprika

1. Cook the potato slices in boiling water for 5 minutes. Drain and set aside.

2. In a large heavy skillet heat the vegetable oil over moderate to high heat. Add the ground beef and brown quickly, crumbling the meat with a spoon as it browns. When the meat has completely lost its pink color, remove it from the pan with a slotted spoon and set aside. Pour off and discard any fat in the pan.

3. Add the olive oil to the pan, then the onion, and sauté over moderate heat, stirring, until the onion begins to turn golden.

4. Stir in the tomato sauce, 1 tsp. of the salt, the pepper, cinnamon, and allspice. Add the browned beef to the tomato sauce, mix well, then cook, uncovered, over low heat for 15–20 minutes.

5. In a blender or food processor combine the cottage cheese, the eggs, the Parmesan, nutmeg, pepper to taste, and the remaining salt. Process until smooth and well blended. Preheat the oven to 350°F.

6. To assemble, spoon half of the meat sauce over the bottom of a buttered 2- to 2½-quart casserole. Spread the potatoes in an even layer over the sauce. Salt and pepper the potatoes lightly. Spoon the remaining meat sauce over the potatoes.

7. Spoon the cottage cheese mixture evenly over the meat layer. Sprinkle it lightly with paprika.

8. Bake the moussaka for 30–40 minutes until the top is firm and lightly browned and the sauce is bubbling up through the topping.

Clay bottle in the form of the "Potato Mother," from pre-Columbian Peru

Potatoes with Clams and Tomatoes

The Portuguese fishermen who settled on the southern coast of New England brought with them a taste for seafood and an already established tradition of tomato sauces. The famous "Manhattan-style" clam chowder was probably of Portuguese origination. This casserole, of a New England staple, potatoes, baked with a richly flavored clam and tomato sauce, is similarly inspired. It is a satisfying earthy dish, and relatively low in fat and calories.

Serves 4–5

2 Tb. olive oil

1 medium onion, chopped

3 large cloves garlic, crushed

1 28-oz. can crushed Italian-style tomatoes

½ tsp. salt

⅛ tsp. pepper

½ cup finely chopped flat-leaf Italian parsley, plus additional
     chopped parsley for garnish

1 cup coarsely chopped fresh clam meat (about ½ lb.)

4–5 medium Russet or other all-purpose potatoes, peeled and thinly sliced

Salt and pepper

10–12 littleneck clams, in shell, well scrubbed

1. In a large skillet heat the oil over moderate heat. Add the onion and the garlic and sauté, stirring, until the onion wilts and begins to turn golden.

2. Add the tomatoes, the salt and pepper, and the chopped parsley. Bring to the simmer, then cook over low heat for 10–15 minutes. Remove from the heat and stir in the chopped clams. Preheat the oven to 350°F.

3. Lightly oil a 2½- to 3-quart casserole. Spoon 3–4 Tb. of the tomato-clam sauce over the bottom of the casserole. Spread ½ of the sliced potatoes in an even layer over the sauce. Salt and pepper the potatoes lightly. Spoon ½ of the remaining tomato-clam sauce over the potatoes. Spread the rest of the potatoes over the sauce, salt and pepper them lightly, then spread the rest of the sauce over the potatoes.

4. Cover the casserole and bake for about 40 minutes until the potatoes are tender when pierced with a sharp knife.

5. Place the clams, hinge side down, over the top of the sauce, pressing them in very lightly. Cover the casserole and bake for 10–15 minutes, or just until the clams have opened.

6. Garnish the casserole with the chopped parsley and serve hot.

Oven-Fried or Roasted Potatoes

French-fried potatoes—*frites* to the French, "chips" to the Brits, "fries" to us—are one of the world's most popular foods, and with good reason. Something wonderful happened when the Incan potato met up with the frying traditions of Europe. Crisp and browned on the outside, soft and melting on the inside, potatoes cooked in hot oil or fat seem to have an almost universal appeal, whether deep fried, panfried or sautéed, or, as in this recipe, oven fried or roasted. It is a very easy dish, a favorite of my sons, who seem to be able to consume unlimited quantities. The recipe works equally well with sweet potatoes.

Serves 4

¼ cup vegetable oil
½ tsp. paprika
4–5 medium Idaho or Russet potatoes, well scrubbed, dried,
and cut in 1-inch cubes (no need to peel)
Salt

1. In a large rimmed baking pan combine the oil and the paprika. Mix well. Preheat the oven to 300–325°F.

2. Toss the potato cubes in the oil, turning them so that all the potato surfaces are coated with oil. Spread the cubes evenly over the pan. Don't worry about excess oil; it will get used.

3. Bake the potatoes for 1½ hours. Turn the cubes with a spatula every 20–30 minutes to insure even browning. When the potatoes are done they will be crisp and browned on the outside, but still soft on the inside, and all the oil will have been absorbed.

4. Sprinkle the potatoes with salt to taste and serve hot.

Note: These potatoes can be additionally flavored if you like. Oregano, cumin, garlic, chili powder, or crushed dried hot pepper are all good. Sprinkle the seasoning over the potatoes for the last few minutes of cooking.

Deluxe Scalloped Potatoes

Besides French-frying, France developed many recipes that have become classics of the potato repertoire. The Gallic talent for butter, cream, and cheese is central to many of the creamed, scalloped, gratinéed potato dishes that are so widely popular. In this recipe, the ingredients and flavors have shifted somewhat to a more American taste. Cheddar cheese, a familiar legacy from our English heritage, also known popularly as "rat" or "coon" cheese, substitutes for the Swiss-type cheeses of French tradition; onions, tomatoes, and bacon contribute their flavor to the homespun character of this rich and hearty dish.

Serves 6–8

6 cups thinly sliced, peeled all-purpose potatoes (about 6–7 medium potatoes)
5–6 slices bacon
4 Tb. butter
2 medium onions, chopped
2 beefsteak-type tomatoes, coarsely chopped
1½ tsp. salt
Several good grinds black pepper
2 Tb. flour
1½ cups milk
⅛ tsp. black pepper
⅛ tsp. cayenne pepper
⅛ tsp. dry mustard
2 cups (8 oz.) shredded sharp Cheddar cheese

1. Cook the sliced potatoes in boiling water until they are just tender when pierced with a sharp knife. Drain thoroughly and set aside.

2. In a medium skillet fry the bacon until it is crisp. Remove the bacon from the pan, crumble, and set aside. Pour off and discard all the fat in the pan.

3. In the same skillet melt 2 Tb. of the butter over moderate heat. Add the onions and sauté, stirring, until they are soft and a light golden color.

4. Add the chopped tomatoes to the onions and continue to cook, stirring occasionally, until almost all of the liquid has cooked away and the mixture is a thick soft puree. Stir in ½ tsp. of the salt and several grinds of pepper and set aside.

5. In a large saucepan heat the remaining 2 Tb. butter over low heat. Stir in the flour to make a *roux*. Cook, stirring, over low heat for 2–3 minutes.

6. Add the milk gradually, stirring briskly. Bring the sauce to the simmer, stirring, until it is smooth and thickened.

7. Remove the sauce from the heat, stir in the black and cayenne peppers, the mustard, the remaining 1 tsp. salt, and the cheese. Stir until the sauce is smooth and well blended. Add the drained potatoes and mix well.

8. Preheat the oven to 350°F. Generously butter a deep 2- to 2½-quart casserole.

9. Spread half of the sauced potatoes in the casserole. Spread half of the onion-tomato mixture over them. Spoon the remaining potatoes into the casserole and top with the remaining onion-tomato mixture.

10. Bake the casserole for 50–60 minutes until it is bubbling throughout. Sprinkle the reserved crumbled bacon over the top.

Turn-of-the-century cheesecake! A promotional photo of a fetching female preparing potato "eyes" for planting.

The Fattening Factor

Somewhere along the line potatoes got the reputation of being fattening, a label that is undeserved but understandable, given the popular traditions of potato cookery in Europe and America. It is not the potato's fault that it tastes so good fried or sautéed, or lavished with such high-fat foods as butter, cream, and cheese. Once those high-calorie additives are stripped away, the potato comes out innocent—and fairly lean. Compared with the kinds of carbohydrate foods that we use in place of the potato, it contains fewer calories per serving than any of them. Consider: a medium-sized (150 grams) baked or boiled potato contains about 100 calories. A serving portion (1 cup) of cooked spaghetti contains 160 calories, a cup of noodles 200 calories, and ¾ cup cooked rice 170 calories. One little innocent hot dog roll (without the hot dog) has 140 calories, while 1 cup of plain regular yogurt has 120 calories. So rethink your diet strategy. The potato is actually a very useful weight-loss food. It provides a satisfying, stick-to-the-ribs experience but is relatively low in calories, provided you avoid the really fattening additives. Steamed, delicate little new potatoes are delicious with just a squeeze of lemon and a sprinkling of fresh herbs; parsley and chives are always good, while dill or rosemary add a special touch. In India they make a spectacular dish of cubed potatoes cooked with yogurt, garlic, and fresh coriander. Try cooking potatoes in stock or zesty tomato sauce, as they do in the Mediterranean, rather than dressing them in cream or cheese sauces. And when you're really hungry, a plain baked potato with a little salt and pepper tastes mighty good and contains fewer calories than ½ cup of—ugh—cottage cheese!

Gratin of Potato and Root Vegetables

Provided you have an electric grater or shredding device, this is an easy and flavorful winter vegetable dish. No extravagant seasonings, just the simple earthy flavors of root vegetables, the combination makes a nice accompaniment to any roast meat or poultry.

Serves 6

3 eggs
½ cup light cream
2 tsp. salt
¼ tsp. black pepper
1 medium onion, grated
2 carrots, grated
1 parsnip, grated
1 medium yellow turnip (rutabaga), peeled and grated
4 medium all-purpose potatoes, peeled and grated
3 Tb. butter, melted

1. In a large bowl whisk the eggs lightly. Stir in the cream, the salt and the pepper, and mix thoroughly.

2. Add all the grated vegetables to the egg mixture and mix very well. Preheat the oven to 400°F.

3. Turn the mixture into a well-buttered large shallow casserole or baking dish, approximately 2 to 3 quarts. Smooth it out with the back of a large spoon to make an even layer. Pour the melted butter evenly over all.

4. Bake the gratin for 40–45 minutes until it is browned and crisp around the edges. Serve hot.

The "micky" vendor with his portable potato baker

Saffron Potato Rolls

In ancient Andean cooking, the potato was used both as a vegetable, and, because of its high starch content, dried and milled into a flour for bread. Although the potato was accepted in most of the Old World primarily as a vegetable, it found its place in a number of breads; both the potatoes themselves and the water in which they were cooked were used to enrich traditional raised wheat and whole-grain loaves, adding moistness and a delicate flavor. These rich golden rolls, fragrant with saffron and honey, have a flavor reminiscent of the traditional Jewish challah.

Makes 30–36 rolls

¼ tsp. saffron threads
¼ cup hot water
¾ cup warm water (can be the water in which the potatoes were cooked)
¼ cup honey
1 Tb. granulated yeast
1 cup plain unseasoned mashed potatoes
½ tsp. salt
2 eggs, lightly beaten
4–5 cups all-purpose flour
3 Tb. butter, melted

1. In a small bowl or cup soak the saffron threads in the ¼ cup hot water for 30 minutes.

2. In a large mixing bowl combine the ¾ cup warm water and the honey; mix well. Sprinkle the yeast over the liquid and let proof for a few minutes. Stir in the saffron water.

3. Add the mashed potatoes, the salt, the eggs, 1 cup of the flour, and the melted butter. Beat the mixture until it is smooth and well blended.

4. Stir in enough additional flour to make a firm, non-sticky dough. Knead the dough thoroughly until it is smooth and elastic.

5. Place the dough in a lightly greased bowl, cover, and let rise in a warm place for about 1 hour or until doubled in bulk. Punch the dough down and knead lightly.

6. Lightly butter three 9-inch cake or pie pans. Pinch off pieces of the dough, about the size of a golf ball. Form into balls and place them, lightly touching each other, in the pans, about 10–12 balls per pan. Cover the pans and let the rolls rise for about 1 hour or until doubled in bulk. Preheat the oven to 350°F.

7. Bake the rolls for about 15 minutes until they are lightly browned. Remove from the oven and cool on a rack. (If you want to freeze some of the rolls, then let them cool completely in the pans; wrap tightly in plastic wrap and freeze.) Serve the rolls warm with plenty of sweet butter.

Potato Latkes

The potato's versatility is clearly evident in the dozens of fritters, cakes, pancakes, and croquettes that developed in cuisines all over the world. They are most commonly made with cold cooked mashed potatoes combined with bits of leftover fish, chicken, or vegetables, and fried in hot fat or oil until golden brown. The latke, or potato pancake, that developed in eastern Europe, is a little different because it uses grated raw potato. It is a traditional dish for the Jewish celebration of Chanukah and is served with either applesauce or sour cream.

Serves 4–6

6 large potatoes (Idaho, Russet, or all-purpose), peeled
1 large onion
3 eggs, lightly beaten
3 Tb. flour
1 tsp. baking powder
2 tsp. salt
⅛ tsp. black pepper
3–4 Tb. vegetable oil
Sour cream or applesauce

1. Soak the peeled potatoes in cold water to cover for 1 hour. Drain and dry well.

2. Grate the potatoes and the onion together. Stir the eggs into the grated mixture, then mix in the flour, the baking powder, the salt, and the pepper.

3. In a large heavy frying pan heat the oil over moderate to high heat. Drop large tablespoonfuls of the potato mixture into the oil and fry until it is golden brown on one side. Turn the pancakes and brown on the other side. Do not crowd the pan while frying the latkes.

4. Serve the latkes hot, with sour cream or applesauce. (The latkes can be made early in the day, then reheated in a 350°F. oven for about 15 minutes.)

Potatoes Vinaigrette

Of the many ways that the potato adapted itself into the culinary traditions of Europe, its combination with the vinaigrette, the classic sauce of oil and vinegar, was one of the simplest and one of the best. It makes an easy and flexible dish that can be served as is, like a potato salad, or as a part of an antipasto or marinated vegetable platter. Any number of seasonings—mustard, garlic, herbs—can be added for variety. Use a firm waxy potato like the Yukon Gold or the Red Bliss that will keep its shape and not fall apart when mixed with the sauce. The cooked potatoes can be sliced or cubed according to personal preference, but should be dressed with the sauce while they are still warm.

Serves 4–6

> 4–5 medium firm, waxy potatoes
> 3 large leeks, white parts only, sliced
> ½ cup olive oil
> ⅓ cup white wine vinegar
> 2 Tb. Dijon mustard
> ¼–½ tsp. salt
> Several good grinds black pepper
> Chopped parsley or snipped chives for garnish

1. Cook the potatoes in boiling water until they are just tender when pierced with a sharp knife. Add the sliced leeks for the last few minutes of cooking. Drain the potatoes and the leeks and cool slightly.

2. In a small bowl or jar with a tight lid combine the oil, the vinegar, the mustard, the salt (start with ¼ tsp.), and the pepper. Whisk or shake to blend thoroughly. Taste for salt and add a bit more if necessary.

3. When the potatoes are just cool enough to handle, peel off the skins, then slice or dice.

4. In a large bowl combine the potatoes, the leeks, and about one third of the vinaigrette sauce. Mix the vegetables lightly but thoroughly with the dressing. Let stand for an hour or two, then taste and add more vinaigrette if desired. Serve the potatoes at room temperature, garnished with the chopped parsley or chives.

Notes: For a nice variation, omit the leeks; dice the cooked potatoes and combine them with 2 lbs. fresh mussels, steamed and shelled. Toss the potatoes and the mussels with the vinaigrette, adding a good handful of chopped fresh dill and a small minced onion.

For a beautiful presentation, cook equal amounts of a golden-fleshed potato and the Peruvian purple potato. Slice the cooked, peeled potatoes and arrange the slices in an attractive pattern on a serving plate. Pour some of the vinaigrette over the potatoes and let stand for an hour or two. Taste and add more sauce if necessary. Garnish the potatoes with a sieved egg yolk and some curly parsley, and serve at the table with an arrangement of purple and yellow irises. It makes a spectacular dish, and it tastes good, too.

Two proud farmers and their prize spuds were captured on film in a tintype, c. 1905, and a 1908 postcard.

All-American Potato Salad

Potato salad is as American as just about anything and is a prime example of how an indigenous New World vegetable was transformed into something uniquely ours through a variety of European influences. Mayonnaise-based salad dressings became very popular here at the end of the nineteenth century and have remained a national favorite. The secret to a successful potato salad of any sort is to mix the dressing with the potatoes while they are still warm so that some of the dressing is absorbed.

Serves 6

6 large all-purpose potatoes
¾ cup mayonnaise
⅓ cup cider vinegar
1 Tb. sugar
¼ tsp. salt, or to taste
¼ tsp. freshly ground black pepper
½ tsp. celery seed
3 stalks celery, diced
1 medium sweet green pepper, seeded and diced
1 small onion, finely chopped, or 6 scallions, chopped

1. Scrub the potatoes thoroughly; then boil them in their jackets until just tender. Do not overcook; the potatoes should pierce easily with a sharp knife but should not be too soft or mushy.

2. While the potatoes are cooking, make the dressing: In a small bowl combine the mayonnaise, vinegar, sugar, salt, pepper, and celery seed. Whisk until smooth and completely blended.

3. When the potatoes are done, drain and rinse them in cold water. Quickly peel off the skin, then cut the potatoes into small cubes.

4. Combine the potato cubes and dressing; mix gently but thoroughly.

5. Mix in the remaining chopped vegetables. Let the salad stand for an hour or two, then taste for salt and pepper. The salad can be served chilled or (as I prefer) at room temperature.

Caribbean Seafood Pie in Sweet Potato Crust

This is an unusual and delicious dish, based on the "batata" or "camote" that Columbus found in the West Indies. It is important to use real sweet potatoes, and preferably the white-fleshed ones. Don't substitute yams, as they are too sweet for this. The seafood can be a mixture of shrimp, prawns, or crabmeat, and scallops are also excellent, if unorthodox. This recipe is an interesting mixture of ethnic traditions—native, Hispanic, Indian, and English—a fine example of Creole cooking.

Serves 4

4 medium sweet potatoes, peeled and cubed
¼ cup milk
1 Tb. butter
1¼ tsp. salt
2 Tb. vegetable oil
1 medium onion, chopped
1 medium sweet green pepper, seeded and diced
1 small fresh hot green chile pepper, seeded and minced,
*   or ¼ tsp. crushed dried hot peppers*
1 tsp. finely minced gingerroot
4–5 small plum tomatoes, coarsely chopped (about 1 cup chopped)
⅛ tsp. freshly ground black pepper
2 tsp. curry powder
½ cup unsweetened coconut milk (see p. 239)
1–1¼ lbs. any one or mixture of peeled raw shrimp or prawns,
*   crabmeat, or scallops*

1. Cook the sweet potatoes in boiling water until very tender; drain, then mash with the milk. Stir in the butter and ¾ teaspoon of the salt and set aside.

2. In a large skillet heat the oil over moderate heat. Add the onion, the green pepper, the chile pepper, and the gingerroot. Sauté, stirring, until the onion begins to turn golden.

3. Stir in the chopped tomatoes and cook, stirring occasionally, until most of the liquid has cooked away and the mixture is soft and thick. This will take about 10–15 minutes, depending on the amount of liquid the tomatoes exude.

continued

Caribbean Seafood Pie continued

4. Stir in the remaining ½ teaspoon salt, the black pepper, the curry powder, and the coconut milk. Simmer over low heat for about 5 minutes, stirring occasionally, until the mixture is slightly thickened.

5. Add the seafood, mix well, and simmer, stirring, for a few minutes.

6. Preheat the oven to 350°F. Butter a deep 9-inch pie dish. Spoon the mashed potatoes into the dish, spreading them evenly with a spoon to form a shell over the bottom and the sides. Spoon the seafood mixture over the potatoes.

7. Bake the pie for about 20 minutes until the seafood mixture is just bubbling. Serve hot.

A Type for Every Taste

Potatoes in America are classified according to four basic types: round white, long white, round red, and long red. These account for most of the potatoes commonly found in our markets, but do not include the many dozens of varieties that exist throughout the world and particularly in the ancient Andean hearth. For most cooks texture is a crucial factor in selecting the proper potato; Idahos and Russets are somewhat mealy, making them a splendid choice for baking or French frying, while the Red Bliss and the newer golden-fleshed varieties have a firmer, more waxy texture that makes them ideal for salads and casseroles. All-purpose potatoes are, as their name suggests, appropriate for almost any treatment—boiling, frying, mashing, or baking. New potatoes are not a separate variety, but simply the first and youngest fruits of the harvest, valued for their sweet delicate flavor and tender skin. As with any other fruit or vegetable, the older the product, the less the flavor. Have fun with a potato tasting. Round up as many varieties as you can and cook them in a number of ways to see the effects that different techniques have on texture and flavor. And try experimenting with some of the more unusual varieties—the buttery little Finnish yellow, for example, or the beautifully colored Peruvian purple.

Sweet Potato Pone

The pone was originally a native North American dish, a flat cornmeal bread baked in hot ashes. The term was eventually broadened to define a variety of baked dishes and, particularly in the South, to include sweet potatoes and yams. This pone is quite elegant and makes a nice accompaniment to a holiday roast or turkey. The flaming with rum at the end is optional but adds good flavor and a bit of drama! As for the choice between cooking syrup or corn syrup (both available in the supermarket), the South prefers cooking syrup, which is based on cane sugar and therefore has a slight molasses flavor. Corn syrup is made from corn sugar and has no significant flavor other than that it is sweet. Sweet potato pone can be served along with the main course or, if you prefer, as dessert.

Serves 6–8

> 2 eggs
> 1 cup milk
> ½ cup cooking syrup or dark corn syrup
> ½ cup firmly packed brown sugar
> 1 tsp. cinnamon
> ¼ tsp. ground allspice
> ½ tsp. salt
> 1 lb. sweet potatoes, peeled and grated (about 4 cups grated)
> 2 medium tart-sweet apples, peeled, cored, and grated
> 3 Tb. butter
> 3–4 Tb. dark or golden rum

1. In a large bowl whisk the eggs thoroughly, then stir in the milk and the syrup.

2. Add the sugar, the spices, and the salt and mix thoroughly.

3. Add the grated potatoes and apples and mix well. Preheat the oven to 350°F.

4. Spread the mixture in a buttered shallow 1½- to 2-quart baking dish or casserole. Dot the top with the butter, cut in small pieces.

5. Bake the pone for about 40 minutes until it is set and lightly browned.

6. Bring the hot pone to the table and pour the rum over the top. Ignite the rum with a match and let it flame until the alcohol burns off.

Sweet Potato Cake with Toffee–Cream Cheese Frosting

The sweet potato was encountered by Columbus on his very first voyage to the West Indies and it reached Europe well before the white potato, which had to wait until the conquistadores reached Mexico and Peru some twenty years later. Although it has no botanic relationship to the yam, which is a native of Southeast Asia and Africa, the sweet potato was so similar in appearance and flavor that it was called the "foreign yam" or the "English tuber" by Asian people, who adopted it as a productive and nourishing food for the poor. Wherever it has traveled, the sweet potato has been valued for its sweet flavor, emphasized here in a moist and spicy cake.

Serves 8–10

1 cup vegetable oil

2 cups sugar

4 eggs

2 cups flour

2 tsp. baking soda

1 tsp. salt

2 tsp. cinnamon

1 tsp. ginger

½ tsp. ground allspice

1 lb. sweet potatoes, peeled and grated (about 4 cups grated)

1. Beat the oil and the sugar together, then add the eggs one at a time, beating well after each addition.

2. Combine the dry ingredients and add them to the sugar-oil mixture; mix until well blended.

3. Add the grated sweet potatoes to the mixture and mix well. Preheat the oven to 350°F.

4. Pour the batter into a buttered 13 x 9 x 2-inch baking pan or a 10-inch bundt pan. Bake the cake for 45–50 minutes until it is lightly browned and firm to the touch. Remove from the oven and cool. When the cake is thoroughly cooled, frost with the Toffee–Cream Cheese Frosting.

TOFFEE–CREAM CHEESE FROSTING

¼ cup butter
½ cup firmly packed brown sugar
2 Tb. strong coffee
½ tsp. vanilla
4 oz. cream cheese, softened
½ cup chopped pecans or walnuts

1. In a small saucepan melt the butter, then stir in the brown sugar. Bring to the boil, stirring constantly. Stir in the coffee and bring to the boil again.

2. Remove the pan from the heat and stir in the vanilla.

3. Cool slightly, then beat the toffee mixture into the cream cheese.

4. Frost the cake with the frosting, then garnish with the nuts.

A sweet potato vendor in Harlem in the 1920s

Five Pepper Soup
Goulash Soup
Vegetable Gumbo
Island Pepper Pot
Southwest Lamb Chili
Texas Red
Indian Spiced Lamb with Peppers
Calves' Liver with Green Chile Sauce
All-American Stuffed Peppers
Dim-Sum Stuffed Peppers
Chicken Paprika
Mushrooms Paprika
Roast Pepper Romesco Sauce
Chicken Pimiento Loaf
Fish Fillets with Chile
Puerto Rican Pepper Sofrito
Pepper, Eggplant, and Walnut Caviar
Tortellini Salad with Mixed Peppers
Pepper Steak
Pepper Hash
Sweet Pepper Focaccia
Chile-Ginger Dessert Sauce

CAPSICUM PEPPERS

Of the many Oriental spices that were coveted by Europe—cinnamon, nutmeg, ginger, cloves—none was so valuable as pepper. Pepper! In the fifteenth century it was a word to evoke exotic climes, luxurious dining, wealth, and prestige. It was literally worth its weight in gold, and it was in large part for the sake of the little black berry, *Piper nigrum,* that the great navigators of Europe vied to find the shortest route to the East Indies. Access to pepper and other spices was money in the bank and it was for this reason that Columbus was able to persuade his Spanish patrons to finance his wild dream of reaching the East by sailing west, a dream that might have been realized but for a large land mass in the way—the New World, with its hitherto undiscovered riches.

One of these treasures was almost immediately evident. Neither gold nor jewels, but the fiery chile, the favorite seasoning of the Caribbean natives, used almost constantly to perk up their diet of fish, beans, maize, and cassava. Called "aji" by these tribes, the chile had pungency and flavor-enhancing qualities that were soon appreciated by the Spanish sailors, whose palates must have been sorely in need of a lift after months of salt pork and hard ship biscuit. Although much more powerful in its effect, chile did the same thing to bland food as the black pepper the Spanish had so fervently hoped to find, and so they called it *pimiento,* the existing Spanish word for pepper. Of course we know now that chile has no botanic relationship to true pepper, but pepper will forever be its name. By around 1700 chiles had been classified botanically as capsicum peppers, and it is by this name that they are known throughout the world today.

Seeds of the capsicum peppers were brought back to Europe by Columbus' crew and were growing in Spanish gardens by about 1500. After only a few decades, the pungent "aji" discovered in the Caribbean had made its way around the world, carried from port to port by Spanish and Portuguese navigators. By the early part of the sixteenth century it was well established in India, Southeast Asia, and parts of Africa, finding enthusiastic acceptance in the cuisines of warm and sub-tropical climates that were already geared to piquancy and pungency.

The whole family of capsicum peppers, and particularly the pungent varieties, had reached a full and complex level of development in the kitchens of the Mayas and the Aztecs of Mexico by the time the conquering Spanish armies arrived. Chroniclers of Aztec culture who traveled with Cortez reported dozens of varieties in the great open market of Tenochtitlán: chiles of every color, size, and piquancy; chiles that were fresh, dried, roasted, and smoked; chiles that were cooked with fish, with game, with beans, with corn; chiles that flavored soups, beverages, sauces, and stews. This elaborate chile tradition, which developed over many thousands of years, continues today, with new varieties being hybridized and new culinary treatments enlarging and enriching the ancient practices. Mexican cooks have had a long and passionate love affair with chiles, carefully exploiting every nuance of pungency and flavor, and achieving in that enterprise a cuisine of great subtlety and refinement.

Largely because the chile pepper was appropriated outside its ancestral home primarily for its pungency, the Old World has never fully appreciated the depth and range of its seasoning capacities. Chiles, in the few centuries since their discovery, have become the single most widely used spice in the world, eaten on a daily basis, it is reported, by at least one quarter of the world's adult population. But this phenomenal success, unprecedented in culinary history, is based almost solely on "hotness" and not on the complex flavors that became so elaborated in the New World tradition. Indeed, it was not until very recent times that Americans have begun to truly appreciate and experiment with the full culinary possibilities of the chile peppers. Where once not so very long ago our national access to chiles was limited to little cans of ground cayenne or crushed dried hot red peppers, our supermarkets are now beginning to stock a variety of peppers in different forms—jalapeños, anchos, serranos, habaneros, fresh, dried, pickled, and canned. And our guide for the use and appreciation of these chile varieties is the ancient culinary tradition of Mexico.

If the chile peppers, the "hot" capsicums, became markedly simplified in their triumphant conquest of the Old World, the experience of the "sweet" capsicums, or what we now call the green or bell peppers, was almost exactly the opposite. Ancient Amerindians grew the sweet pepper and ate it, as the Spanish reported, whole and fresh, like a piece of fruit. It does not seem to have played a major role in the cooking or flavoring practices. But when it hit the cuisines of the Old World all sorts of marvelous and innovative things began to happen. Imagine if you will Mediterranean food without its underpinning of roasted and sautéed peppers in olive oil, Hungarian cuisine without its identifying hallmark of paprika, Middle Eastern food without its stuffed peppers, its savory salads and relishes. The sweet bell pepper, from its relatively simple origins, became elaborated into a myriad of new forms, most of which have returned to play a central and intrinsic role in American cooking.

The culinary development of the sweet pepper took four basic forms, the first two of which occurred in its original port of entry, Spain. Here, perhaps in imitation of the Mexican practice of chile-roasting, sweet peppers were charred over open fires, then peeled and marinated in olive oil. So was born the pimiento, that delectable component of sauces, salads, and antipasto platters, and so was consummated the marriage of peppers and olive oil, an intimate relationship symbolized by that most familiar of Spanish products, the olive stuffed with a bit of red pimiento. The second Spanish innovation was the addition of sweet peppers to the *sofrito,* the slow stewing of onions in olive oil, a flavoring technique that underlies much of the cooking of the Mediterranean today.

The two other major elaborations of sweet pepper cookery came from the east, through Turkey, which was at the time the primary cultural and mercantile disseminator of goods from the New World. From Turkish cuisine itself came the practice of stuffing sweet peppers with rice and ground meat and vegetables. For a Middle Eastern tradition that was already rich in stuffed vegetables—eggplant, cabbage, vine leaves—the bell pepper appeared on the scene as a ready-made container, its sweet characteristic flavor blending easily with familiar ingredients. And from Hungary, which was introduced to the peppers by the Turks through their Balkan provinces, came the development of what is now an indispensable and commonplace coloring and seasoning agent—paprika—the dried ground powder made from sweet and pungent red capsicums.

Every one of these novel ways of cooking with sweet peppers has come back to the New World to play a fundamental part in American cuisine, and America herself has devised a number of ingenious uses for the sweet pepper in relishes, pickles, and salads. What left these shores a simple vegetable, eaten out of hand, has returned as an ingredient of marvelous complexity, with culinary possibilities that are still being explored. Columbus probably never really knew what he had discovered, but most of the world today knows, and appreciates. The capsicum peppers, both hot and sweet, can truly be called the culinary gold of the New World. They pique the palate and flavor the food of millions; they have transformed and shaped cuisines the world over. And they continue to develop as a beloved and integral force in the unique character of American cooking. From deviled eggs to chili dogs, from Tabasco sauce to spaghetti sauce, from the *dim sum* tea house to the neighborhood pizzeria, peppers are a large part of what we eat.

Five Pepper Soup

An early Spanish observer wrote of chile peppers: "...if you mix an almond sauce with them, you will taste nothing more delicious, you can devour nothing more appetizing." This richly flavored and highly colored soup does just that, combining toasted almonds with no less than five forms of pepper. It is a tribute to the Spanish genius for pepper cookery, containing sweet peppers sautéed in olive oil, roasted peppers, and paprika, as well as cayenne and the Mexican ancho.

Serves 4–6

2 Tb. olive oil
1 medium onion, coarsely chopped
1 large clove garlic, crushed
2 large sweet red peppers, seeded and coarsely chopped
3 roasted red peppers, homemade or jarred (see p. 95)
4 cups chicken stock
1 dried ancho chile, seeded and torn in pieces, or 1 Tb. ground ancho chile
1 tsp. paprika
Good dash cayenne pepper
⅓ cup whole roasted almonds, lightly toasted
Garlic croutons for garnish, if desired

1. In a medium saucepan heat the oil over moderate heat. Add the onion, the garlic, and the chopped fresh peppers and sauté, stirring, for about 15 minutes, until the onions and the peppers are very soft.

2. Stir in the roasted peppers, the stock, the ancho chile, the paprika, and the cayenne. Bring to the simmer, then cook over low heat, uncovered, for about 20–30 minutes.

3. With a slotted spoon remove the vegetables from the soup and place in a blender or food processor. Add the toasted almonds and a little liquid from the soup, and process until the mixture is smooth. (The almonds will remain slightly grainy; this is fine, as it provides texture for the soup.)

4. Return the puree to the soup and heat just to the simmering point. Serve hot, garnished with garlic croutons, if desired.

At the turn of the century, food trade cards were as popular as baseball cards are today. This one depicts a sweet pepper "plantation" and harvest in Spain.

Goulash Soup

The goulash is an ancient dish of the Hungarian Magyars, a hearty stew of meat and sausage cooked in an iron pot over an open fire. When peppers arrived in Hungary they were incorporated into goulash, both in fresh form and powdered as paprika. When goulash came to America, it changed character once again, joining forces with beef and tomatoes to constitute a whole new tradition of filling, flavorful soups and stews that became a mainstay of the home kitchen and the roadside diner. One of the endearing qualities of this soup, like so many of its type, is that it improves with age, so don't be afraid to make it a day or two in advance.

Serves 6–8

2 Tb. vegetable oil
1 large onion, chopped
2 carrots, sliced or coarsely chopped
2 large cloves garlic, crushed
2 sweet red and/or green peppers, seeded and diced
½ lb. lean boneless beef, diced
1 Tb. paprika (preferably Hungarian sweet)
10 cups water
3 Tb. tomato paste
¼ tsp. black pepper
1 medium all-purpose potato, peeled and diced
2 tsp. salt, or to taste

1. In a large heavy pot heat the oil over moderate heat. Add the onion, the carrots, the garlic, and the sweet peppers. Sauté, stirring, until the onion and peppers are soft and the onion is beginning to brown.

2. Add the diced beef and the paprika and sauté, stirring, for another few minutes. There is no need to brown the beef completely.

3. Add the water, the tomato paste, and the pepper. Mix well, bring to the simmer, then cook, uncovered, over low to moderate heat for about 3 hours. Skim off any scum that may rise to the surface while the soup is cooking.

4. Add the diced potato and cook until tender.

5. Add the salt to taste and mix well.

Confusing Nomenclature

The best-known term for capsicum peppers, particularly those of the pungent variety, is chile, variously spelled chili or chillie. It comes directly from Nahuatl, the language of the Aztecs, in which *chil* or *chili* was the generic root term for all the capsicum peppers. To this root was appended a suffix or prefix designating the specific type; the same linguistic process endures today, except that the adjectival suffix has become separated from the root, resulting in such terms as chile ancho, chile poblano, chile verde, and so on. The word *chile*, meaning the pungent capsicums, is to be distinguished from the word *chili*, now commonly accepted as the name of a dish of North American invention, a stew of meat or beans or both heavily seasoned with chile peppers. Chili powder is the seasoning compound typically used to flavor various kinds of chili. To add to the confusion, commercial chili sauce has very little to do with either chili or chile. Although it may originally have been made with a heavier dose of the hot stuff, it has come today to designate a chunkier, unstrained version of its cousin, ketchup, a spicy sweet tomato condiment.

The name paprika derives from the Latin word for pepper, *piper.* When the capsicums were introduced into Eastern Europe by the Turks, the diminutive suffix *-ke* was added to the Latin root; the resulting *piperke* gradually changed into *paprika.* In Hungary this term is used to designate all forms of capsicum peppers, but elsewhere it is more specifically applied to the brilliant red powder made from ground dried red peppers. Much the same thing occurred in Spain, where the original Spanish word for pepper, *pimienta*, was applied to all the capsicums. In English pimiento more narrowly refers to the roasted, marinated sweet red peppers that stuff olives, flavor cream cheese, and can be bought whole or diced in little glass jars.

Vegetable Gumbo

Gumbo gets its name from an African word for okra, the vegetable that was one of the many contributions of black Americans to the unique character of Creole cooking. The indigenous American contribution to this dish was the peppers, both sweet and hot, and the characteristic flavor of liquid hot pepper sauce. Serve this very hearty vegetable stew in soup bowls with hot cooked rice and pass the hot pepper sauce to taste.

Serves 6–8

2 Tb. vegetable oil
1 large onion, coarsely chopped
3 large cloves garlic, crushed
1 medium sweet red or green pepper, seeded and diced
3 stalks celery, with leaves, diced
2 large tomatoes, coarsely chopped
½ lb. okra, sliced (about 2 cups sliced)
½ lb. mustard, kale, or collard greens, coarsely chopped
½ tsp. crushed dried hot peppers
4 cups chicken stock
1 tsp. cumin
1 tsp. dried thyme
¼ tsp. salt
Good handful chopped flat-leaf Italian parsley
½ cup fresh or frozen corn kernels
½–1 tsp. Tabasco sauce
Hot cooked rice

1. In a large pot heat the oil over moderate heat. Add the onion and the garlic and sauté, stirring, until the onion is wilted.

2. Add the sweet pepper, celery, tomatoes, okra, greens, hot peppers, stock, cumin, thyme, and salt. Bring to the simmer, then cover and cook over low heat for 1½ hours.

3. Uncover the gumbo and add the parsley, corn, and Tabasco sauce. Cook for 15 minutes. Taste for salt and hot pepper.

4. Place a spoonful or two of hot cooked rice in each soup bowl and ladle the gumbo over it. Pass additional Tabasco sauce.

Island Pepper Pot

History and linguistics have conspired to make a mess of the distinction between black pepper and the capsicums. The famous Philadelphia pepper pot soup, said to have been invented by a cook in George Washington's army, was so named because of a heavy infusion of black pepper. Nowadays pepper pot is more often than not spiced with some variety of hot chile; this is certainly true of the soups and stews of the West Indies, where chiles were known and used long before black pepper appeared on the scene. The chile of choice in this chicken and vegetable pepper pot is the habanero, a fiery little devil that is also known as the Scotch Bonnet or Bonnie pepper; other less pungent types can be substituted if you want a milder dish.

Serves 4–6

2–3 lbs. chicken breasts, cut in quarters

2 Tb. olive oil

1 large onion, coarsely chopped

1 large sweet green pepper, seeded and coarsely chopped

3 cloves garlic, crushed

1–2 fresh habanero peppers, seeded and minced
        (or any fresh hot chile to taste, seeded and minced)

2 medium ripe tomatoes, coarsely chopped

½ cup chicken stock

½ tsp. salt

1 tsp. dried thyme

1 Tb. capers

1 Tb. wine vinegar

2 medium potatoes or sweet potatoes, peeled and cubed

1–2 small green or yellow summer squash, cubed

1–2 carrots, sliced

2–3 cups hot cooked rice

Hot pepper sauce (preferably Barbadian or Jamaican) to pass

1. In a large heavy pot or Dutch oven brown the chicken in the oil over moderately high heat. Remove the chicken from the pot as it browns, salt and pepper it lightly, and set aside.

2. Add the onion, the green pepper, the garlic, and the chile peppers to the pot. Sauté, stirring, until the onion begins to brown.

3. Add the tomatoes, the stock, the salt, thyme, capers, and vinegar. Mix well, then return the chicken pieces to the pot, cover, and cook over low heat for about 30–35 minutes.

4. Uncover the pot and add the potatoes, squash, and carrots. Continue to cook, uncovered, until the chicken is very tender and the vegetables are soft.

5. Serve the pepper pot in large soup bowls with the hot cooked rice. Pass the hot pepper sauce to add to taste.

Stirring the mash for Tabasco sauce. The mixture of ground peppers and salt is aged for several years in oak barrels, then mixed with vinegar, and strained.

The Sexy Spice

"A hot chile is a macho chile." From the earliest times chile peppers have been associated with masculinity. In Mexico, the origin and site of the chile's most elaborate development, folklore is saturated with puns and word-plays that refer to the relationship between peppers and the male sexual organ. Size, shape, and color all seem to be implicated in this popular association, but hotness or pungency seems to be the most critical factor. While one variety is actually called the Penis or Peter Pepper because of its characteristic shape, any chile with its seeds removed is referred to by Mexicans as emasculated or "caponized." The reason for this is clear, as capsaicin, the chemical responsible for the hotness, is frequently present in the seeds of the pepper; once they are removed, the chile loses its "macho" qualities.

The eating of chile peppers is also linked to machismo. This is perhaps nowhere else so directly expressed as in the annual chile-eating contest in Laredo, Texas. In the yearly ritual, grown men compete to determine who can consume the greatest number of jalapeño peppers in the shortest amount of time. The agonizing consequences, beginning with the mouth and proceeding the entire length of the digestive tract, defy description, but for the winner, public acknowledgment of his superior machismo is apparently worth the pain.

The Aztecs believed the chile pepper to be a powerful sexual stimulant, and early Spanish priests cautioned against its use, claiming that it "inciteth to lust." Given the frequently puzzling and somewhat bizarre connections that human beings make between their food and their sexuality, the one involving chile peppers is perhaps not so far-fetched as most. After all, many of the symptoms produced by eating chile—flushing, tearing, sweating, and increased body heat—are very much the same as those produced by sexual arousal.

Southwest Lamb Chili

Chili in its original connotation meant any dish of meat or vegetables cooked with chile peppers. This version, from the Pueblo tradition of the Southwest, uses neither the beans, the beef, nor the tomatoes of the more familiar Tex-Mex or mainstream American chilis. Its unique flavor comes from lamb, a domestic animal introduced by the Spanish, and juniper berries, a traditional seasoning ingredient. It should be fairly spicy, but the hotness can be adjusted to personal taste.

Serves 4–6

2 Tb. vegetable oil
1 large onion, chopped
2 large sweet green peppers, seeded and finely chopped
3 cloves garlic, crushed
6–8 juniper berries, crushed
2 small fresh hot green chile peppers, seeded and minced
2 lb. lean boneless lamb, diced or cut in very small chunks
1 tsp. oregano
3–4 medium potatoes, peeled and diced or cut in small cubes
½ cup chopped fresh coriander leaf (cilantro)
1–2 tsp. salt

1. In a large heavy skillet or Dutch oven heat the oil over moderate heat. Add the onion and the green peppers and sauté, stirring, until the onion begins to wilt. Add the garlic, the juniper berries, and the chile peppers, and sauté a few minutes more.

2. Add the lamb in small batches and brown quickly. Stir in the oregano.

3. Cover the pot and cook over low heat for about 2–2½ hours until the lamb is very tender. The meat and vegetables should provide enough liquid, but if the stew should begin to dry out, add a little water during cooking.

4. When the lamb is tender, stir in the potatoes, cover, and cook until the potatoes are done, about 20–30 minutes.

5. Stir in the chopped coriander and 1 tsp. of salt. Mix well, then taste for salt and chile pepper and add more if necessary.

Texas Red

When beef-eating Anglo ranchers, cowboys, and frontiersmen met up with the bean and chile-eaters of the Southwest, a great tradition was born. Chili, the dish of meat and beans stewed with chile peppers and spices, became one of the enduring classics of the American table. Chili, of course, means many things to different people, most of whom, it would seem, are ready to argue quite loudly about what real chili is and where it originated. Whatever the merits of the various points of view, it is clear that there are regional differences, and Texas, which has made chili its state dish, lays claim to one of the best, though for the record it must be stated that not all Texans agree about what makes a good chili. The consensus seems to be a mixture of beef chunks, spices, and plenty of hot chile—no beans and no tomatoes. The red in Texas Red comes from the peppers. Chili powder, the seasoning blend for most chili dishes, was first produced commercially by a German immigrant living in Texas; like the original, most chili powders are a blend of chile peppers, garlic, cumin, and oregano. Texas Red, like the chuckwagon and campfire stews from which it came, should simmer for long fragrant hours.

Serves 4–6

2 Tb. vegetable oil
2 large onions, coarsely chopped
5 cloves garlic, crushed
2–2½ lbs. lean boneless beef, cut in small cubes, about ½-inch
3 Tb. chili powder
1 Tb. paprika
1 tsp. crushed dried hot peppers
2 tsp. cumin
2 tsp. oregano
1 cup hot water
1 tsp. salt
1–2 Tb. masa harina (corn tortilla flour)

1. In a large heavy pot or Dutch oven heat the oil over moderate heat. Add the onions and garlic and sauté until very lightly browned.

2. Add the beef cubes in several batches and brown on all sides.

3. When all the beef is browned, add all the remaining ingredients except the masa harina. Bring to the simmer, then cook, covered, over low heat for 3–4 hours until the

meat is very tender. If too much of the liquid cooks away, add some more hot water during the cooking. Taste for salt and chili powder, adding more to taste if desired.

4. To thicken the chili, mix the masa harina with a little cold water, then add this to the chili while it is still simmering. Cook the chili 10–15 minutes longer.

5. Serve the chili in bowls with crackers and cooked pinto or kidney beans on the side, if desired.

Judges at a chili contest in Laredo, Texas. Their faces tell it all!

Indian Spiced Lamb with Peppers

The cuisine of India has been for thousands of years the acknowledged center of an elaborate herb and spice tradition. When capsicum peppers were introduced by the Portuguese early in the sixteenth century, they were enthusiastically incorporated into the existing seasoning practices. Interestingly, the hot chiles, which have become so fundamental a part of Indian cookery, were not selected primarily for their flavoring capacities, but for their hotness or pungency. It is almost as though the chiles were seized upon as a super stimulus, to heighten or enhance familiar traditional flavors without providing any significant flavor variation of their own other than hot. If one combines the complex spicing practices of Indian cuisine with the more subtle chile flavoring traditions of the New World, some marvelous new flavor experiences can result. In this lamb dish with its characteristically Indian herbs and spices, the flavor and pungency of the fresh habanero are used to great advantage; the flavor of the fresh serrano chile also works very well. Note also the use of fresh sweet peppers.

Serves 4

2 Tb. cumin seed
2 Tb. vegetable oil
1 medium onion, minced
4 cloves garlic, finely minced
2 tsp. finely minced gingerroot
1–2 habanero chiles, seeded and finely minced or slivered, or 1–2 serrano
*   chiles, seeded and finely minced or slivered*
1½ lbs. lean boneless lamb, cut in thin strips or small thin slices
1 cup coarsely chopped plum tomatoes
1 tsp. salt
⅛ tsp. black pepper
1 tsp. ground coriander
1 medium onion, thinly sliced
1 large sweet red or green pepper, seeded and cut in thin strips
Chopped fresh coriander leaf (cilantro) for garnish
2–3 cups hot cooked rice

1. In a small skillet heat the cumin seeds over moderate heat, shaking the pan, until they are lightly browned and aromatic. Cool slightly, then grind the seeds in an electric spice grinder and reserve.

2. In a large heavy skillet heat the oil over moderate heat. Add the minced onion, the garlic, the gingerroot, and the minced chiles. Sauté, stirring, until the onion is soft and the mixture is aromatic.

3. Turn the heat up a bit and add the lamb strips in several batches and brown quickly.

4. Stir in the tomatoes, the salt and pepper, the coriander, and 2 teaspoons of the reserved ground cumin. Mix well, then cover and cook over low heat for 40–45 minutes, until the lamb is tender.

5. Uncover the skillet and add the sliced onion and sweet pepper. Mix well, then cook, uncovered, for another 15–20 minutes until the onion and pepper are soft.

6. Stir in 1 additional teaspoon of the reserved ground cumin. Taste for salt, then garnish with the chopped coriander. Serve the lamb with hot cooked rice.

Calves' Liver with Green Chile Sauce

This is a French-style sauce whose flavor is reminiscent of certain Mexican green *moles* or of the fresh chile sauces of our own Southwest. The sauce may be used on sautéed chicken, turkey, or pork cutlets, but it is particularly good with calves' liver.

Serves 4–6

GREEN CHILE SAUCE

1 medium onion, finely chopped
1 large or 2 medium sweet green peppers, seeded and finely chopped
2 large cloves garlic, crushed
1 small fresh hot green chile, seeded and minced
2 Tb. olive oil
1 Tb. flour
¾ cup beef stock
½ tsp. oregano
¼ cup finely chopped fresh coriander leaf (cilantro)

1½–2 lbs. sliced calves' liver
Flour for dredging
2–3 Tb. olive oil
Salt and pepper

1. Make the green chile sauce: In a medium skillet sauté the onion, the peppers, the garlic, and the chile in the olive oil over moderate heat, stirring occasionally, until the vegetables are soft, about 15–20 minutes.

2. Stir in the flour and cook, stirring, another 2–3 minutes.

3. Add the stock and the oregano and bring to a simmer, stirring. Cook over low heat until thickened and smooth. Stir in the coriander. Taste the sauce; it should be fairly piquant. If it doesn't seem perky enough, add a dash or two of cayenne pepper.

4. In a large skillet heat the remaining olive oil over moderate to high heat. Dredge the liver slices in flour, shaking off the excess.

5. Sauté the liver in the oil until it is just lightly browned on both sides. Salt and pepper the liver lightly.

6. Spoon the hot sauce over the sautéed liver. Serve with steamed new potatoes.

Note: This sauce is also excellent with poached or fried eggs—a nice variation on huevos rancheros and its traditional red chile sauce.

Chile Plus

Wherever chile peppers were accepted into Old World cuisines, they were used both fresh and dried; frequently they were incorporated as well into condiment sauces or seasoning pastes that combined the pungent chile with already familiar ingredients. In the Orient there developed a variety of hot soybean pastes and sauces, often seasoned with garlic or sesame oil. In Southeast Asia, India, and Indonesia there were any number of curry pastes to use as seasoning in cooking, and a raft of chutneys and sambals, pungent spiced relishes to eat with cooked food. In North Africa there was the *harissa,* fresh chile pounded with olive oil, cumin, and coriander, and in Portugal the *piri-piri,* a chile-seasoned olive oil. The tradition came full circle back to the New World with the development of America's own hot pepper sauce, Tabasco. Named for the region in Mexico from which the seeds for the tiny hot red chile originally came, Tabasco is compounded of hot peppers, salt, and vinegar, aged and strained. Made today as it has always been on Avery Island, off the southern coast of Louisiana, it has become one of the distinctive seasonings in Creole cooking. It is surely the grandaddy of many of the hot pepper sauces found throughout the South and the West Indies, where a number of different varieties have emerged. In Jamaica and Barbados hot pepper sauce is made from the habanero chile, and flavored with onion, mustard, and vinegar. All these chile-based sauces, pastes, and relishes confirm once again the observation of one of the earliest Spanish explorers on the native Mexicans: "Without chile," he said, "they do not think they are eating."

All-American Stuffed Peppers

Americans love the combination of ground beef, tomatoes, and cheese, whether in the form of cheeseburgers, chili, spaghetti, or meat loaf. Small wonder, then, that we stuff peppers with the same triad, in a recipe that combines elements of Italian, Middle Eastern, and English cuisines, and turns out wholly American.

Serves 3–4

6–8 small blocky sweet green and/or red peppers, or 3–4 large peppers
1 medium onion, finely chopped
1 small sweet green pepper, finely chopped
1 Tb. oil
1 lb. lean ground beef
2 cups canned crushed tomatoes or thick tomato sauce
½ tsp. salt
⅛ tsp. pepper
½ tsp. basil
½ tsp. oregano
2 Tb. freshly grated Parmesan cheese
2 cups cooked rice
1–1½ cups shredded Cheddar or Monterrey Jack cheese

1. If using small peppers, slice off the tops and remove the inner membranes and seeds. For large peppers, cut out the core end, slice the peppers in half lengthwise, and remove the membranes and seeds. Blanch the peppers in boiling salted water for 3–4 minutes. Drain and cool.

2. In a large skillet brown the onion and chopped green pepper in the oil. Add the beef and brown quickly, stirring to break up lumps. When the beef is completely browned, carefully pour off all liquid and fat in the pan and discard.

3. To the beef add 1½ cups of the tomatoes, salt, pepper, basil, and oregano. Bring to a simmer and cook over moderate heat about 15 minutes. Remove from heat and stir in the Parmesan. Preheat the oven to 350°F.

4. Add the rice to the beef and mix thoroughly. Spoon the mixture into the pepper shells. Place the stuffed peppers in a lightly greased casserole or baking dish, stuffing side up. Spoon the remaining ½ cup of tomatoes over the tops. Add a few Tb. of water to the bottom of the pan.

5. Cover the casserole lightly with foil and bake for about 30–40 minutes. Remove the foil for the last 10 minutes of baking; cover the tops of the peppers with the shredded cheese. Bake until the cheese is melted and bubbly.

Dim-Sum Stuffed Peppers

Wherever sweet peppers were accepted as a fresh vegetable, they were inevitably stuffed with traditional ingredients and familiar seasonings. Here in America the Chinese-style stuffed pepper has become a regular feature of the *dim sum* meal, an endless round of savory appetizer and snack foods. These shrimp-stuffed peppers make a fine hors d'oeuvre or appetizer. In typical Chinese fashion they are made in two-bite-sized pieces that can be picked up with the fingers or chopsticks.

Makes 16 stuffed pepper pieces

1 cup raw peeled and deveined shrimp (about ½ lb. with shells)
1 egg white
4 scallions, chopped
2 tsp. soy sauce
2 tsp. finely minced gingerroot
½ tsp. sugar
1 tsp. sesame oil
⅛ tsp. white pepper
2 large or 4 small blocky sweet green peppers
Cornstarch
¼ cup peanut oil or vegetable oil

1. In a food processor combine the raw shrimp, the egg white, the scallions, the soy sauce, gingerroot, sugar, sesame oil, and pepper. Process into a coarse, not fine, puree; there should be some bits of shrimp and scallion evident in the mixture.

2. If the peppers are large cut them in eighths, if small cut them in quarters. Remove the seeds and membranes.

3. Dust the inside of the pepper pieces with cornstarch. (The easiest way to do this is to spoon in some cornstarch, then tap out the excess.)

4. Spoon the shrimp mixture into the pepper pieces.

5. Heat the oil in a heavy skillet over moderate to high heat. Place the stuffed peppers, stuffing side down, in the hot oil. Fry them about 2 minutes until the stuffing side is nicely browned. Turn the stuffed pepper pieces and fry for 2 minutes on the other side.

6. Drain the fried stuffed peppers on paper towels and serve hot.

Chicken Paprika

Although paprika is produced in many areas of concentrated pepper cultivation—California, Mexico, Spain, Morocco—it is Hungary that gave us both the name and the most elaborate tradition of paprika cookery. The brilliant red powder that serves so beautifully as a garnish and coloring agent functions in Hungarian cuisine as a distinctive flavoring in its own right. Combined with onions and lard, it forms the seasoning hallmark for a variety of soups, stews, sausages, and, of course, goulash. Hungarian paprikas are generally available here in two basic varieties, rose sweet and hot. The hot is simply the sweet from which the pungent seeds have not been removed in the grinding process.

Serves 4–6

3- to 3½-lb. frying chicken in parts
2 Tb. vegetable oil
1 large onion, finely chopped
1 medium sweet red pepper, seeded and finely chopped
2 large cloves garlic, crushed
2 Tb. Hungarian sweet paprika
1 lb. fresh mushrooms, sliced
⅓ cup dry white wine
½ cup tomato sauce
½ cup sour cream
¼ tsp. salt

1. In a large heavy skillet or Dutch oven brown the chicken parts in the oil over moderately high heat, turning the parts to brown evenly. As the chicken browns, remove it from the pot, salt and pepper lightly, and set aside.

2. Pour off and discard all but about 1 tablespoon of the fat remaining in the pan. Add the onion, the sweet pepper, and the garlic, and sauté over moderate heat until the onion is just beginning to turn golden.

3. Stir in the paprika and the mushrooms and sauté, stirring, for another few minutes.

4. Stir in the wine and the tomato sauce and mix well. Return the chicken to the pan, cover, and cook over low heat about 30–40 minutes until the chicken is very tender.

5. Remove the chicken from the pan and set aside. Turn the heat up to moderately high and cook the sauce for about 10–15 minutes until it is reduced by about one third. Lower the heat and stir in the sour cream and the salt; blend thoroughly.

6. Return the chicken parts to the sauce and cook until they are completely heated through, but do not let the sauce boil. Serve with freshly cooked hot buttered noodles or dumplings.

Mushrooms Paprika

Like chicken paprika, the preceding recipe, this dish came to the American table from Hungarian immigrants who settled in the upper Midwest. It can be served as is, on toast, or with rice or buttered noodles, and a few spoonfuls will turn a plain baked potato into a really memorable dish.

Serves 4

2 Tb. butter
1 medium onion, finely chopped
1 lb. fresh mushrooms, sliced or coarsely chopped
2 tsp. Hungarian sweet paprika
Good dash cayenne pepper
2 Tb. tomato paste
2/3 cup sour cream (If you're counting calories, a reduced-fat sour cream is fine.)
1/2 tsp. salt
2 Tb. finely snipped fresh dill, or 2 tsp. dried dillweed

1. In a large skillet heat the butter over moderate heat. Add the onion and sauté, stirring, until it just begins to turn golden.

2. Add the mushrooms and sauté, stirring, until they are just very lightly browned. Stir in the paprika and the cayenne and sauté a few minutes more.

3. Stir in the tomato paste, the sour cream, and the salt. Mix well, then bring to the simmer and cook over low heat for a few minutes.

4. Stir in the dill and mix well.

Hungarian girls stringing paprika peppers to dry

Roast Pepper Romesco Sauce

The Romesco sauces of Spain are similar to the *pesto* sauces of Italy, thick pastes made of garlic, olive oil, ground nuts, and seasonings. They are ancient sauces that were in use long before the discovery of the New World. But some New World ingredients— the tomato, and more particularly peppers—had an enormous impact, especially in the tradition of Spain. Use as a sauce for cooked vegetables or fish and as a dip for raw vegetables on the buffet table.

Makes about 1¼ cups

½ cup roasted almonds (not blanched or salted)*
2 roasted sweet red peppers (see p. 95), or 6 oz. (about ½ cup jarred) roasted
        peppers, thoroughly drained
3 cloves garlic
½ tsp. salt
Good pinch cayenne pepper, or ¼ tsp. crushed dried hot peppers
¾ cup olive oil
2 Tb. sherry vinegar

1. In a food processor combine the almonds, peppers, garlic, salt, and cayenne pepper. Process into a coarse paste.

2. While the machine is running, add the olive oil in a slow stream. Blend into a smooth paste.

3. Add the vinegar and process a few seconds more.

*To roast almonds: Spread whole unpeeled almonds in a single layer in
a pie tin or baking pan. Place in a 300°F. oven for 10–15 minutes, stirring occasionally, until the nuts are very lightly browned.

Roasted Peppers and Pepper Puree

It is the Spanish to whom we are indebted for the glory of the roasted pepper, and although it has only recently been rediscovered as a trendy new ingredient, it has been around for quite a long time. It is a marvelous vegetable, not only beautiful to look at, but filled with a rich sweet flavor. Roasted peppers can be bought in jars, usually imported from Spain, Italy, or Mexico, and these are fine for most purposes. When sweet red peppers are in season, however, you can make your own quite easily. Here's how:

Choose firm, unblemished, fully ripe sweet red peppers. Roast them on a grill over a wood or charcoal fire, turning them until they are blackened on all sides. (If they are not blackened the skins will not peel off easily.) Have ready a large container of ice water. As you remove the charred peppers from the grill, place them in the water. When the peppers are cool enough to handle, slip off the skins with your fingers, then remove the stem and the seeds. Drain the peppers thoroughly. They are now ready for whatever you want to do with them—eat them as is, in salads or sandwiches, or drizzle them with a little olive oil or vinegar or both and marinate them for a few hours or overnight. Peppers are best roasted over an open fire, but they can also be broiled, or held on a long fork and turned over a gas fire, or roasted in a pan in a very hot (450°–500°F.) oven and turned occasionally until black on all sides.

The Hungarians make a puree out of stewed, sieved sweet red peppers; called paprika lekvar, it is a rich, thick, red paste that is used to flavor soups and stews, or it can be spread on bread as a tasty sandwich filling. To make the best of both Spain and Hungary, you can puree roasted peppers to make an extremely useful flavoring ingredient. It can be used in tomato sauces, in soups, and in delicate cream sauces for pasta and seafood. Because it is nothing but pepper, it is low in calories and contains no fat. If you substitute half the mayonnaise in egg salad with pepper puree, for example, you will substantially lower the calories while upping the flavor. You can also mix some olive oil, salt, and a bit of garlic into the puree; spread the puree on slices of French bread, top with cheese, if desired, and bake in a 400°F. until just hot and bubbly.

Chicken Pimiento Loaf

Remember chicken à la king? It used to be a rather fashionable dish—chunks of chicken in white sauce that was studded with bits of red pimiento. Nowadays we tend to use the pimiento more for its flavor than as a colorful garnish. It still goes well with chicken. This simple loaf is good hot, with a light tomato sauce, but it works especially well chilled and sliced thin for sandwiches.

Serves 4

1 6- to 7-oz. jar pimientos or roasted peppers, drained,
        or 3 homemade roasted peppers (see p. 95)
1 egg
1/3 cup light cream
1 small onion, coarsely chopped
1 lb. ground raw chicken
1 tsp. salt
1/4 tsp. nutmeg
1/8 tsp. pepper
Good dash cayenne pepper
2 Tb. freshly grated Parmesan cheese
1/4 cup flavored bread crumbs

1. In a blender or food processor combine the pimientos, the egg, the cream, and the onion. Puree until smooth.

2. In a large bowl combine the puree with the chicken, the salt, the nutmeg, the peppers, the cheese, and the bread crumbs. Mix together very thoroughly. Preheat the oven to 350°F.

3. Spoon the chicken mixture into a buttered 9 x 5 x 3-inch loaf pan. With the back of large spoon smooth and level the mixture, pressing down to eliminate air bubbles.

4. Bake the loaf for 40–45 minutes. Remove from the oven and pour off any accumulated liquid and fat. Serve the loaf hot, with a simple tomato sauce, if desired, or chill the loaf and slice for sandwiches.

Fish Fillets with Chile

In traditional Mexican cookery, dried or roasted chile peppers are soaked, ground with other ingredients, then fried in oil or lard to form a seasoning paste for meat, poultry, or fish. Today's adventurous cooks are experimenting with this ancient technique, using different combinations of chiles and a variety of seasonings.

Serves 4–6

2 dried ancho chiles, seeds and stem removed
1 dried pasilla chile, seeds and stem removed
1 medium onion, chopped
2 Tb. olive oil
2 cloves garlic
1 large sweet red or yellow pepper, seeded and coarsely chopped
Juice 1 lime (about 2 Tb.)
Good handful fresh coriander leaf (cilantro)
¼ tsp. salt, or to taste
2 lbs. fish fillets (flounder, sole, perch, or red snapper)
Additional limes and fresh coriander for garnish

1. Soak the dried chiles in warm water to cover for about 20 minutes.

2. In a medium skillet sauté the onion in the olive oil until just lightly browned. Remove from heat.

3. Drain the chiles; combine them in a food processor with the onions and all other ingredients except the fish and the garnish. Process into a paste.

4. Return the paste to the skillet in which the onions were cooked. Fry, stirring over moderate heat until slightly thickened, about 4–5 minutes. Preheat the oven to 400°F.

5. Place the fish fillets in a single layer in a lightly oiled shallow baking dish. Spread the chile paste evenly over the fillets.

6. Bake for 10–20 minutes or until the fish flakes easily when tested with a fork. (Baking time will depend on thickness of fillets.)

7. Serve the fish with the lime wedges and fresh chopped coriander leaf sprinkled over the top.

Capsaicin

Capsaicin is the chemical compound responsible for the hotness or pungency of chile peppers. It is produced primarily in the placenta, the whitish membrane inside the pepper, but may also be present in lesser amounts in the flesh and seeds. Depending on the type of pepper, the method of preparation, and the amount ingested, capsaicin can produce the familiar burning sensation on the lips, tongue, palate, and throat, facial sweating, tearing of the eyes, and increased motility of the gut. It is for these reasons that a heavy use of chile peppers is clearly associated with vegetable-based cuisines, where the diet consists largely of starchy, mealy, or fibrous plant foods—a daily diet that seems to require, for many people, both the gastric and the gustatory stimulation that chile peppers so generously provide.

Because of its potent effects on the skin and mucous membranes, capsaicin has also long been used for medicinal purposes. The ancient Mexicans had a large body of remedies based on chile, and through the centuries the curative powers of the pungent peppers have been claimed for such various ailments as fever, dropsy, vomiting, diarrhea, toothache, and colic. In modern pharmacology capsaicin is used in cold and cough remedies and in plasters, poultices, and rubs for joint and muscle pain.

Not all the uses of the chile pepper have been so benign. The very substance that enabled it to perk up bland food or to produce a soothing heat for an aching muscle could also produce severe pain. Both the Mayas and the Aztecs possessed a whole armament of insidious punishments based on the pain-producing properties of chile peppers: Chile was rubbed into raw or open wounds, or into the genitalia of adulterous women; disobedient children, servants, and wives were suspended over fires of chile peppers, the smoke from which produced excruciating pain and temporary blindness. Even in more modern times chile, rubbed on the nipples, has been used as a way to encourage weaning, and smeared on the fingers as a way to discourage thumb-sucking.

Puerto Rican Pepper Sofrito

A *sofrito* can mean many things. In classical Spanish tradition it referred to onions sautéed slowly in olive oil. When sweet peppers and tomatoes arrived in Spain they joined the onions in the *sofrito,* becoming the basis of many familiar Spanish-style sauces. In the New World, and particularly in Puerto Rico, *sofrito* means an uncooked seasoning sauce, similar in form and flavor to the raw *salsas* of Mexico, but with sweet peppers instead of tomatoes. In Puerto Rican cuisine it is typically used as a seasoning sauce for soups and stews, with diners adding it to taste. It is also very good on grilled meat and hamburgers and as a dip for corn chips.

Makes about 2½ cups

2 large sweet green or red peppers, seeded and coarsely chopped
1 medium onion, coarsely chopped
1 small fresh hot chile pepper, seeded
2 large cloves garlic
Good handful fresh coriander leaf (cilantro)
1 Tb. wine vinegar
¼ tsp. salt

In a blender or food processor combine all the ingredients and process until the mixture is coarsely pureed. It should not be too fine but should retain some texture.

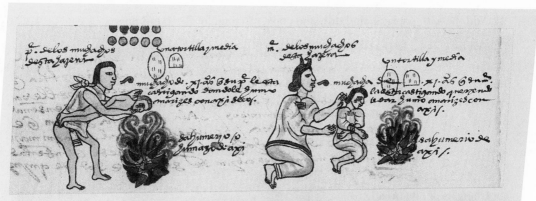

From a sixteenth-century Aztec manuscript, this picture shows children punished by being suspended over fires of hot capsicum peppers. After exposure to the burning smoke, the child on the right is in obvious pain and his eyes tear.

Pepper, Eggplant, and Walnut Caviar

Vegetable "caviars" are traditional in the Balkans and eastern Europe, where inexpensive, plentiful vegetables, highly seasoned and coarsely pureed, substitute for the scarcer and more expensive fish roe. Three forms of pepper—fresh sweet, hot dried, and ground paprika—give this caviar its rich and satisfying flavor.

Makes about 2 cups

1 medium eggplant, peeled and diced
2 medium sweet red peppers, seeded and diced
2 medium sweet green peppers, seeded and diced
1 large onion, finely chopped
4 cloves garlic, crushed
¼ tsp. crushed dried hot peppers
¼ cup olive oil
½ tsp. salt
¼ tsp. sweet paprika (preferably Hungarian)
2 Tb. fresh dill, finely snipped
½ cup walnuts, freshly toasted
1–2 Tb. olive oil

1. In a large heavy saucepan combine the eggplant, the peppers, the onion, the garlic, the dried peppers, and the olive oil. Mix well, then cook uncovered over low to moderate heat for 40–45 minutes, stirring occasionally, until the mixture is soft and dark.

2. Add the salt, paprika, and dill, and cook, stirring, for 5–10 minutes.

3. Combine the vegetable mixture and the walnuts in a food processor, and process to a coarse puree, adding the olive oil as you process. Let the mixture cool, taste for salt, and serve as a spread with crisp crackers or triangles of pita bread.

Display of paprika cans in Hungary. Szeged, in the rich central valley, is the center of paprika production.

Tortellini Salad with Mixed Peppers

You've had your fill of multicolored pasta. How about plain old-fashioned white pasta with multicolored peppers? We may wonder what pasta would be like if the tomato had never made it to the Mediterranean; we can speculate equally about sweet peppers, with their unique flavor and visual beauty. While the inspiration for most of our pasta dishes comes from Italy, pasta salads are as American as apple pie.

Serves 4–6

1 large onion, finely chopped
3 Tb. olive oil
2 medium sweet green peppers, seeded and diced
2 medium sweet red peppers, seeded and diced
2 medium sweet yellow or orange peppers, seeded and diced
¼ cup pine nuts
2 Tb. capers
2 Tb. balsamic vinegar
1 lb. fresh or frozen cheese tortellini
Several grinds black pepper
Salt to taste

1. In a medium skillet sauté the onion in the olive oil over moderate heat until the onion just begins to wilt.

2. Add the peppers and sauté, stirring, until they just begin to wilt. Stir in the pine nuts and remove from the heat.

3. Cook the tortellini in boiling salted water for 8–10 minutes until just tender but still firm. Drain thoroughly.

4. Combine the tortellini, peppers, capers, vinegar, and black pepper. Mix gently but thoroughly. Add a little salt to taste, if desired.

Pepper Steak

The Chinese, masters of the culinary art for thousands of years, exhibited the same flair with New World foods as they did with their traditional ingredients. Neither beef nor peppers were part of their ancient tradition, but when the Chinese came to America they turned these two foods into a dish that has become a national favorite. Like chop suey and a host of other "made up" dishes, pepper steak demonstrates the Chinese artistry with technique and flavoring and an extraordinary flexibility in dealing with a variety of ingredients.

Serves 3–4

1 lb. lean boneless round or sirloin steak, cut in thin slices
1 Tb. finely minced gingerroot
3 cloves garlic, crushed
1 Tb. sesame oil
2 Tb. soy sauce
2 Tb. rice wine (sake *or dry sherry may be substituted)*
2 Tb. bottled commercial chili sauce
1 tsp. sugar
2 tsp. hoisin sauce
1 Tb. cornstarch
2 Tb. peanut oil
1 large onion, thinly sliced
1 large sweet green pepper, seeded and cut in strips
1 large sweet red pepper, seeded and cut in strips
Good pinch crushed dried hot peppers
2 cups hot freshly cooked rice

1. In a bowl combine the beef strips, the gingerroot, the garlic, and the sesame oil. Mix thoroughly and set aside.

2. In a small bowl combine the soy sauce, the wine, the chili sauce, the sugar, the hoisin, and the cornstarch. Mix thoroughly, smoothing out the little lumps of cornstarch, and set aside.

3. In a wok or large frying pan heat the oil over high heat. When the oil is very hot add the onion and stir-fry for a few minutes. Add the peppers and the dried hot peppers and stir-fry a few minutes more.

4. Add the beef strips and stir-fry just until the beef loses its pink color.

5. Stir the sauce mixture well, then add it to the beef and peppers, stir-frying until the sauce thickens and the ingredients are evenly coated.

6. Serve the pepper steak immediately with the hot cooked rice.

Pepper Hash

Pepper hash is an old-fashioned dish, made by thrifty farm housewives to preserve sweet peppers for winter use when fresh vegetables were not available. On the East Coast it is traditionally eaten with broiled or fried seafood, but it is very good for any meal where a sweet/sour relish is appropriate. You don't have to process endless jars. Just make up a small batch of this to keep in a covered jar in the refrigerator. The flavor of sweet peppers in pickles and relishes is unique and delicious, which is no doubt why Peter Piper picked a peck of 'em.

Makes about 2 cups

2 large sweet green and/or red peppers, seeded
1 medium onion
1 small fresh hot chile pepper, seeded (optional)
½ cup cider vinegar
¼ cup sugar
½ tsp. celery seed
¼ tsp. mustard seed
¼ tsp. salt

PEPPER.
Large Bell, or Bull Nose.   5c

1. Finely chop the peppers, the onion, and the chile, if desired. Place the chopped vegetables in a colander or strainer to drain.

2. In a small saucepan combine the vinegar, the sugar, the celery and mustard seeds, and the salt. Bring to the simmer and cook for about 5 minutes. Remove from the heat and cool.

3. Combine the chopped vegetables and the sauce and mix well. Let stand a couple of hours before serving. Store the relish in a covered jar in the refrigerator.

Sweet Pepper Focaccia

Focaccia is a flat hearth bread, best eaten hot from the oven. It can be made very simply, brushed lightly with olive oil and sprinkled with coarse salt, or it can be dressed up with a variety of herbs, dried tomatoes, or cheese. This version uses sweet red peppers, which taste wonderful and look beautiful.

Makes one 9- or 10-inch loaf

2 tsp. sugar
1 Tb. dry granulated yeast or cake compressed yeast
1 cup very warm water
2½–3½ cups all-purpose flour
1 tsp. salt
1 large sweet red pepper, seeded and cut in thin strips
1½ Tb. olive oil
Coarse (Kosher) salt

1. In a bowl dissolve the sugar and yeast in the warm water, and let stand a few minutes. Add 2 cups of the flour and the salt and beat until smooth.

2. Add enough additional flour to make a smooth, elastic, nonsticky dough. Knead thoroughly. Form the dough into a ball, brush lightly with olive oil, place in a bowl, then cover with a cloth and let it rise in a warm place for about 1 hour or until it doubles in bulk.

3. Punch the dough down, then spread it in a rimmed 9- or 10-inch round baking pan. If you have a stone or earthenware baking dish, use it.

4. Combine the pepper slivers with the olive oil and mix thoroughly. With your fingertips, press the pepper strips into the dough. Sprinkle it with the coarse salt. Let the loaf rise for 40–45 minutes. As it rises, preheat the oven to 400°F.

5. Bake the bread for 20–25 minutes or until nicely browned.

6. Remove the bread from the pan and let it cool slightly. Serve it warm, cut in wedges.

Chile-Ginger Dessert Sauce

This recipe takes the chile pepper about as far from its original use as can be imagined. The hot capsicums are not traditionally used with sweet foods and desserts, although they certainly play an important role in the sweet and pungent sauces of the Orient. This sauce was a deliberate exercise, designed to pit the heat and pungency of chile against the cold and sweetness of ice cream. It works very nicely and makes an unusual and appropriate dessert for an Oriental meal. Any extra sauce can be stored almost indefinitely in the refrigerator.

Makes about 2½ cups

2 cups sugar
2 cups water
3 Tb. Japanese-style pickled ginger, drained and finely chopped
¼ cup dried apricots, coarsely chopped
¼ cup raisins
¼ cup slivered blanched almonds
¼ cup walnuts, coarsely chopped
¼–½ tsp. crushed dried hot peppers
Good splash grenadine syrup
Vanilla or coconut ice cream

1. In a medium saucepan combine the sugar and water and bring to a boil. Cook, uncovered, over moderate heat for about 15 minutes.

2. Add the remaining ingredients, including enough grenadine to make a pleasant rosy color. Simmer 5–10 minutes. Let cool, then serve over vanilla or coconut ice cream.

Chile *ristras* hung to dry in the Jemez Pueblo of New Mexico. Note also corn drying in the foreground.

Creamy Tomato and Crab Soup

Fresh Tomato Avgolemono

Tarascan Tomato Soup

Southern-Style Chicken, Tomato, and Vegetable Soup

Gazpacho

Tomato Chutney

Spiced Tomato Vinaigrette

Barbecue Pork

Creole Spaghetti Sauce

Spiced Tomato Eggplant Casserole

Lisbon Burgers

Chicken in Double Tomato Sauce

A Trio of Italian Tomato Sauces

1. The Marinara

2. Tomato Sauce with Peppers and Mushrooms

3. Tomato Cream Sauce

Braised Salmon Provençal

Spicy Tomato Aspic

Tomato Rice Salad

Tomato Salad with Chick-Peas and Tuna

Sun-Dried Tomato Pesto

Tomato Herb Bread

Spiced Fried Green Tomatoes

Tomato and Apple Pie

TOMATOES

The local supermarket is as accurate an index as any of the trends, the traditions, the fads, and the fashions of American eating habits. It takes no more than a quick run through the neighborhood market to confirm what we already know—that the tomato is a crucial and fundamental part of American cuisine, as much, if not more, as hot dogs and apple pie. Just think of the number of tomato products that are routinely available, that we take for granted as part of the basic cooking repertoire. In addition to the fresh varieties in the produce section, there are canned whole tomatoes, stewed tomatoes, crushed tomatoes, tomato puree, tomato sauce, and tomato paste. There are dried tomatoes, tomato juice, tomato soup, tomato ketchup, chili sauce, spaghetti sauce, barbecue sauce, and Mexican salsa. And that doesn't even begin to include the prepared foods that have tomatoes as one of their important ingredients—baked beans, chili, beef stew, and the Beefaroni and SpaghettiOs of the young set.

This evidence of our national dependence on the tomato in all its many forms is not in itself so remarkable, except when one realizes that the whole phenomenon occurred only in the last one hundred years or so. Unlike other New World foods that traveled abroad and then returned in fairly quick order, the tomato took its own sweet time to come back to us. But it seems to have been worth the wait, for of all the foods that originated here, it is the tomato, gone and come home again, that has most deeply affected our cuisine.

History is curiously silent about the tomato. Unlike the other new foods that were to have a major impact on the cuisines of the Old World—capsicum peppers, chocolate, the potato—the tomato was scarcely noted by early observers. Indeed, one of the very first mentions was fairly sinister: Bernal Diaz del Castillo, a priest who traveled with Cortez on his first expedition to Mexico, wrote: "So in return for our having come to treat them like brothers and to tell them what Our Lord God and the King have ordained, they wished to kill us and eat our flesh, and had already prepared the pots with salt and peppers and tomatoes."

Hardly an auspicious beginning, and the story was not to get much better. In central and northern Europe, at least, tomatoes were viewed with grave suspicion, thought to be poisonous because they are members of the Solanacae, a large group of plants that includes the deadly nightshade. Of course, the same people who objected to the tomato didn't seem to be bothered by the fact that other New World foods, including the potato, peppers, and that fashionable novelty, tobacco, were also members of the nightshade family, as was the familiar Old World eggplant. But the tomato, perhaps because of its vibrant color, perhaps because of the pungent odor of its leaves, was damned by a large part of Europe as unfit for human consumption. It was grown as an ornamental plant, recorded in early herbals and botanic works, but on the historic level, at least, rejected as food.

However, on another less-public level, unnoticed and undocumented, the tomato was quietly revolutionizing the cuisines of southern Europe and the Mediterranean during the first two centuries after its introduction. From Spain and Portugal, southern Italy and France, east to Greece and Turkey, and around the rim of North Africa—indeed, everywhere that the olive and olive oil were entrenched—the tomato established itself in the kitchen gardens of the common folk, forming an indissoluble union with olive oil and other traditional ingredients to produce the savory tomato sauces and the fresh tomato salads that are so fundamental a part of Mediterranean cuisine.

It is difficult to imagine today what Spanish or Sicilian or Turkish or Moroccan cooking would be like without the tomato; so integral has it become that one can hardly believe it wasn't always there. There are few written records, but the culinary evidence suggests that the Mediterranean was in some profound ways "ready" for the arrival of the tomato. Perhaps it was the climate, so favorable for the easy growth of this prolific garden crop; perhaps it was the tomato's vivid color, unmatched by any other readily available ingredient; perhaps it was the flavor, round, slightly salty, and mildly acidic, that melded so gracefully into existing seasoning traditions. And perhaps it was the fact that the tomato, when cooked, provided a thick coating sauce that was a source of great visual and gustatory richness, red and meaty, filling both the mouth and the eye with savor. However it happened, the marriage between olive oil and the tomato was a brilliant unprecedented culinary match, and because of it the world's table, and our own, was forever changed.

While the tomato was strengthening its position in the Mediterranean, it was making small forays back to its native shores. It had long been used in Mex-

ico where, it must be assumed, it functioned as more than just a sauce for belea-
guered missionaries. It returned to Mexico in a variety of Spanish-style sauces.
Indeed, everywhere the Spanish and Portuguese settled in the New World, the
tomato followed, now inexorably bound with olive oil, with onions and peppers,
with oregano and basil and parsley and garlic. In California, in the Southwest, in
the West Indies, and the Creole country of Louisiana, even on the coast of New
England, the tomato was grown and used on the tables of immigrants from southern Europe. But these were limited groups on the fringes of mainstream America,
still in its heritage largely of northern European background, and not yet ready
for the exotic and dangerous tomato.

It is amusing, then, and perhaps inevitable, that the tomato's first major
impact on the American table came from the English, in the form of ketchup.
Ketchups had developed in England in the sixteenth and seventeenth centuries
from British contact with the East Indies; the strained piquant sauces that were
made in England from locally available ingredients such as mushrooms, walnuts,
and grapes were an imitation of a variety of Oriental-style condimental sauces.
Our word "ketchup" seems to be of Malaysian derivation, meaning a sweet condimental soy sauce, and it is interesting that tomato ketchup is today sometimes
referred to in England as "tomato soy." (The Chinese term "*k'e-tsiap*" is a Can-
tonese word for tomato sauce that appeared after the tomato was introduced into
China, and appears to be a more recent term than the Malaysian *ketjap*.)

But ketchup as we know it, a strained spicy sweet tomato condiment,
was born here in America, the offspring of English tradition and an abundant
local fruit. For the tomato is technically a fruit, and it was as such that the
English regarded it, sweetening it and seasoning it with the aromatic spices—
cinnamon, nutmeg, ginger, cloves—that were traditionally used for fruit pies,
jams, relishes, and sauces. In this form the tomato became acceptable to mainstream America, and there was a proliferation of tomato ketchups in the farm
kitchens of eighteenth- and nineteenth-century America. In 1876 the Heinz
Company produced the first commercially available ketchup; it was to become
one of the greatest success stories the sauce world has ever known. Indeed,
ketchup was the forerunner of a whole complex of sweetened tomato preparations—soups, barbecue sauces, salad dressings—that were to become so much
a part of the American table.

Gradually, toward the end of the nineteenth century, the tomato came to
be eaten on the farm as a raw salad vegetable and in a variety of stewed and scalloped dishes. The savory sauces of the Mediterranean, which existed in small

regional pockets throughout America, slowly began to infiltrate the mainstream; these nonsweetened tomato-flavored or tomato-sauced recipes were invariably labeled "Spanish." Spanish rice, Spanish omelets, Spanish meatballs, Spanish-style sauce—all were so designated because they were perceived, not unreasonably, as having originated in the kitchens of Spain. If the tomato had initially to overcome its reputation as a poison, it had yet, at the turn of the century, the need to rise above its status as an "ethnic" ingredient. And that development occurred, curiously, with the overwhelming acceptance into American cuisine of two blatantly ethnic traditions, southern Italian and Mexican.

Although Italian emigration to America was well under way in the nineteenth century, the American experience of Italian food was limited pretty much to spaghetti and meatballs and veal Parmigiana. Americans were for the most part largely unaware of the stunning complexity of Italian cuisine. It was not really until the end of World War II that Italian cooking, and particularly the food of southern Italy, swept across this country and conquered the mainstream palate. The emissary of this onslaught was the American GI, returned from the south of Italy with his taste buds newly awakened to the delights of pizza and pasta; the conquering hero the tomato, returned to its native shores in a host of robust sauces, redolent with garlic and herbs. To the already familiar spaghetti and elbow macaroni were added dozens of novel varieties of pasta—rotini and fettuccine and fusilli and radiatore—and the simple tomato sauces burgeoned into a multitude of different forms. Pizza parlors and hoagie houses, as well as three-star Italian restaurants, joined the neighborhood spaghetti joint in opening up the vast exciting and innovative traditions of Italian and subsequent Italian-American food. And we gobbled it all up! In the fifty or so years since the end of World War II the tomato-sauced food of Italy has become as familiar, as loved, as American, as anything that came before.

And finally, if a little late, we have learned to love what was here from the start, a pot with "salt and peppers and tomatoes," the ancient Mexican tomato-chile tradition, rejuvenated and refashioned through the prism of the Southwest and California. As the Mediterranean enabled us to appreciate the tomato in a new way, Mexico has given back what was always ours; while pizza and spaghetti and meatball hoagies have become an integral part of the American experience, so too have chili and tacos and enchiladas. Can there be any doubt that Tomatoes are US?

Creamy Tomato and Crab Soup

One of the earliest ways tomatoes were used, once northern Europe decided they were safe to eat, was to make soup. Characteristically, both their brilliant color and stalwart flavor were tempered by the dairy products that were so widely used in England and America. Butter, milk, and cream work very well with tomatoes, mellowing their acidity, smoothing out the flavor, and providing a lovely blush color that goes very nicely with seafood.

Serves 6

2 Tb. butter
1 medium onion, finely chopped
1 large stalk celery, with leaves, finely chopped
1 cup coarsely chopped plum tomatoes
2 Tb. flour
4 cups chicken stock
2 Tb. tomato paste
Several good grinds black pepper
Good dash cayenne pepper
⅛ tsp. ground mace
2 Tb. cream (sweet) sherry
½ lb. crabmeat, picked over to remove any bits of cartilage
½ cup light cream

1. In a large heavy pot heat the butter over moderate heat. Add the onion and the celery and sauté, stirring occasionally, until the onion is soft and just beginning to turn golden.

2. Stir in the tomatoes and cook, stirring occasionally, until the tomatoes are soft and most of the liquid has cooked away.

3. Stir in the flour and cook, stirring, for 2–3 minutes.

4. Add the stock, the tomato paste, the black and cayenne peppers, and the mace. Bring to the simmer and stir until the soup is smooth and very slightly thickened.

5. Stir in the sherry and the crabmeat, mix well, and cook until very hot.

6. Stir in the cream and heat just to the simmer. Serve hot.

Fresh Tomato Avgolemono

In 1898 a New Jersey chemist named John T. Dorrance decided to market a line of condensed canned soups, drawing on the ample harvest of the Garden State's rich truck farms. So was born Campbell's Tomato Soup, a product that was to become the standard for tomato soup for many generations of Americans. It reflected the original flavor profile—slightly sweet and cinnamon-spiced—that first made the tomato acceptable to the American palate. It was used not only as soup, but as a component of sauces, salad dressings, and casseroles, and even as an ingredient in chocolate cake. Here is a very different tomato soup, with an eastern Mediterranean influence.

Serves 6

2 Tb. olive oil
1 medium onion, finely chopped
4 cups coarsely chopped plum tomatoes (about 12 tomatoes)
4 cups chicken stock
1/8 tsp. freshly ground black pepper
2 Tb. finely snipped fresh dill, or 1 tsp. dried dillweed
1/3 cup small seed-shaped pasta (orzo or seme di mellone)
1 egg
1 Tb. lemon juice

1. In a medium saucepan heat the oil over moderate heat, add the onion, and sauté until it begins to turn golden.

2. Add the tomatoes and cook, stirring occasionally, over moderate heat until the mixture is thick and soft, almost a puree, and most of the liquid has cooked away.

Campbell's tomato soup ads from the 1920s

3. Cool the mixture slightly, then puree in a blender or food processor.

4. Return the tomato puree to the pan; add the stock, the black pepper, and the dill. Bring to the simmer, then add the pasta and cook over low heat for about 15 minutes or until the pasta is tender.

5. In a small bowl whisk the egg, then add the lemon juice and whisk it lightly into the egg.

6. Remove the soup from the heat. Slowly pour some of the soup into the egg mixture, whisking as you pour. When you have added enough soup to warm the egg well, stir the egg mixture back into the pot.

7. Bring the soup just to the simmer, but do not let it boil. Taste for salt.

What's in a Name?

The ancient Aztec word for tomato was *xi-tomate,* which survives in the modern Mexican *jitomate* (pronounced hee-to-máh-tay). It is a term that differentiates the common tomato from the little green husk tomato, the tomatillo, which is widely used in the familiar Mexican salsa verde, or green sauce, but which never left its native home. When the tomato traveled abroad it kept its original Aztec name, simply dropping the prefix and shortening to some form of *tomate* in most of the languages of the Old World. Only in one language was the name of the tomato completely and irrevocably changed. The Italian word for its most beloved adopted food is *pomodoro,* a name that evolved from a number of early descriptive terms for the tomato— *pomo di oro,* apple of gold; *pomo di amore,* apple of love; and *pomo di Mori,* apple of the Moors. (The Moors were associated with Spain, the tomato's first port of entry into Europe.) The comparison of tomatoes with apples is not difficult to understand, given similarities of size, shape, and color; the other designations are somewhat more fanciful, but it is perhaps not inappropriate that the language of Italy should have provided a brand-new name for a food that was so profoundly to affect the cuisine of Italy.

Tarascan Tomato Soup

A classic soup from the state of Michoacán, west of Mexico City, this recipe clearly shows the origin of our own Tex-Mex and chili flavoring traditions. The combination of tomato, ancho chile, oregano, and garlic provides a fundamental seasoning profile that pervades much of Mexican and derivative Mexican cuisine. Here is a rich, smooth, flavorful soup.

Serves 6–8

2 Tb. vegetable oil
1 medium onion, chopped
3 cloves garlic, crushed
2 medium sweet green and/or red peppers, seeded and chopped
1 1-lb. can dark red kidney beans, with juice
1 cup fresh or canned tomatoes, coarsely chopped
4 cups chicken stock
1 6-oz. can tomato paste
2 large ancho chiles, seeded and cut in thin strips
1 tsp. oregano
¼ tsp. crushed dried hot peppers
1–1½ cups shredded mild Cheddar cheese
2 cups crisp corn chips or tortilla chips, coarsely broken

1. In a large heavy pot heat the oil over moderate heat. Add the onion, the garlic, and the peppers and sauté until the onion is just beginning to brown.

2. In a blender or food processor combine the beans and their juice with the tomatoes. Blend until smooth.

3. To the vegetables in the pot add the stock, the pureed beans, the tomato paste, the chile strips, the oregano, and the hot peppers. Cook uncovered over low heat, stirring occasionally, for about 45 minutes.

4. To serve, place a small handful of the grated cheese on the bottom of individual soup bowls. Ladle the hot soup over the cheese, then garnish the soup with corn chips. Serve immediately.

Southern-Style Chicken, Tomato, and Vegetable Soup

The tomato came back to America not just from the Mediterranean, but from Africa as well, a continent sorely impoverished by its peculiar climate and geography and eagerly receptive to many of the valuable New World plant foods. Returned to the American South with black slaves, the tomato became an important ingredient in many savory soups and stews. This flavorful, chowderlike soup is a fine example of how the traditions of the Anglo-American and the African-American came together to produce the undeniable glory of Southern food.

Serves 6–8

2 Tb. vegetable oil
1 medium onion, coarsely chopped
2 cloves garlic, crushed
1 medium sweet green pepper, seeded and diced
2 stalks celery, with leaves, diced
3 oz. cured country-style ham, diced
4 cups coarsely chopped plum tomatoes
4 cups chicken stock
Several good grinds black pepper
½ tsp. dried thyme
½ cup fresh or frozen baby lima beans
½ cup diced cooked chicken
½ cup fresh or frozen corn kernels
Good dash Tabasco sauce

1. In a heavy pot or Dutch oven heat the oil over moderate to high heat. Add the onion, the garlic, the green pepper, the celery, and the ham. Sauté, stirring, until the vegetables are wilted and the onion is beginning to turn golden.

2. Add the chopped tomatoes, the stock, the black pepper, and the thyme. Bring to the simmer, then cook, uncovered, over low heat for 40–45 minutes.

3. Stir in the lima beans, the chicken, the corn, and the Tabasco. Cook for 15–20 minutes. Taste for salt and hot pepper and add more, if desired.

Gazpacho

It is hard to imagine gazpacho without tomatoes or peppers, but, in fact, it is an ancient dish that developed in dozens of varieties throughout Spain long before the discovery of the New World. These so-called "white" gazpachos are made with olive oil, bread, almonds, or eggs, and serve as either a thick soup or a soupy main dish. The gazpacho we know and love can be described as either a cold vegetable soup or a liquid salad, and it shows clearly the impact that tomatoes and peppers had on an Old World tradition. It is one of the most refreshing and satisfying summer dishes ever invented.

Serves 6

1 cucumber, peeled and chopped
¼ cup chopped parsley
1 sweet green pepper, seeded and chopped
2 scallions, or 1 small onion, chopped
2 cloves garlic
½ tsp. oregano
2 Tb. lemon juice
3 Tb. red wine vinegar
1 tsp. Tabasco sauce (more or less to taste)
2 cups tomato juice (fresh strained or bottled)
¼ cup olive oil
Salt and freshly ground pepper to taste

Garnish

1 cucumber, peeled and diced
1 large sweet red or green pepper, seeded and diced
3–4 scallions, chopped
1 avocado, sliced (optional)

1. In a blender or food processor combine the cucumber, parsley, green pepper, scallions, garlic, oregano, lemon juice, vinegar, Tabasco, and enough tomato juice to make the blending easy. Blend until smooth.

2. Pour the pureed mixture and the remaining tomato juice into a serving bowl. Stir in the olive oil and salt and pepper to taste. Chill thoroughly, then taste for seasoning.

3. In a small bowl combine the chopped garnish vegetables. Top with avocado slices, if desired. Serve the gazpacho in bowls and pass the vegetable garnishes.

Tomato Chutney

Sweet, sour, spicy, and pungent—this Indian-style tomato relish is a clear prototype for our own beloved ketchup. Our favorite tomato condiment is tamer and more finely textured, but its affinities with the spiced relishes of the East are obvious. Like ketchup, this chutney is excellent with any grilled meats or kabobs, or as a dip for fried snacks. It will also enliven any recipe that calls for ketchup or chili sauce, as, for example, Russian dressing or cocktail sauce for shrimp.

Makes about 1½ pints

4–5 large red ripe tomatoes, finely chopped
1 large onion, finely chopped
4 large cloves garlic, minced
¼ cup cider vinegar
⅓ cup sugar
1 tsp. ground ginger
½ tsp. crushed dried hot peppers
½ tsp. salt
2 Tb. lime juice
¼ cup raisins

1. In a large heavy enamel or stainless steel pot combine the tomatoes, the onion, the garlic, and the vinegar. Bring to a boil, then cook, uncovered, over moderate heat for 45–60 minutes until it is reduced by about half and most of the liquid has cooked away.

2. Stir in the remaining ingredients and cook, stirring occasionally, for about 15 minutes more until the mixture is quite thick.

3. Store in a covered jar in the refrigerator.

A seventeenth-century English engraving of "apples of love," an early term for tomatoes

Spiced Tomato Vinaigrette

It was Fannie Farmer who, early in the century, was apparently responsible for originating one of the more dubious of American culinary traditions. She stirred some ketchup into a classic oil and vinegar dressing and thus created what the food industry latched on to and stubbornly perpetuated ever since as "French Dressing." I have never met a Frenchman, nor ever hope to meet one, who would claim allegiance to that sweet, gluey, orange concoction. But here is an updated version of Fannie's original idea, a robust, tangy sauce that is nice on lightly cooked, crisp green beans or wax beans or strips of raw zucchini.

Makes about 1 cup

½ cup salad oil
¼ cup cider vinegar
3 Tb. tangy, high-quality ketchup or chili sauce, preferably homemade
¼ tsp. salt
½ tsp. dry mustard
Good dash cayenne pepper
1 tsp. ground freshly toasted cumin seed*

Combine all the ingredients in a jar, cover tightly, and shake vigorously to blend.

*To toast cumin seed: Place the seeds in a small frying pan and heat over moderate heat, shaking the pan constantly, until the seeds are just lightly browned and starting to become aromatic. Remove from heat, cool slightly, then grind in an electric grinder.

| 1876-1870 | 1883-1905 | 1888-1895 | 1889-1910 | 1914-1920 | 1944 to Present | 1983 to Present | 1985 to Present |

Heinz ketchup bottles from 1876 to the present. Although there has been a switch from glass to plastic and from "catsup" to "ketchup," the basic formula remains the same.

Barbecue Pork

In America barbecue means several things, both a way of cooking, usually out-of-doors over fire or hot coals, and a way of seasoning or saucing grilled or roasted foods. There are dozens of regional varieties of barbecue sauce, from the tangy thin vinegar marinades of the South to the sweet-and-sour sauces of the Midwest to the spicy chile mixtures of the Southwest. In this sauce, as in so many others, the tomato acts as a mediator, combining a number of different traditions into a sauce with zesty flavor that is equally good on chicken or beef. Serve this pork thinly sliced or coarsely shredded, smothered in sauce, and heaped on fresh rolls—a sloppy heartwarming sandwich, wonderful with onion rings, creamy cole slaw, and corn on the cob.

Serves 4–6

2 Tb. vegetable oil

2–2½ lbs. lean boneless pork roast, in one piece

1 large onion, chopped

1 large sweet green pepper, seeded and chopped

2 large cloves garlic, crushed

1 cup canned crushed tomatoes or thick tomato sauce

¼ cup cider vinegar

1 Tb. Worcestershire sauce

1½ Tb. brown sugar

¼ tsp. salt

2 tsp. chili powder

*2 whole dried chipotle peppers (if not available substitute 1 tsp. liquid smoke
    and ½ tsp. crushed dried hot peppers)*

1. In a large heavy pot or Dutch oven heat the oil over moderate heat. Add the pork and brown slowly on all sides.

2. While the meat is browning, add the onion, the pepper, and the garlic, and sauté them, stirring.

3. When the meat is nicely browned on all sides, add the remaining ingredients. Mix well, then bring to a simmer. Cover the pot and cook over low heat for 2½–3 hours until the meat is very tender. Remove and discard the chipotle peppers.

4. Remove the meat from the pot and let it stand for about 10 minutes. Continue to cook the sauce over low heat to thicken slightly. Cut the meat in thin slices or shred it coarsely. Return the meat to the sauce and cook over low heat for 20–30 minutes.

5. Serve the meat hot as is or on fresh rolls.

Animal or Vegetable?

In 1820 a Colonel Robert Johnson stood on the courthouse steps in Salem, New Jersey, and ate a raw tomato. To the crowd's amazement he did not drop dead on the spot. He was not the first to eat a raw tomato, but his act marked the beginning of the tomato's emergence into the mainstream as a common salad vegetable. Modern seed catalogues list about two dozen varieties of tomato, most of which were hybridized only within the last century. Though all tomatoes can be eaten raw or cooked, a number of different types have been developed to suit a variety of needs: The tiny cherry tomato is best as a garnish or salad component, while the fleshy plum and pear types are more suitable for cooking because they keep their shape better when heated. Perhaps the most familiar of the American tomatoes is the beefsteak, a large, heavy-fleshed juicy type that represents the flavorful best of the summer harvest. No one is certain who gave the beefsteak its name, but it first appeared under that label in the 1920s, and growers agree that it was called beefsteak because it was so tasty and meaty, almost like a slice of rare juicy steak. The redness and meatiness of tomatoes, unique among fruits and vegetables, may account for its initial rejection by certain Orthodox Jewish sects in eastern Europe; though they recognized it as a fruit, its red meaty quality offended the sacred prohibition against eating blood.

Creole Spaghetti Sauce

Our national passion for pasta with tomato sauce, originally the gift of southern Italy, takes yet another form in this combination that is unique to southern Louisiana. Its flavoring shows once again the complex multi-ethnic makeup of Creole cooking. An interesting change from the more familiar Mediterranean-style tomato sauces, this sauce can be eaten as is on plain cooked spaghetti, or, as is frequently done, combined with the pasta, spooned into a large buttered casserole, topped with grated cheese, and baked.

Serves 4–5

4–5 slices bacon, coarsely chopped
1 large onion, chopped
3–4 stalks celery, with plenty of leaves, diced
1 medium sweet green pepper, seeded and diced
1 medium sweet red pepper, seeded and diced
3 large cloves garlic, crushed
1 28-oz. can crushed tomatoes
2 bay leaves
½ tsp. dried thyme
1 Tb. Worcestershire sauce
⅛ tsp. freshly ground black pepper
½ tsp. Tabasco sauce (more or less to taste)
½ tsp. salt
Good handful flat-leaf Italian parsley, finely chopped
1 lb. hot freshly cooked spaghetti

1. In a large heavy pot fry the bacon over moderate heat until it is crisp and brown. Remove the bacon from the pot with a slotted spoon, drain on paper towels, and reserve. Discard all but about 2 tablespoons of bacon fat from the pot.

2. Add the onion, the celery, the peppers, and the garlic to the pot. Sauté over moderate heat, stirring, until the vegetables are soft and the onion is beginning to turn golden.

3. Add the tomatoes and all the seasonings, mix well, then cook, uncovered, over low heat for about 1 hour. Add the reserved bacon for the last few minutes of cooking. Remove the bay leaves before serving.

4. Taste the sauce for salt and piquancy. Serve over hot cooked spaghetti.

Spiced Tomato Eggplant Casserole

The eggplant, native to Southeast Asia, is the only major food plant of the nightshade family that was not indigenous to the New World. It is perhaps for this reason, a separation of close relatives for untold generations, that the ultimate reunion between the eggplant and the tomato would prove to be so harmonious and so intense. One has only to look at the cuisines of the Mediterranean, the Middle East, and the Balkans to see how closely the eggplant and the tomato work together—sisters under the skin. (Indeed, the Chinese quickly recognized the relationship, calling the tomato, when it was first introduced, the "barbarian eggplant.") This casserole has an unusual flavor, with a hint of both India and the Middle East. The yogurt topping is optional but very good.

Serves 6

5–6 Tb. olive oil
2 medium eggplants, peeled and cut in ½-inch slices
Salt and pepper
1 large onion, coarsely chopped
3 cloves garlic, crushed
2 cups canned crushed tomatoes
½ tsp. salt
Several good grinds black pepper
½ tsp. cinnamon
½ tsp. cumin
3–4 Tb. each of finely chopped flat-leaf Italian parsley,
     fresh dill, and fresh coriander leaf (cilantro)
1 cup plain yogurt (optional)

1. Put 2 Tb. of the olive oil in a large heavy frying pan and heat over high heat. Place the eggplant slices in the pan and turn them over almost immediately so that both sides absorb a small amount of the oil. Sauté the slices quickly, turning frequently, until lightly browned on both sides. As the slices brown remove them to a shallow (about 10 x 12-inch or 13 x 9-inch) casserole. Continue sautéing, adding a little more oil as necessary, until all the eggplant is sautéed. Salt and pepper the slices.

2. To the same pan add 2 more Tb. olive oil. Sauté the onion and the garlic over moderate heat, stirring, until the onion just begins to brown.

3. Stir in the tomatoes, salt, pepper, cinnamon, and cumin. Simmer over low heat for about 30 minutes. Preheat the over to 350°F.

4. In a small bowl combine the chopped fresh herbs and mix well. Reserve 2 Tb. of this mixture for garnish; mix the rest into the tomato sauce.

5. Spread the tomato sauce over the eggplant slices. Bake uncovered for 30–40 minutes until bubbling. Turn off the oven.

6. Spread the yogurt, if desired, over the casserole, and return it to the still-hot oven for about 5 minutes. Remove the casserole from the oven and garnish the top with the reserved chopped herbs. Serve the casserole warm or at room temperature.

The New Jersey tomato harvest on its way to the Campbell's soup factory in the 1940s

Lisbon Burgers

The Portuguese took to the tomato as enthusiastically as did their Spanish neighbors, turning it into a classic sauce, the *tomatada*, used on everything from eggs to vegetables to the national favorite, *bacalhao*, dried salted codfish. It is a robust and versatile sauce, marvelous on hamburgers, if you can pry your family away from the ketchup bottle! It's also excellent on meatloaf, omelets, or almost any cooked vegetable.

Serves 6

2 Tb. olive oil (for best flavor use a ripe, fruity variety)
1 large onion, finely chopped
2 cloves garlic, crushed
4 cups finely chopped fully ripe tomatoes (about 6–7 medium tomatoes)
½ tsp. salt
several good grinds black pepper
small handful flat-leaf parsley, finely chopped
12 oil-cured black olives, pitted and coarsely chopped
several good dashes of piri-piri (chile-seasoned olive oil), or Tabasco sauce, or
*   a generous pinch of crushed, dried hot peppers*
1½–2 lbs. lean ground beef
3–4 large, crusty Kaiser or sourdough rolls, sliced in half

1. In a heavy skillet sauté the onion in the oil over low to moderate heat, stirring occasionally, until the onion is soft and a deep golden color. Add the garlic and cook a few minutes more.

2. Add the tomatoes and cook over moderate heat, stirring occasionally for 40–45 minutes or until most of the liquid has cooked away and the mixture is thick and soft.

3. Stir in the salt, pepper, parsley, olives, and hot pepper. Mix well and cook a few minutes more.

4. Form the beef into 6 large patties and grill or pan-fry to desired doneness. Place each pattie on half a roll, spread generously with the tomato sauce, and serve open-face, accompanied by home-fried potatoes and a green salad.

Chicken in Double Tomato Sauce

The sun-dried tomato is one of the exquisite elaborations of the tomato tradition for which the cuisine of Italy must be gratefully acknowledged. Although it has been somewhat overused in recent times as a trendy new ingredient, there is no doubt that it provides a rich, intense, and unparalleled tomato flavor.

Serves 4–6

3–4 lbs. cut-up chicken fryer parts
2 Tb. olive oil
1 medium onion, finely chopped
8 sun-dried tomatoes (dry packed, not oil packed)
1 tsp. oregano
⅛ tsp. freshly ground black pepper
2 cups tomato sauce or crushed Italian-style tomatoes
2 Tb. balsamic vinegar
Salt to taste

1. In a large heavy skillet or Dutch oven brown the chicken parts in the olive oil over moderately high heat. Remove the chicken from the pot, salt and pepper lightly, and set aside.

2. In the same skillet sauté the onion until it is golden brown.

3. Return the chicken to the pot, add the dried tomatoes, oregano, pepper, and tomato sauce. Bring to a simmer, then cover and cook over low heat about 30–40 minutes or until the chicken is just tender.

4. Remove the cover, add the vinegar, and simmer a few minutes. Taste for salt. Serve the chicken with a simple rice or pasta.

The Inside Story

Slice a large ripe tomato horizontally and behold one of nature's marvels of symmetry. In a beautiful flower-like design lines of red tomato flesh enclose segments of a lucent jelly-like substance that contains the tiny tomato seeds. This inner part of the tomato is as important as the brilliant red outer shell. The jelly contains the highest concentrations of vitamin C in the fruit and much of the tomato's flavor. (You can test this yourself by spooning out a bit of the jelly and comparing it with a bite of the flesh.) The jelly is also responsible for a good deal of what we value the tomato for—its juiciness. Flavor and juice are what make the ripe raw tomato so delectable in salads and sandwiches. Can you imagine a BLT without the T? Or a barbecue without a platter of thick-sliced beefsteak tomatoes, filled with the flavor of summer and so juicy that your hamburger or steak needs no other dressing?

Tomato jelly is wonderful stuff, and its only flaw is that it contains the seeds, which some fastidious cooks find offensive; in an effort to remove the seeds they frequently do away as well with the flavorful jelly. That is a big mistake. If you want to get rid of the seeds in a tomato sauce, strain the sauce after it has cooked, so that the juice is retained as a part of the flavor.* So if you run into a recipe that instructs you to squeeze out the juice and discard it, throw away the recipe and keep the tomato with its insides intact.

*Or if you need a tomato shell with the flesh scooped out, strain the seeds from the inside material and save it for use in soups or sauces.

A Trio of Italian Tomato Sauces

Although Columbus sailed under the flag of Spain, he was Italian by birth; it is ironic that he was never to know that, of the many gifts of the New World, one was to become the national treasure of his own homeland. Would he have relished a plateful of pasta with zesty tomato sauce? or a hearty seafood marinara? We will never know and neither will he, unless, of course, there is an explorers' heaven and its clouds are lined with chicken cacciatore and spaghetti Bolognese! Tomato sauces—for meat, for vegetables, and especially for pasta—have become a truly integral part of the American table, and most of what we know and love about them comes from the cuisine of southern Italy. Here is a trio of Italian-style tomato sauces to fit a variety of needs.

1. The Marinara

In America marinara is frequently used as a kind of generic term for any Italian-style tomato sauce. In Italy the name refers more specifically to a tomato sauce used for seafood by coastal people or fishermen. It is a robust, simple sauce that complements the salty-fresh tang of the day's catch, and it does well with almost any ocean fish or shellfish, alone or in combination. This one makes a fine base for steamed mussels in red sauce or a San Francisco-style *cioppino*.

Serves 4

> *3–4 Tb. olive oil*
> *4–5 large cloves garlic, crushed*
> *1 28-oz. can crushed tomatoes*
> *½ cup finely chopped Italian flat-leaf parsley, plus additional for garnish*
> *½–¾ tsp. salt*
> *⅛ tsp. black pepper*
> *⅓ cup dry white wine (optional)*

1. In a large heavy pot heat the olive oil over low to moderate heat. Add the garlic and cook, stirring, until the garlic is just starting to turn a pale gold color and is very aromatic. Do not brown or overcook the garlic.

2. Add the tomatoes, the parsley, ½ tsp. salt, pepper, and the white wine, if desired. Bring to the simmer, then cook, uncovered, over low heat for about 20 minutes stirring occasionally, until slightly thickened. Serve with hot cooked spaghetti or linguine and garnish with the remaining parsley.

2. Tomato Sauce with Peppers and Mushrooms

This hearty, chunky sauce has the flavor we most closely identify as "Italian." Served over hot cooked pasta, it is fine as is, or you can add meatballs, cooked ground beef, or sausage, if desired.

Makes about 4 cups sauce, enough for 1 lb. cooked pasta

Serves 4–6

4 Tb. olive oil

1 large onion, coarsely chopped

1 large sweet red or green pepper, seeded and coarsely chopped

3 cloves garlic, crushed

1 28-oz. can crushed tomatoes

1 cup tomato sauce

1½ tsp. dried crumbled oregano

1½ tsp. crushed dried basil

1 tsp. salt

⅛ tsp. freshly ground black pepper

½ lb. fresh mushrooms, sliced

1. In a heavy pot heat 2 Tb. of the oil over moderate heat. Add the onion, the peppers, and the garlic and sauté, stirring, until the onion starts to turn golden.

2. Stir in the tomatoes, the tomato sauce, the oregano, basil, salt, and pepper. Bring to the simmer, then cook, uncovered, over low heat for 30–40 minutes, stirring occasionally.

3. In a medium skillet heat the remaining 2 Tb. olive oil over moderate to high heat. Add the sliced mushrooms and sauté quickly, stirring or tossing them in the pan, until just lightly browned.

4. Add the sautéed mushrooms to the sauce and cook a few minutes more. Serve the sauce over hot cooked pasta and pass freshly grated Parmesan or Romano cheese.

3. Tomato Cream Sauce

Here is a rich but delicate sauce, fine with pasta but especially good with sweet little scallops or shrimp. Its butter and cream reveal a northern Italian influence. As an interesting flavor variation with seafood, add ½ tsp. fennel seed and 2 tsp. grated orange zest to the tomatoes while they are cooking. As in any tomato sauce, it is important to use fine, fully ripe tomatoes. If high-quality fresh tomatoes are not available, substitute 2 cups of canned crushed.

Makes about 2½ cups, enough for about 1–1½ lb. seafood

Serves 4

1 Tb. olive oil
1 Tb. butter
1 medium onion, finely chopped
4–5 medium, fully ripe tomatoes, coarsely chopped
        or coarsely processed in the food processor
1 cup light cream
½ tsp. salt
½ tsp. crushed dried basil
¼ tsp. nutmeg
Several good grinds black pepper
2 Tb. freshly grated Parmesan
        cheese

1. In a medium heavy skillet or saucepan heat the olive oil and the butter over moderate heat. Add the onion and sauté, stirring, until the onion wilts and begins to turn golden.

2. Add the tomatoes, mix well, then cook, uncovered, over moderate heat, stirring occasionally, until most of the liquid has cooked away and the tomatoes are soft and thick.

3. Stir in the cream, the salt, basil, nutmeg, and pepper. Bring just to the simmer, then cook over low heat for about 5 minutes.

4. Stir in the cheese and mix well.

In the 1950s, pizza transformed the American landscape.

Braised Salmon Provençal

Here again is the alliance of olive oil and tomatoes, this time with the distinctive flavor profile of southern France. Salmon is not commonly used in Mediterranean cooking, but it is a fish Americans are very fond of, and it lends itself well to this simple but elegant treatment. The dish can be served either hot or cold.

Serves 4

2 Tb. olive oil
1 medium onion, finely chopped
2 cloves garlic, crushed
1 lb. ripe plum tomatoes (about 6–8), coarsely chopped,
        or 2 cups canned crushed tomatoes
½ tsp. dried basil
¼ tsp. dried thyme
¼ tsp. salt
Several good grinds black pepper
2–3 Tb. dry white wine
1 Tb. capers
4 small salmon steaks (about ⅓–½ lb. each) of uniform thickness
Fresh chopped parsley for garnish

1. In a medium to large skillet heat the oil over moderate heat. Add the onion and the garlic and sauté until the onion wilts and begins to turn golden.

2. Add the tomatoes, the herbs, the salt, and the pepper, and simmer, uncovered, over moderate heat about 20–30 minutes, stirring occasionally, until the mixture is soft and thick and most of the liquid has cooked away.

3. Stir in the wine and the capers, mix well, then place the salmon steaks in the sauce. Bring to a simmer, cover, and cook over low heat for 10–15 minutes or until the salmon is just cooked through. (Test for doneness with a small sharp knife in the thickest part of the steak.)

4. Remove from the heat and garnish with the chopped parsley. Serve hot with steamed new potatoes, or chill, if desired.

Spicy Tomato Aspic

Aspics and molded fruit and vegetable salads were once very popular but have declined in fashion in the last few decades. I predict a revival, minus the canned fruit cocktail and mini-marshmallows. Aspics are refreshing and versatile and, properly flavored, can deliver a low-calorie, nonfat dish that is very satisfying, tastes good, and can be exciting visually. This aspic, with its robust south-of-the-border flavor, can be served simply as a salad, on a plate of greens with a few slices of avocado and a dollop of sour cream. Or, for a more extravagant first course or lunch entrée, garnish it with cooked shrimp or crabmeat, hard-boiled egg wedges, or strips of smoked turkey or ham.

Serves 4–6

2½ cups canned or bottled tomato juice
1 dried smoked chipotle chile*
¼ tsp. ground ancho chile
⅛ tsp. oregano
Dash salt
1 Tb. (1 envelope) unflavored gelatin
1 Tb. fresh lime juice
3 Tb. chopped fresh coriander leaf (cilantro)
4–5 scallions, mostly white part, minced
½ cup finely chopped sweet green pepper

1. In a small saucepan combine 1½ cups of the tomato juice and the chipotle chile. Let stand 1 hour.

2. Add the ancho chile, oregano, and salt. Bring to a simmer, then cook over low heat about 6–7 minutes. Remove the chipotle pepper and discard.

3. In a small bowl soften the gelatin in the remaining 1 cup tomato juice.

4. Add the gelatin mixture to the hot tomato-chile mixture and stir until the gelatin is completely dissolved. Stir in the lime juice and coriander.

5. Refrigerate the mixture until partially set. Stir in the scallions and the green pepper.

6. Pour the mixture into a 3- or 4-cup mold. Refrigerate for several hours or until set.

*If not available, substitute ½ tsp. liquid smoke and ½ tsp. Tabasco sauce.

Tomato Rice Salad

Here is that old American favorite, Spanish rice, newly garnished and chilled and with its flavor dressed up, to serve as a hearty salad or a light main course. It is also very good as a stuffing for peppers.

Serves 6–8

1 medium onion, finely chopped
1 medium sweet red or green pepper, finely chopped
2 Tb. olive oil
1½ cups converted long-grain rice
2 cups chicken stock
1 cup (8-oz. can) tomato sauce
¼ tsp. black pepper
6–8 sun-dried tomatoes, cut or torn in small pieces
½ cup cooked fresh or frozen peas
1 cup cooked or canned chick-peas, drained
1 medium zucchini, diced
1 large ripe tomato, coarsely chopped
½ cup finely chopped flat-leaf Italian parsley
3 Tb. lemon juice
2 Tb. olive oil

1. In a medium saucepan sauté the onion and pepper in the olive oil over moderate heat, stirring occasionally, until they are soft and the onion is golden brown.

2. Add the rice and stir into the onion-pepper mixture.

3. Add the stock, tomato sauce, pepper, and dried tomatoes. Bring to a boil, then cover and cook over low heat about 20 minutes until the rice is tender and all the liquid is absorbed. Remove from heat and let cool completely.

4. Add the remaining ingredients to the cooled rice and mix gently but thoroughly. Chill, then taste for salt and pepper.

Tomato Salad with Chick-Peas and Tuna

The same people of the Mediterranean who cooked the tomato into a wide variety of sauces also seem to have appreciated early on its value as a fresh salad ingredient. In the mid-eighteenth century an English horticulturist noted—with some skepticism—that the Spanish and Italians ate tomatoes "as we doe cucumbers, with pepper, oil, and salt." It took another hundred years for northern Europe and America to eat the tomato raw, but that belated acceptance has turned into an overwhelming appreciation for the juicy and flavorful fruit. This salad, with its clear Middle Eastern affinities, makes a refreshing light main course; it can be served as is or stuffed into pockets of pita bread.

Serves 4–6

1 6½- to 7-oz. can tuna (water-packed), drained
2 cups cooked chick-peas, or 1 1-lb. can chick-peas, drained,
*   rinsed in cold water, and drained again*
3 large ripe tomatoes, coarsely chopped
5–6 scallions, minced
½ cup Kalamata or other oil-cured black olives
½ cup chopped flat-leaf Italian parsley
1½ tsp. oregano
¼ cup olive oil
2 Tb. lemon juice
½ tsp. salt
⅛ tsp. freshly ground black pepper

1. In a large bowl mix together the tuna, lightly flaked, the chick-peas, the tomatoes, the scallions, the olives, the parsley, and the oregano.

2. In a small bowl or cup combine the olive oil, the lemon juice, the salt, and pepper. Whisk to blend thoroughly.

3. Pour the dressing over the salad and blend lightly but thoroughly. Serve on a bed of greens with pockets of pita bread.

Sun-Dried Tomato Pesto

As Spain and Hungary were centers of sweet pepper elaboration, southern Italy was the focus of tomato cookery, and the Italian practice of sun-drying tomatoes was described in English herbals as early as the eighteenth century. This is a very richly flavored *pesto;* a little goes a long way. Serve it as a sauce or dip for cold cooked vegetables and shrimp, or as a sauce for grilled lamb. I like it for little hot tomato croustades. Spread lightly on thin slices of French or sourdough bread, top with mozzarrella cheese, and bake for about 10 minutes in a 350°F. oven until the cheese is melted and bubbly. Or use in a fragrant Tomato Herb Bread (see facing page).

Makes about 1 cup

1 cup (lightly packed) sun-dried tomatoes (not oil packed)
4 cloves garlic
½ tsp. salt
Good handful flat-leaf Italian parsley
½ cup olive oil
1 Tb. lemon juice

1. Cover the dried tomatoes with hot water and let stand for 15–20 minutes. Drain thoroughly.

2. In a blender or food processor combine the drained tomatoes, the garlic, the salt, and the parsley. Process until the mixture is coarsely pureed.

3. Continue to process while adding the olive oil in a slow steady stream.

4. When all the olive oil has been incorporated, blend in the lemon juice.

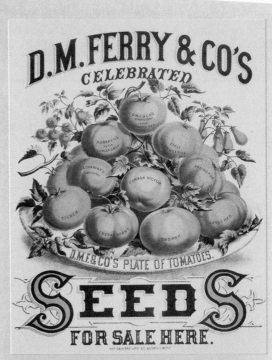

Early seed advertisement showing a variety of tomatoes. During the nineteenth century the tomato experienced a dramatic turnabout, from a fruit suspected of being poisonous to a popular food for the American table.

Tomato Herb Bread

The tomato seems to have found a special affinity for the herbs of the Mediterranean—garlic, basil, sage, thyme, oregano. We tend to think of oregano as an Italian seasoning, but actually, it existed in pre-Columbian Mexico before the Spanish arrived. Stronger and somewhat more pungent than its Mediterranean counterpart, it was called "Mexican sage" by the conquistadores. In this recipe the tomato combines with old and new seasoning allies for a fragrant, tasty loaf.

Makes 1 loaf

1 cup very warm water
2 tsp. sugar
1 Tb. granulated yeast or 1 cake compressed yeast
2½–3½ cups flour
1 tsp. salt
4–5 Tb. Sun-Dried Tomato Pesto (see preceding page)
¼ tsp. dried crumbled oregano
1 Tb. fresh rosemary leaves
6–8 fresh sage leaves (tear in half if very large)

1. In a large mixing bowl combine the water and the sugar; mix until the sugar is dissolved. Sprinkle the yeast over the water and let proof for 5 minutes.

2. Stir in 1 cup of the flour and the salt and beat the mixture for 2–3 minutes.

3. Stir in enough additional flour to make a thick dough. Knead the dough until it is smooth, elastic, and nonsticky.

4. Place the dough in a lightly oiled bowl, cover with a towel, and let rise in a warm place for about 1 hour until it is doubled in bulk.

5. Punch the dough down, then roll it out on a floured surface into a rectangle about 15 x 6-inches. Spread the tomato pesto evenly over the surface, to within 1-inch of the edges. Sprinkle the oregano over the pesto, then place the rosemary and sage leaves over the top.

6. Roll up the dough from the long side, as you would roll a jelly roll. Taper the ends of the loaf and pinch the dough to seal. Place the loaf, seam side down, on a baking tray or a baking stone. With a sharp knife make a few slashes in the top of the loaf. Cover the loaf with a towel and let rise in a warm place for about 1 hour until doubled in bulk.

7. Preheat the oven to 400°F. Bake the loaf for about 20 minutes until it is brown and crusty and sounds hollow when tapped sharply with the fingers. Cool slightly on a rack before slicing.

Spiced Fried Green Tomatoes

Although the red tomato was widely accepted in other parts of the world, and particularly in the Mediterranean, the use of the unripe, or green, tomato seems to be a largely American phenomenon. And even here green tomatoes rarely appear outside the home kitchen, where a tradition of their cookery developed in response to the prolific harvest of the summer garden. Because of their firm texture and agreeable tartness, green tomatoes are frequently pickled, either whole or in relish, or sugared and sliced, like apples, for pie. Fried green tomatoes are a Southern specialty; they make a very nice brunch or vegetable side dish. Serve hot from the pan.

Serves 3–4

1 cup cornmeal
½ tsp. salt
½ tsp. cumin
¼ tsp. oregano
⅛ tsp. cayenne pepper
1 Tb. freshly grated Parmesan cheese
3–4 large green tomatoes
3–4 Tb. vegetable oil

1. In a shallow dish or pie pan combine the cornmeal, the salt, the cumin, oregano, cayenne, and Parmesan. Mix thoroughly.

2. Cut the ends off the tomatoes, then cut the tomatoes in 3–4 slices, each about ½-inch thick.

3. In a heavy skillet heat the oil over moderately high heat.

4. Dredge the tomato slices in the cornmeal mixture, then fry in the hot oil, turning once, until nicely browned and crisp on both sides. Place on a platter and serve immediately.

Tomato and Apple Pie

Tomato pie in America was an early name for pizza, a flat Italian bread topped with tomato sauce and cheese. In England, tomato pie meant something quite different; the tomato's original use by the English was as a fruit, sweetened, spiced, and combined with other fruits. This pie is an adaptation of an early English pie in which the tomato appears as part of a sweetened fruit mixture, lending an interesting and unusual flavor to a traditional apple pie. It is important to use high-quality, fleshy, fully ripe tomatoes.

Serves 6–8

Pastry for 1 deep 9-inch pie
4–5 medium fully ripe red tomatoes, coarsely chopped
6 cups peeled thinly sliced Granny Smith apples (about 8 medium apples),
*   or other tart-sweet pie apples*
⅔ cup sugar
1 tsp. cinnamon
½ tsp. ginger
¼ tsp. nutmeg
2 Tb. flour
¼ cup heavy cream, plus additional heavy cream to pass

1. In a blender or food processor puree the chopped tomatoes. Pour the puree into a medium skillet or saucepan and cook, uncovered, over moderate to high heat, stirring occasionally, until all the liquid has cooked away and the tomatoes are a thick, soft puree. This will take 15 minutes or so, depending on the amount of liquid in the tomatoes. Preheat the oven to 400°F.

2. In a large bowl combine the sliced apples, the sugar, the spices, and the flour. Mix thoroughly.

3. Spoon the tomato puree into the apples and mix thoroughly.

4. Line a 9-inch pie pan with pastry dough, trim, and crimp the edges.

5. Spoon the apple mixture into the pie shell, mounding it slightly in the center. Dribble the ¼ cup heavy cream over the apples.

6. Bake the pie for 15 minutes at 400°F., then reduce the heat to 350°F. Bake for an additional 30–35 minutes until the apples are bubbling and tender.

7. Serve the pie with the heavy cream.

Smoky Bean Soup

Chili Bean Soup

Curried Lima Bean Chowder

West Indian Pumpkin Soup

Cuban Black Beans and Rice

Creole Red Beans and Rice

Gingered Barley, Bean, and Bulgur Pilaf

Pasta Fazool

Bean-Stuffed Pasta Shells Primavera

Barbecue Butter Beans

Black Bean Quiche

Dill-Pickled Green Beans

Stir-Fried String Beans with Elephant Garlic

Mock Chopped Liver

Beer-Baked Beans with Apples and Sausage

Pumpkin Seed Pesto

Gratin of Summer Squash

Tex-Mex Vegetable Casserole

Summer Garden Sauté

Fresh Cranberry Bean Salad with Herb Vinaigrette

Zucchini Bread

BEANS, PUMPKINS, AND SQUASHES

No matter what its outer appearance, a bean is just a bean. Of all the foods discovered in the New World, beans initially received almost no press; they made their way to Europe without seeming to evoke any response whatsoever. This experience was very different from that of the other new foods, which were greeted with a mixed bag of reactions, from fear to delight to repugnance, but which were acknowledged at some level for their novelty. Tomatoes, as we have seen, were shunned as poisonous and potatoes were thought to cause leprosy, while chocolate and vanilla were eagerly accepted and turkey prized as a bird for the tables of the rich. But no one said a word about the beans—beans of every size, shape, and color; beans that had never before been seen.

The lack of excitement is not surprising, given that beans of one sort or another have been known and utilized from the earliest periods of human history. Wherever in the world people roamed or settled there has been some variety of legume to nourish and sustain when animal foods were scarce. Beans have been called "poor man's meat" because they are filling, satisfying, and relatively high in protein. Unremarkable and unglamorous, but steadfast and reliable, they formed the nutritional backbone of many cuisines. In Southeast Asia, and particularly in China, it was the soybean, elaborated into a number of different forms—soy pastes, soy curd (*tofu*), soy sauce—that was from earliest days an important feature of Oriental cooking. In India it was pulses—all manner of lentils and split peas—that took the place of meat for folk who couldn't afford it or who wouldn't eat it because of religious taboo. In Africa there were cow peas and black-eyed peas that were eventually to come to the American South; and in the Middle East and Europe, chick-peas, fava (broad) beans, as well as a variety of dried peas and beans that turned up as daily sustenance in soups, pilafs, porridges, and stews.

So beans as a generic food were nothing really new. But here in the New World an entirely new cast of characters was discovered—black beans, pinto beans, teppary beans, kidney beans, string beans, lima beans, runner beans, navy beans, cranberry beans, and dozens more. A whole new range of colors, shapes, and textures, a whole new set of possibilities for adding variety to traditional bean cookery. Some seem never to have made a truly successful crossing; perhaps differences in color or texture made black beans, speckled beans, and limas less acceptable to Old World tastes. Others, like red and white kidneys, pea and marrow beans, made the journey with ease and were absorbed quietly into the beanpots of the world. Indeed, the green bean or string bean, which is simply the immature green pod of the kidney bean, was so quickly enfolded into the cuisine of France that it became known as the "French" bean, an inaccuracy reflected in Gilbert and Sullivan's operetta, *Patience:*

> *Then a sentimental passion of a vegetable fashion must*
> *excite your languid spleen,*
> *An attachment* à la *Plato for a bashful young potato, or*
> *a not-too-French French bean!*

If Native Americans were dedicated bean-eaters before Columbus, immigrant Americans remained afterward faithful to the tradition, simply adding new flavors and new ingredients that were a part of their Old World cultures. Where North American tribes had sweetened their beans with maple syrup and enriched them with bear fat, New Englanders frequently substituted sugar or molasses and ham or bacon. Baked beans, the dish that has always been emblematic of Anglo-American home cooking, is a genuine amalgam of Old and New World traditions, and is as esteemed today as it was in the times of the early settlers. Boston will forever be known as "bean town" because of its dependence on this dish that was both satisfying and frugal. Customarily eaten with Boston brown bread (a loaf of cornmeal, rye or wheat flour, and molasses), it provided a complete meal that was tasty, filling, and very nourishing, requiring no supplement of meat or other animal foods.

And this brings us to what it is that is so remarkable about all these humble little beans. Wherever in the world they have turned up, they function in exactly the same way in the human diet: Whatever the variety, beans are consistently cooked and eaten together with another plant or vegetable food, usually a cereal grain. Both beans and cereal grains are seeds and as such contain a large amount of the plant's proteins. But no single bean or grain contains the full complement of amino acids necessary for human nutrition, such as are found in meat or animal foods. We don't know how human beings learned about combining complementary plant proteins to achieve a satisfactory balance of amino acids, but it is a phenomenon that occurred at many different times in many diverse areas. It was one of those pieces of nutritional wisdom, learned over centuries through careful observation, and passed on from generation to generation.

In the New World the cereal grain was corn, a food low in two essential amino acids, lysine and tryptophan; the many beans supplied these two acids, while corn provided zein, a protein lacking in the beans. The two foods, consistently eaten together in the same meal, provided a nutritionally satisfactory balance of proteins, equal to any slice of steak or hunk of cheese. The pervasive combination of corn and beans resulted in culinary traditions that are alive and well today: stewed or mashed beans eaten with tortillas in Mexico, a variety of corn and bean stews that are known in North America as succotash, and, yes, baked beans and brown bread. When Old World grains were introduced to America, they too combined happily with the many indigenous beans, and so was begun a whole new complex of bean and grain dishes; beans with barley, beans with rice, and beans with wheat, in the form of both bread and pasta. Nowadays when we savor our minestrone, brimming with kidney beans and macaroni, our spicy Creole red beans and rice, our crunchy corn chips with garlicky bean dip, we are participating in an age-old tradition that has its roots in the need for proper nourishment. But we are enjoying as well the gastronomic pleasures of the homely little bean, a genuine food of the people. Nearly two thousand years ago the Roman poet Martial said it as well as it has ever been said:

If pale beans bubble for you in a red earthenware pot
You can oft decline the dinners of sumptuous hosts.

Completing the triad of basic foods that nourished pre-Columbian America from the most ancient times are the squashes and pumpkins. The intimate relationship between the "three sisters" of the New World began in the gardens and fields, where the corn and beans were planted in the same mound of earth, the corn stalks providing a support for the twining bean plants. And between the rows grew the winter squashes, ripening on the vine after the corn had been harvested in the fall. Though not as nutritionally power-packed as corn and beans, the large variety of squashes provided a welcome addition of fresh vegetables from summer well into winter. They were cooked much as they are today, baked (in the hot ashes rather than an oven) and then sweetened with maple syrup or honey, or simmered in soups and combined with other vegetables. Squashes and pumpkins were extraordinarily useful and versatile; not only was their flesh eaten as a vegetable, but their blossoms, *flores de calabeza* in Spanish, were cooked and eaten as a great delicacy, as they are still today in Mexico. Their seeds, a rich source of oil and protein, were toasted and eaten out of hand or ground into pastes and thickeners for sauces. And the shells of some varieties were used as bottles, containers, ladles, and spoons. It's not every plant that can provide, in one handy package, the food, the bowl to put it in, and the spoon to eat it with!

Of the many varieties of squash and pumpkin that were indigenous to the New World, the most widely used today are the hard-shelled winter squashes (acorn, hubbard, butternut) and the soft-shelled summer squashes (the yellow and the green, better known as zucchini, courgette, or calabacita). All these have remained a vital part of the American tradition, while new varieties like the tender little pattypan and the sweet golden dumpling have been hybridized to add interest and novelty to the traditional cast of characters.

And, of course, the best known and best beloved of all is the Halloween pumpkin, tangible symbol of the abundant autumn harvest. Its succulent orange flesh was transformed by early settlers into a rich, sweet custard, fragrant with cinnamon and nutmeg, and baked, as the English prepared so much of their food, "in a pye." Its seeds were roasted and salted for a crunchy snack on cold winter nights. And the shell was carved into the grinning jack-o'-lantern of All Hallow's Eve, an ancient festival that marked the death of summer and the passage into winter. In America it has become a special holiday for children, and the pumpkin is used more for fun and decoration, while its distinctive shape and color are mimicked in a variety of sweets more acceptable to the juvenile palate.

The beans, pumpkins, and squashes that grew so abundantly in the New World were accepted with ease and with gratitude, if with little fuss. They remain today what they have always been—homely foods, foods of the earth—and it is very likely that this is why they have come to be more surely appreciated in contemporary cuisine.

Smoky Bean Soup

The simplest is often the best, as this combination amply proves. An unassuming traditional classic of the American table, it combines a rich smoky flavor we like so well with beans in a hearty stick-to-the-ribs soup.

Serves 6–8

1 lb. dried navy beans
6 whole cloves
1 large onion, peeled and left whole
2 carrots, sliced
2 stalks celery, with leaves, coarsely chopped
2 bay leaves
3 Tb. tomato paste
1–1½ lb. smoked turkey parts
3 quarts water
2–2½ tsp. salt
¼ tsp. black pepper

1. Soak the beans in cold water for 4 hours or overnight. Drain.

2. Stick the cloves into the ends of the onion.

3. In a large pot combine the drained beans, the clove-stuck onion, the carrots, celery, bay leaves, tomato paste, turkey parts, and the water. Bring to the simmer, then cook, uncovered, over moderate heat for 1½–2 hours or until the beans are very tender.

4. Stir in the salt and pepper and taste for seasoning. Remove the onion, the bay leaves, and the turkey parts before serving (the turkey will have given all its flavor to the soup).

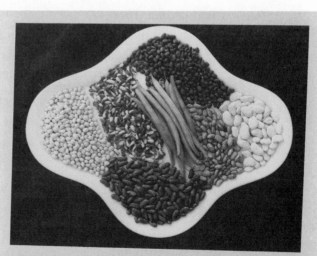

Some of the more familiar New World beans. From the top, clockwise: black beans, limas, kidneys, navy beans. In the center, left to right: speckled beans, string beans, pinto beans.

To Soak or Not To Soak

Except for the few varieties that we consume fresh, most of the beans we use are mature, dried seeds, and require long cooking in liquid to make them palatable as well as digestible. Tradition has it that before they are cooked beans should be soaked in water overnight or for at least four hours. There is nothing mysterious about the soaking process; it simply shortens the subsequent cooking time. It is interesting, however, that in Mexico, the ancient hearth of bean cookery, beans are not customarily soaked before they are cooked. The reason may be that beans, even those of the same variety, differ widely in their permeability—that is, their capacity to absorb water. Mexican cooks claim that because of this variability, with some beans absorbing more water than others, prior soaking results in an unevenly cooked pot of beans. With today's modern harvesting and processing, however, this variability may not be as significant a factor as it is on the village or market level. The packaged beans we buy in supermarkets frequently come with "quick soak" instructions; this too can shorten the cooking time. To soak or not to soak remains an individual decision, then; my recipes call for soaking, but if you choose not to, readjust your calculations for a somewhat longer cooking time. There is one rule about bean cooking that is worth observing: Salt should not be added to the cooking liquid before the beans are almost fully cooked, as salt severely inhibits the softening process.

Here are the basic bean cooking directions: Rinse the beans thoroughly in cold water, drain, then place in a large pot. Cover them with 3 to 4 times their volume in cold water. Soak them for at least 4 hours or overnight. Drain them again, then cover them with the same amount of fresh cold water. Add any seasonings except salt. Simmer the beans, uncovered, until they are tender, then proceed with any particular recipe. The cooking time will vary according to the type of bean (kidneys and large limas require more time than marrows or pintos); the finished dish (beans for soups or purees should cook longer than beans for salads or casseroles); and the freshness of the dried bean—beans that have sat too long on the pantry or supermarket shelf will require longer cooking and may cook unevenly.

Canned beans, which come in many varieties, are frequently a useful shortcut. Always rinse them well in cold water and drain thoroughly before using.

Chili Bean Soup

The legendary scout, Kit Carson, is reported to have said on his deathbed: "I'm just sorry I haven't got time for one more bowl of chili!" This one's for you, Kit; a spicy forthright soup to share with friends on a snowy Taos night.

Serves 6

1 medium onion, chopped
1 medium sweet red pepper, seeded and chopped
2 Tb. vegetable oil
2 large cloves garlic, crushed
¼ tsp. crushed dried hot peppers (more or less to taste)
2 cups canned crushed tomatoes
3 cups water
2 cups dried red kidney beans, soaked and cooked (see p. 144)
*   or canned red kidney beans, drained*
½ tsp. salt
½ tsp. oregano
1 tsp. cumin
3–4 oz. chorizo, or other spicy garlic sausage, cooked and crumbled
Finely chopped onion, shredded Monterrey Jack or mild Cheddar cheese,
*   sour cream, and unsalted corn chips for garnish*

continued

Chili Bean Soup continued

1. In a medium saucepan sauté the onion and pepper in the oil until the onion wilts and starts to turn golden.

2. Stir in the garlic and the crushed dried peppers and sauté a few minutes more.

3. Add the tomatoes, water, beans, and seasonings and simmer over low heat for about 30–40 minutes.

4. Add the chorizo and cook for 15 minutes more.

5. Serve the soup very hot with an assortment of the garnishes.

Curried Lima Bean Chowder

Like corn, its ancient partner, the lima bean can be eaten both fresh and dried. Treated with respect in its immature green state it can be a wonderful crunchy vegetable, with none of the mealiness of the mature dried bean. If fresh limas are not available, use frozen baby limas. Canned beans are too salty and overcooked to work in this soup.

Serves 4

1 Tb. butter
1 medium onion, chopped
1 carrot, diced
1 rib celery, chopped
1 tsp. curry powder
2 cups chicken stock
¾ cup fresh green small lima beans or frozen baby lima beans
1 medium potato, peeled and diced
¼ tsp. mace
Good dash cayenne pepper
½ cup light cream

1. In a medium saucepan heat the butter over moderate heat. Add the onion, the carrot, and the celery and sauté until the onion is soft.

2. Stir in the curry powder and sauté for another few minutes.

3. Add the stock, the beans, the potato, the mace, and the cayenne. Bring to the simmer and cook, uncovered, over low heat until the beans and the potato are just tender.

4. Stir in the cream and bring just to the simmer.

West Indian Pumpkin Soup

The cooking of the West Indies is a blend of many elements—Spanish, English, African, Native American. This richly flavored soup is no exception; its beautiful color and creamy texture are provided by the pumpkin, an ancient New World food.

Serves 6

4–5 slices bacon, diced
1 medium onion, chopped
1 sweet green pepper, chopped
1 large carrot, diced
2 cloves garlic, mashed
3 cups ham stock (chicken stock may also be used)
1 cup fresh or canned tomatoes, with juice, coarsely chopped
1 large bay leaf
1 cup pureed unsweetened pumpkin (cooked or canned)
⅛ tsp. ground allspice
Good pinch crushed dried hot peppers
Several good grinds black pepper
1 Tb. cream (sweet) sherry
Salt to taste

1. In a heavy pot cook the bacon until crisp. Remove the bacon from the pot with a slotted spoon and reserve. Pour off the fat, leaving just enough to film the bottom of the pot.

2. Add the onion, green pepper, carrot, and garlic and sauté over moderate heat until the vegetables are soft.

3. Add the remaining ingredients except the sherry and bring to a simmer. Cook, uncovered, over low heat for about 30 minutes.

4. Just before serving, stir in the sherry. Taste for salt. Garnish the soup with the reserved bacon pieces.

Cuban Black Beans and Rice

There are as many beans-and-rice dishes in the West Indies as there are cooks, and they are similar in many ways. All are highly seasoned with garlic, thyme, and peppers; they are generally flavored with some kind of pork or smoked ham; and when combined with rice they form a complete meal. Note the similarity of this recipe to the Creole dish of red beans and rice. Both come from the same tradition, one that encompasses elements of Spanish, African, and New World cuisines, but they taste significantly different. This dish is nicknamed "Moros y Christianos," black beans for the Moors, white rice for the Christians. Integration occurs in cuisine, if not in real life.

Serves 4–6

4 cups soaked and cooked (see p. 144) black beans,
    or 2 1-lb. cans, drained, rinsed, and drained again
1 large onion, chopped
1 large sweet green pepper, seeded and chopped
2 large cloves garlic, crushed
2 Tb. olive oil
½ cup finely chopped smoked ham
4 plum tomatoes, chopped, or 1 cup tomato sauce
2 Tb. wine vinegar
1 tsp. dried thyme
Several good dashes West Indian hot pepper sauce (or Tabasco,
    or a good pinch of crushed dried hot peppers)
Good handful chopped flat-leaf Italian parsley
Salt to taste
2–3 cups freshly cooked hot rice

1. In a large skillet or pot sauté the onion, pepper, and garlic in the olive oil until the onion is soft. Add the ham and sauté a few minutes more.

2. Add the tomatoes and all the other seasonings and mix well.

3. Stir in the beans and cook over low heat, stirring occasionally, until the mixture is thick, about 15 minutes.

4. Serve the beans over hot rice. Pass additional hot pepper sauce.

Note: This dish is traditionally served hot with rice, but it is very good served chilled, without rice, as a salad or vegetable.

Creole Red Beans and Rice

From southern Louisiana, this is one of America's great regional bean dishes. It combines many influences—the smoked pork of Europe, the rice of the Mediterranean, the seasonings of Africa and the Caribbean, and, of course, the kidney beans and chile peppers of the New World. The secret to its success lies in a liberal hand with the seasoning and long slow cooking. The finished dish should be thick and creamy, with a melt-in-the-mouth texture that is complemented by its zesty flavor.

Serves 6–8

2½ cups (1 lb.) dried red kidney beans
1 very large onion, coarsely chopped
3 large cloves garlic, crushed
3–4 bay leaves
2 small dried whole hot red peppers
1 tsp. dried thyme
1–1½ lb. smoked pork hock
½ tsp. salt
⅛ tsp. black pepper
2–3 cups hot cooked rice
Tabasco sauce to pass

1. Soak the beans in 6 cups cold water for at least 4 hours or overnight. Drain.

2. In a large pot combine the drained beans, 8 cups cold water, the onion, garlic, bay leaves, dried peppers, thyme, and smoked pork. Bring to the boil, then simmer, uncovered, over low to moderate heat for 2½–3 hours, until the beans are very soft and the mixture is thick and creamy.

3. Remove and discard the smoked pork, the bay leaves, and the chile peppers. Stir in the salt and pepper and mix well. Taste for salt and add a little more if necessary.

4. Serve the beans over hot cooked rice; pass Tabasco sauce for diners to add to taste. Cooked spicy garlic sausage can be added to the beans, if desired.

Gingered Barley, Bean, and Bulgur Pilaf

Two of the oldest grains cultivated in the Old World, barley and wheat, team up with the American kidney bean in a pilaf that is both very traditional and very new. Don't be put off by the ginger—it adds an unusual and delicious flavor accent. This pilaf is good with roast pork, ham, or poultry.

Serves 4–6

1 onion, minced
1 carrot, finely diced
2 Tb. butter
2½ cups chicken stock
½ cup pearl barley
½ tsp. ground ginger
½ cup bulgur
⅛ tsp. freshly ground black pepper
2 cups soaked and cooked (see p. 144) red kidney beans
       or canned red kidney beans, drained and rinsed
2 Tb. finely minced crystallized ginger
1 Tb. orange zest, finely shredded

1. Sauté the onion and carrot in the butter until the onion just begins to turn golden.

2. Add the stock, barley, and ground ginger. Bring to a simmer, then cook, covered, over low heat, for ½ hour or until the barley is just tender.

3. Stir in the bulgur and pepper, mix well, then cover and cook over low heat for about 20 minutes.

4. Stir in the kidney beans and crystallized ginger, cover, and cook for a few more minutes. Remove from heat and stir in the orange zest. Let stand 5–10 minutes, then fluff with fork and serve.

Ceramic bean pod whistle from pre-Columbian Peru

Pasta Fazool

When I was a kid growing up in New York, one of the favored epithets of the street was PASTA FAZOOL!!, uttered in a loud and menacing tone of voice. If you skinned your knee roller-skating, you shouted PASTA FAZOOL!! and felt better. If a nasty boy ran off with your books, you shouted PASTA FAZOOL!! and shook your fist at him. How surprised—and disappointed—we would all have been to know that PASTA FAZOOL!! meant nothing more scurrilous than "macaroni and beans," the American corruption of *pasta e fagioli*. The Italians have always been great bean fanciers, combining pasta and beans with grace and savvy, and raising poor man's food to the level of gourmanderie. There are dozens of such pasta and bean combinations; here is one that is easy and delicious. If you are in a hurry it can be assembled in half an hour from ingredients on your pantry shelf.

Serves 4–6

1 large onion, chopped
3 large cloves garlic, crushed
2 Tb. olive oil
4 cups soaked and cooked (see p. 144) white kidney beans (cannellini),
      or 2 1-lb. cans, drained, rinsed, and drained again
1 28-oz. can Italian-style tomatoes
1 tsp. dried sage
½ tsp. salt (more or less to taste)
⅛ tsp. freshly ground black pepper
½ cup chopped flat-leaf Italian parsley
1 lb. pasta, freshly cooked and drained*
Additional olive oil for garnish
Freshly grated Parmesan cheese to pass

1. In a large skillet sauté the onion and garlic in the olive oil until the onion is soft and just beginning to brown.

2. Add the beans, tomatoes, sage, salt, and pepper. Simmer gently, stirring occasionally, for about 15–20 minutes until thick.

3. Stir in the parsley, and taste for seasoning.

4. Serve the bean mixture hot over cooked pasta, with an additional Tb. or two of olive oil on the top. Pass a bowl of the Parmesan.

*Spaghetti, linguine, or ziti.

Bean-Stuffed Pasta Shells Primavera

The affinities between Italian and Mexican food are many and strong, due primarily to an intense use of tomatoes and peppers and a love of similar seasoning ingredients such as garlic and oregano. This dish is a true cousin of a Mexican baked enchilada casserole, with stuffed pasta substituting for stuffed corn tortillas. And like lasagna or enchiladas, there is a fair amount of assembly, but it can be prepared well ahead of time.

Serves 4–5

THE STUFFING

2 cups soaked and cooked (see p. 144) or canned white beans,
        any type, drained
1/3 cup light cream
2 Tb. freshly grated Parmesan cheese
1/4 tsp. nutmeg
3 Tb. finely chopped flat-leaf Italian parsley
Dash salt, or to taste
1/8 tsp. freshly ground black pepper

THE SAUCE

1 medium onion, chopped
1 medium sweet green pepper, chopped
1 medium carrot, diced
2 Tb. olive oil
1 28-oz. can crushed Italian-style tomatoes
1/2 tsp. salt
1 tsp. dried basil
1/4 tsp. oregano
1/8 tsp. freshly ground black pepper
1 small zucchini, diced
1/2 cup fresh or frozen peas
2 Tb. finely chopped flat-leaf Italian parsley

15–20 jumbo macaroni shells
2 cups (8 oz.) shredded mozzarrella cheese

1. Make the stuffing: Puree the beans with the cream in a food processor until smooth. Mix in the Parmesan cheese, nutmeg, parsley, salt, and pepper and set aside.

2. Make the sauce: In a large skillet sauté the onion, pepper, and carrot in the oil until the onion just begins to turn golden. Add the tomatoes, salt, basil, oregano, and pepper. Simmer over low heat for about ½ hour. Add the zucchini, peas, and parsley, and simmer another few minutes.

3. Cook the shells in boiling salted water for about 10–12 minutes or until almost but not completely cooked. Drain and rinse in cold water. Preheat the oven to 350°F.

4. To assemble: Lightly butter a large shallow casserole or baking dish—about 13 x 9 inches or 12 x 10 inches. Place half of the tomato sauce evenly over the bottom of the casserole. Lightly stuff each shell with a heaping teaspoon of the bean mixture. Do not overstuff or mound the filling. Place the stuffed shells, stuffing side up, in a single layer on the sauce. Spoon the remaining sauce evenly over the stuffed shells. Sprinkle the shredded cheese over the sauce.

5. Lightly cover with foil and bake for about 30 minutes. Uncover and bake 10 minutes more or until the cheese is melted and bubbly.

Childhood memories: Barbara and Nanette choosing the Halloween pumpkin

The Flatulence Factor

Beans, beans the musical fruit,
the more you eat, the more you toot!
Beans, beans, they're good for your heart,
the more you eat, the more you fart!

Beans are a terrific food, no doubt about it. They are high in fiber, rich in protein and carbohydrate, low in fat. They're cheap, easy to store, and can be prepared in an almost unlimited variety of dishes, combining easily with any number of seasonings and ingredients. But there's no getting around the fact, known and acknowledged as long as they have been eaten, that beans cause flatulence. The reason is no mystery: Beans contain large amounts of complex sugars called oligosaccharides that react potently when they meet up with certain bacteria found abundantly in the human digestive system. The problem is that there is no sure way of getting rid of the oligosaccharides without at the same time leaching out many of the valuable nutrients in the beans. And to complicate the issue, not all people react the same way to beans; some folks are more sensitive than others, and digestive systems seem to be very individualistic. The National Aeronautics and Space Agency apparently came to the same conclusion. After extensive research on flatulence, it recommended screening for potential astronauts on this delicate issue. So if you like 'em, eat 'em. Whatever the consequences, you'll be in good company.

Barbecue Butter Beans

Butter beans are another name for the large lima beans that originated in Peru and take their name from that country's capital city. They require a little extra work at the onset to remove the outer skins, but are well worth the effort. This dish is a flavorful accompaniment to a mixed grill, a platter of sausages, or hot dogs. And as a bonus for vegetarians and dieters, it is made without meat or animal fat of any kind.

Serves 6

2 cups dried large limas (butter beans)
½ cup firmly packed dark brown sugar
½ cup cider vinegar
¼ cup soy sauce
1 large onion, chopped
¼–½ tsp. crushed dried hot peppers (more or less to taste)
2 tsp. dry mustard
3 oz. tomato paste
Reserved cooking liquid

1. Soak the beans in water for 4 hours or overnight.

2. Drain the beans, then place them in a large pot with 6 cups water.

3. Rub fingertips lightly through the beans: this will cause outer skins to come off and rise to the top of the water. Skim off the skins and discard.

4. Simmer the beans over moderate heat for about ½ hour. Skim off any additional skins that may rise to the top.

5. Drain the beans, reserving the cooking liquid. Preheat the oven to 300°F.

6. In a large casserole or baking dish, approximately 2½ to 3 quarts, combine the remaining ingredients and 1 cup of the reserved liquid. Add the beans and mix well.

7. Cover the casserole and bake for about 2 hours. Stir occasionally; if the mixture becomes too dry, add more of the cooking liquid, about ½ cup at a time. When done, the beans should be meltingly soft, almost buttery in texture, and the sauce should be thick without being either too dry or too soupy.

Black Bean Quiche

A bit of Spain, a touch of Mexico, and a soupçon of France combine in a dish that is a little out of the ordinary and very good. The bean mixture is really nothing more than the Mexican standard, *frijoles refritos*, refried beans, flavored with fresh coriander.

Serves 6–8

Pastry for 1 8- or 9-inch fluted quiche pan
1 medium onion, finely chopped
2 Tb. olive oil
2 cups soaked and cooked (see p. 144) black beans or canned black beans
  (reserve a little cooking liquid)
¼ tsp. salt
⅛ tsp. cayenne pepper
Good handful fresh coriander leaf (cilantro), finely chopped
2 eggs
½ cup light cream
¼ tsp. salt
Good dash cayenne pepper
2 roasted red peppers (see p. 95) or 6 oz. jarred roasted peppers, cut in strips
2 cups shredded Monterrey Jack cheese

1. In a medium skillet sauté the onion in the olive oil until it just begins to turn golden.

2. Puree the beans in a food processor, adding just enough cooking liquid to facilitate the pureeing.

3. Spoon the pureed beans into the onion, add the salt and cayenne, and cook, stirring, over moderate heat for about 5 minutes. Stir in the chopped coriander and remove from the heat. Cool slightly.

4. Whisk 1 of the eggs, stir it into the cooled beans, and mix well.

5. In a small bowl beat the remaining egg thoroughly, then stir in the cream, salt, and cayenne, and mix well. Preheat the oven to 350°F.

6. Fit the pastry into the quiche pan. Spread the bean mixture evenly over the bottom of the pastry shell.

7. Lay the pepper strips evenly over the bean layer. Sprinkle the shredded cheese evenly over all.

8. Carefully pour the egg-cream mixture into the pan.

9. Bake the quiche for 40–45 minutes until the top is nicely browned. Remove from the oven and let stand 5–10 minutes before cutting into wedges to serve.

Dill-Pickled Green Beans

The green bean, or string bean, is a familiar part of American cooking, turning up in soups and stews and as a simple boiled vegetable. The ancient bean-eaters of the Southwest threaded fresh green beans on long strings and dried them for winter use. Called "leather britches," they were reconstituted by long cooking in savory meat and dried corn soups. And who can forget Julia Child demonstrating on TV in the 1960s the proper way, the *French* way, to cook beans—by plunging them briefly into rapidly boiling water, then slathering them with butter and parsley? I suspect it was she who turned on a great many people to the gastronomic pleasures of this old-fashioned vegetable. Because of its lovely crisp texture, the green bean was quickly adopted in America as a vegetable for pickling, particularly by German and other northern European immigrants, for whom pickling was a way of preserving the summer harvest for winter use. The beans can be stored in the refrigerator for several months.

Makes 2 quarts

2 lbs. fresh green beans of fairly uniform size and length
1 large onion, thinly sliced
2 large cloves garlic
5–6 stalks fresh dill
2 cups white vinegar
½ cup sugar
1 tsp. salt
1 tsp. celery seed

1. Snap off the ends of the beans, then cook the beans in rapidly boiling water for 3–4 minutes until they are just tender but still crisp. Drain thoroughly.

2. Distribute the sliced onion, the garlic, and the dill stalks between two 1-quart jars, or place them in one 2-quart jar. Pack the drained green beans vertically into the jar(s).

3. In a saucepan combine the vinegar, the sugar, the salt, and the celery seed. Bring to the simmer and cook for a few minutes until the sugar is thoroughly dissolved.

4. Pour the vinegar mixture over the green beans. Cover and refrigerate for at least 1 week before serving. Serve the beans, drained, as is, like pickles, or as part of an antipasto platter or a composed salad.

Stir-Fried String Beans with Elephant Garlic

The Chinese did not wholeheartedly embrace the full range of New World beans, probably because they already had beans of their own, including the all-important soybean. But the string bean, as a green vegetable, was enthusiastically accepted, in large part because of its wonderful texture, and now appears frequently in stir-fried dishes. This is an easy and tasty preparation that is equally good hot or cold.

Serves 4

1 lb. string beans of uniform size, ends removed
2 Tb. peanut oil
1 small onion, thinly sliced
1–2 large cloves elephant garlic, cut in julienne strips (about ½ cup)*
⅛–¼ tsp. crushed dried hot peppers
2 Tb. soy sauce
1 Tb. rice vinegar
½ tsp. sugar
1 tsp. cornstarch
1–2 tsp. sesame oil

1. Blanch the string beans in boiling water for 2 minutes. Drain, rinse in cold water, drain again, and dry thoroughly.

2. Heat a wok or frying pan over high heat. Add the oil, then the onion, garlic, and dried peppers. Stir-fry a few minutes until the vegetables are just starting to brown.

3. Add the string beans and stir-fry another few minutes.

4. In a small bowl or cup combine the soy sauce, vinegar, sugar, and cornstarch. Blend thoroughly.

5. Pour the sauce mixture into the string beans and stir-fry until the sauce is thickened and the vegetables are coated.

6. Remove from heat and stir in the sesame oil. Serve hot or cold.

> **Elephant garlic, as its name implies, is jumbo-sized garlic, one clove of which equals 4 or 5 normal cloves. Julienned, it serves as both seasoning and vegetable. Don't be afraid to use it generously.*

Mock Chopped Liver

The Jews, like other people with strong beliefs and constraints involving meat and animal foods, have evolved a long tradition of sophisticated vegetable cookery that mimics meat preparations. Where once in the Old World eggplant or mushrooms might have substituted for the chicken livers and eggs of the original recipe, American Jews used the New World string bean. Theirs is an interesting treatment. The Sephardic (Spanish or Mediterranean) influence is evident in the use of olive oil and the *sofrito* of onions and peppers.

Makes about 2½ cups

1 lb. string beans
3 Tb. olive oil (a strong fruity Spanish variety is best)
2 large onions, coarsely chopped
1 medium sweet green pepper, seeded and coarsely chopped
3 cloves garlic, crushed
1 cup walnuts, lightly toasted*
1 tsp. salt
⅛ tsp. freshly ground black pepper
Good dash cayenne pepper
3–4 Tb. finely minced flat-leaf Italian parsley

1. Cook the string beans in boiling water until very tender; drain and set aside.

2. In a skillet slowly sauté the onions and the pepper in the olive oil over low to moderate heat, stirring occasionally, until the onions are very soft and turn a deep golden brown. Add the garlic and sauté another few minutes.

3. Grind the beans, walnuts, and onion mixture together. (Grinding produces a better texture than pureeing.) Or chop the mixture fine. Stir in the salt, peppers, and parsley and mix thoroughly.

4. Serve chilled or at room temperature as a spread or dip with crisp crackers, rye bread, or raw vegetables.

*To toast walnuts: Place the nuts in a single layer in a pie tin or baking sheet. Heat in a 350°F. oven for about 10 minutes, or until the nuts are just beginning to turn lightly brown. Watch carefully as they burn easily.

Beer-Baked Beans with Apples and Sausage

A nice flavor variation on an oldtime national favorite. Apples, beer, and sausage, three traditional European foods, combine to make this bean dish rich, dark, and delicious.

Serves 6–8

1 lb. dried pinto beans
6 whole cloves
1 medium onion
8 cups water
1½ cups (12 oz.) beer
1 medium onion, coarsely chopped
2–3 medium apples, peeled, cored, and diced
¼ cup soy sauce
½ cup firmly packed dark brown sugar
4 cloves garlic, crushed
1 tsp. dry mustard
1 lb. smoked sausage (hot, garlic, or Polish), sliced

Two American classics—the Boston bean pot and the Boston Terrier, both from the author's collection

1. In a large pot soak the beans in 6–8 cups cold water for at least 4 hours or overnight. Drain thoroughly. Return beans to pot.

2. Stick the whole cloves into each end of the onion. Add the onion to the beans and pour in 8 cups cold water. Bring to the simmer, then cook, uncovered, over moderate heat for 1½–2 hours until the beans are tender.

3. Drain the liquid from the beans and reserve it. Discard the clove-studded onion. Preheat the oven to 300°F.

4. Transfer the beans to a beanpot or large casserole with a cover. Add all the remaining ingredients, plus 2 cups reserved bean liquid. Mix well, cover, then bake for 2–2½ hours until the beans are very soft and most of the liquid has been absorbed. Check occasionally while the beans are baking; if the liquid seems to be cooking away too quickly, add more of the reserved bean liquid as necessary. The finished dish should be soft, dark, and moist without being too soupy.

Pumpkin Seed Pesto

Pesto, as we commonly understand it, is an Italian seasoning paste made of fresh basil, pine nuts, olive oil, and garlic. It is used as a sauce for hot pasta or to flavor soups, sauces, and cold meats. It is the best known of a number of such seasoning pastes common throughout the Mediterranean; the Spanish use almonds and peppers to flavor theirs. Mexican cuisine had its own seasoning pastes, developed long before the Spanish conquest, and theirs were more likely to be made of ground pumpkin or squash seeds. This updated version contains the pumpkin seeds that were originally called for with a number of Old World ingredients. It is delicious on cooked hot string beans or zucchini, spread on baked or broiled fish fillets, or as a flavoring for soups.

Makes about 1¼ cups

½ cup unsalted hulled pumpkin seeds (pepitas)
1 medium plum tomato, coarsely chopped
2 cloves garlic
1 small fresh hot green chile, seeded, or a good pinch crushed dried hot peppers
Generous ¼ tsp. salt
Good handful fresh coriander leaf (cilantro)
½ cup olive oil
2 Tb. lemon juice
2 Tb. orange juice

continued

Pumpkin Seed Pesto continued

1. In a small heavy skillet heat the pumpkin seeds over moderate heat, stirring constantly, until they are lightly browned. Take care, as the seeds will pop as they heat; do not overbrown them. Remove from heat and cool.

2. In a food processor combine the seeds, tomato, garlic, chile, salt, and coriander. Process until coarsely ground.

3. Slowly add the olive oil, processing until the mixture is smooth.

4. Add the lemon and orange juices and process until well blended.

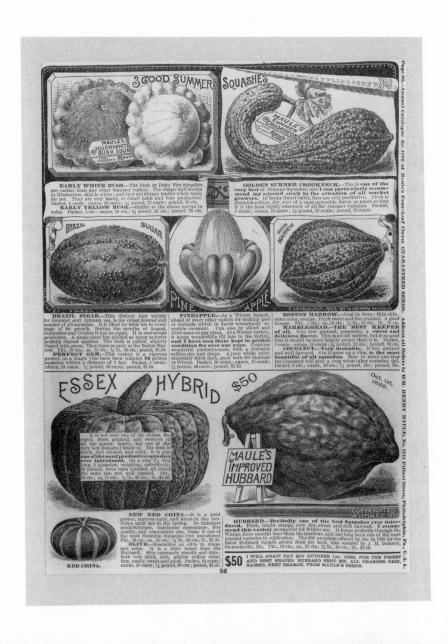

Gratin of Summer Squash

Select the youngest, freshest, yellowest squashes for this delicate dish.

Serves 4–6

1 medium onion, finely chopped
1 small sweet red pepper, seeded and finely chopped
2 Tb. butter
2 eggs
1 cup light cream
2 Tb. flour
½ tsp. salt
Several good grinds black pepper
Dash cayenne pepper
4 oz. (½ cup) feta cheese, finely crumbled
1 Tb. finely snipped fresh rosemary leaves
4 cups grated yellow summer squash

1. In a small skillet sauté the onion and the sweet pepper in the butter until the vegetables are just wilted. Remove from the heat and set aside.

2. In a large bowl whisk the eggs thoroughly. Stir in the cream, flour, salt, and pepper and whisk to blend thoroughly. Preheat the oven to 350°F.

3. Add the cheese, rosemary, grated squash, and the reserved sautéed onion and pepper. Mix gently but thoroughly.

4. Spread the mixture in a large shallow buttered casserole, approximately 1½ to 2 quarts. Bake for 30–35 minutes until the custard is set and very lightly browned on the top. Serve hot.

Tex-Mex Vegetable Casserole

Two kinds of squash, two kinds of beans, plus potatoes, tomatoes, peppers, and corn make this a superb hodge-podge of the American harvest. It is similar to other dishes in cuisines throughout the world, where mixtures of vegetables, legumes, and grains cooked together in savory sauces provide tasty and nutritious one-dish meals. This is a very full-flavored but not very spicy mixture; if you prefer it hotter, add some fresh or dried hot chile to taste. After cooking, the casserole can be eaten just as is, or it can be topped with shredded cheese and baked in the oven.

Serves 6–8

3 Tb. olive oil

1 large onion, coarsely chopped

4 cloves garlic, crushed

1 medium acorn squash, peeled, seeded, and cut in small cubes
    (about 3 cups cubes); slice the squash first to make peeling easier.

1 large potato, cut in small cubes (no need to peel)

2 cups green beans, cut in 1-inch lengths

2 large tomatoes, coarsely chopped

1 medium sweet green or red pepper, seeded and cut in small squares

1 dried mild red chile pepper (New Mexico, ancho, or pasilla),
    seeded and torn into small pieces

1 cup tomato sauce

1 tsp. oregano

2 small zucchini, cut in small cubes

2 cups soaked and cooked (see p. 144) or one 1-lb. can red kidney
    or pinto beans, drained

1 cup fresh, frozen, or canned corn kernels

1 large handful fresh coriander leaf (cilantro), chopped

1 tsp. salt

2 cups shredded mild Cheddar or Monterrey Jack cheese (optional)

1. In a large heavy pot, Dutch oven, or stove-to-oven casserole combine the oil, the onion, garlic, squash, potato, green beans, tomatoes, sweet and dried peppers, tomato sauce, and oregano. Mix together thoroughly, then cook, uncovered, over low to moderate heat, stirring occasionally, for 35–45 minutes or until the squash, the potatoes, and the green beans are just tender.

2. Stir in the zucchini, the kidney or pinto beans, the corn, the coriander, and the salt. Mix thoroughly, then bring to the simmer and cook for 5–10 minutes. Serve as is, or top with shredded cheese and bake in a preheated 375°F. oven for about 15 minutes or until the cheese is melted and bubbly.

Summer Garden Sauté

Beautiful to look at, lovely to eat, this is a very simple dish whose delicate flavor depends on the youngest, tenderest, freshest vegetables of the summer garden. Choose the most richly colored little squashes; they will require only very brief cooking.

Serves 4–6

1 bunch (6–8) scallions, chopped
1 medium sweet green or red pepper, seeded and chopped
1 Tb. butter
1 Tb. olive oil
5–6 medium very ripe plum tomatoes, chopped
3–4 small green squash (zucchini), thinly sliced
3–4 small yellow squash, thinly sliced
2 Tb. chopped fresh basil leaves
2 Tb. chopped flat-leaf Italian parsley
Good squeeze fresh lemon juice
Salt and pepper to taste

1. In a medium skillet sauté the scallions and sweet pepper in the butter and olive oil over moderate heat until the vegetables just begin to wilt.

2. Stir in the chopped tomatoes and sauté until most of the liquid has cooked away.

3. Add the green and yellow squash and sauté, stirring, until the squash is just heated thoroughly but still crisp.

4. Add the remaining seasonings and stir to blend well.

Note: Fresh corn kernels and/or tender little cooked string beans may also be added at the last minute.

Fresh Cranberry Bean Salad with Herb Vinaigrette

The cranberry bean, like the lima, is one of the few American beans that is used fresh as well as dried. It is very attractive, both the pod and the beans themselves a creamy white speckled with pink. Unfortunately, the pretty mottling disappears in cooking and the beans turn a uniform pinkish beige color. No matter. They have a wonderful flavor that is enhanced by this simple herb-flavored vinaigrette.

Serves 4–6

3 cups fresh shelled cranberry beans (about 2 lbs. in the shell)
¼ cup olive oil
3 Tb. red wine vinegar
¼ tsp. salt
Several good grinds black pepper
1 large clove garlic, crushed
1 small onion, finely chopped
1 Tb. chopped fresh sage
1 Tb. chopped fresh rosemary
2–3 Tb. chopped fresh flat-leaf Italian parsley

1. Cook the beans in boiling water for about 15 minutes until they are tender but still have a very slight crunch. Drain the beans thoroughly and set aside.

2. In a small bowl combine the oil, vinegar, salt, pepper, and garlic. Whisk to blend thoroughly.

3. Place the warm drained beans, onion, and the herbs in a bowl. Pour the vinaigrette over them and mix thoroughly. Let the beans marinate for a couple of hours, stirring occasionally.

4. Serve the beans at room temperature, with a couple of extra grinds of black pepper.

Note: Although fresh cranberry beans are especially good in this salad, almost any cooked or canned bean can be substituted.

Zucchini Bread

Anyone who has grown summer squash in the garden knows that the problem is not getting the stuff to grow, but getting rid of it once it does. It is a prolific vegetable, frequently producing much more than any family can use. American cooks have always been ingenious at devising novel ways of using the excess, and this bread is a good example. Really more a cake than a bread, it is moist and delicately flavored and needs no frosting or other adornment.

Makes one 10-inch Bundt cake
or two 9 x 5-inch loaves

1 cup vegetable oil
2 cups sugar
4 eggs
2 cups all-purpose flour
1 tsp. baking soda
½ tsp. baking powder
1 Tb. cinnamon
1 tsp. ginger
¼ tsp. nutmeg
½ tsp. salt
4 cups shredded zucchini
2 tsp. vanilla

1. In a large mixing bowl beat the oil and sugar until well blended.

2. Beat in the eggs one at a time, beating well after each addition.

3. Mix together all the dry ingredients and add to the batter, stirring to blend thoroughly. Preheat the oven to 350°F.

4. Stir in the shredded zucchini and vanilla and mix thoroughly.

5. Pour the batter into a well-buttered 10-inch Bundt pan or divide it between two 9 x 5 x 3-inch loaf pans.

6. Bake for 50–60 minutes or until firm to the touch and lightly browned. Cool on a rack in pan for 20–30 minutes, then unmold onto a serving plate.

Leftover Turkey Stock
Turkey Soup with Wild Rice and Dried Corn
Smoked Turkey Stock
Vermont Smoked Turkey and Creamy Cheddar Soup
Herbed Turkey Breast with Chestnut Risotto Stuffing
Braised Turkey Provençal
Spicy Turkey Sausage Patties
Turkey in Red Chile Sauce (Turkey Mole)
Turkey Cutlets with Onion-Dijon Puree
Turkey Gumbo
Taverna Turkey
Hickory Grilled Breast of Turkey
Curried Turkey Hash
Turkey in Double Mushroom Sauce
Turkey Bobotie
Cincinnati Hot Shots
Turkey Pibil
Smoked Turkey Salad with Chutney

TURKEY

"Poultry is for the cook what canvas is for a painter....It is served up boiled, roasted, fried, hot or cold, whole or in parts, with or without sauce, boned, grilled, stuffed, and always with the same success." So proclaimed the renowned eighteenth-century French gastronome Jean Anthelme Brillat-Savarin, and went on shortly to say: "The turkey is certainly one of the most beautiful presents which the New World has made to the Old." This high opinion of the all-American bird was enthusiastically shared by the rest of Europe, which immediately appropriated the turkey as a distinguished addition to the festive board—not surprising, as roasted fowl of all sorts had been highly prized in Europe since Roman times.

Notwithstanding the turkey's immediate popularity, a certain confusion existed about its origin, a confusion reflected in the nomenclature that arose to describe the novel fowl. The French, eloquent if inaccurate, called the turkey "Coq d'Inde," Cock of India, a name that shortened in time to its present form, *dinde,* which designates a hen turkey. (The term *dindon* refers to a tom turkey, while *dindonneau* means a young turkey.) The Germans, with their penchant for detail, further refined the Cock of India into the Rooster of Calcutta, Calcuttishe Hahn. And the English, who had long referred to anything new and exotic as Turkish, adopted a no-nonsense approach and simply called the bird Turkey, after its supposed origins in the lands of the mysterious East. This name not only reflected an initial misinformation about the origin of the turkey, but indicated as well the role of the Turks as mercantile middlemen in the spread of Oriental and New World products, a role reflected in an early English term for maize, Turkish wheat.

The turkey was the only domesticated food animal contributed by the New World. Unknown here were the pigs, the chickens, the cows, the sheep, and goats so heavily utilized by the rest of the world. Unknown as well, therefore, were the derivative products of these animals—the eggs, the dairy products, the animal fats. Small wonder, then, that the inhabitants of both North and South America embraced so ardently the beef, the chicken, and particularly the pork

introduced by European settlers, and integrated them into their culinary traditions. So the New World got much more in terms of animal foods than it gave;
nonetheless, the turkey was no small gift.

The center of turkey domestication was in Mexico, site of the New
World's most highly developed, settled agrarian culture. The tribes of North
America were well acquainted with wild turkey, which abounded in the hills and
woodlands of the continent and which was hunted as a game bird but not bred in
captivity. So it seems that the famous fowl, emblematic of our history, brought
by Chief Massasoit and his tribe to the Pilgrims at Plymouth for that first harvest dinner in November of 1621, was almost certainly a wild turkey.

It is a curious fact, then, that although Mexico was the hearth of the
domesticated turkey and of a highly developed and elaborate tradition of turkey
cookery, its culinary practices for the preparation of the bird were rejected by
Europe while turkey itself was eagerly accepted.

European notions of superior dining had for centuries revolved around
great hunks of roasted meat, and whole roasted fowl was considered perhaps the
most elegant of all. The turkey arrived on the scene as a kind of super bird, bigger,
meatier, more impressive than anything else available. Indeed, the reaction of
Europe was perhaps not very different from that of my youngest son who, as a very
small boy, wandered into the kitchen while I was preparing the Thanksgiving
turkey. "Oh!," he exclaimed, and his eyes grew very wide. "What a BIG chicken!"

So there was never any doubt about the turkey's role in European, and
subsequent American, cuisine. It was to be stuffed, roasted whole, and served as
the dramatic focus of festive and celebratory entertaining, and it has continued to
function in that fashion through the centuries. The American Thanksgiving feast
is the archetype of the turkey dinner, but it is a model that has its roots in Europe
and not in the New World. Indeed, the differences in Europe from cuisine to
cuisine in the preparation and presentation of the roast turkey lie in the details of
the stuffing and accompanying dishes and not in the treatment of the bird itself.

Lost, or more likely ignored, by European and American tradition, was
the Mexican treatment of the turkey. This too was an elaborate and festive tradition, but very different from that of the whole roasted bird. Turkey in high Aztec
culture was cut into parts and then stewed in spiced sauces of marvelous complexity. Nuts and seeds, spices and herbs, tomatoes, and chiles of an amazing
variety were blended into seasoning pastes in which the turkey parts were slowly
simmered. These *moles* (from the Aztec word *molli*, meaning combination or
mixture and pronounced "mo-lay") were an important part of the elaborate cook-

ing for holidays and celebrations and not the ordinary fare of daily life, for much time, care, and expense were required for their preparation. There are today as many *moles* in Mexico as there are cooks, and turkey *moles* are probably the most esteemed of all. The famous *mole* Poblano or *mole* of Puebla, in which chocolate figures as one of the seasoning ingredients, is just one regional variation on this widespread Mexican tradition.

But for European taste, the cutting up of this noble new bird and stewing it in a liquid, no matter how tasty, seemed inappropriate, and it would take another couple of centuries after the turkey's introduction for cooks to entertain the possibility of techniques other than roasting. Innovation in turkey cookery arose, as so much culinary innovation arose, from the cuisines of France and Italy. Turkey dishes appeared in a myriad of new forms—the rich meaty thighs, wings, and drumsticks braised or poached in savory sauces, the breasts marinated and grilled, or sliced into steaks and fillets. The turkey had finally emerged from the Middle Ages.

Except, that is, in America. Here the original traditions of the Pilgrims remained entrenched, with turkey cooking consisting of the roasting of the Thanksgiving bird and the subsequent preparation of its leftovers for innumerable days thereafter. Turkey hash, turkey croquettes, creamed turkey, turkey salad —all these standard dishes of the American repertoire had their roots in the frugal housewife's desire to utilize every edible scrap, and a fundamental conservatism that prevented her from dealing with turkey in "foreign" ways.

But all that has changed, and in very recent times. The impetus for opening the door to a whole new world of turkey preparation came, interestingly enough, not primarily from an interest in gastronomy but from a burgeoning concern with nutrition and diet and, of course, from an aggressive turkey marketing industry. Americans were finally taking heed of the cost of centuries of indulgence, an overconsumption of red meat, animal fat, and dairy products. Cholesterol and saturated fats became household words, and no longer were thick sirloins, pork chops, hamburgers, ham and eggs considered appropriate for daily consumption. Meat-loving America was feeling the necessity to change her eating habits.

And there, waiting in the wings, was an old favorite, the turkey, with its tasty and familiar meat now more highly appreciated because it is leaner, lower in calories and saturated fats than beef, pork, or lamb. Ground, it substitutes for beef in meatballs, meat loaf, casseroles, and pasta dishes; cut up in parts, it simmers in gumbos and stews; its delicate breast meat performs beautifully in a variety of sauté and scallopini dishes. Turkey, it turns out, is wonderfully versatile: Its dark meat can taste almost like beef, its white meat, properly prepared, like veal or chicken. And turkey smokes very successfully; its smoked white meat is a delicacy, while smoked turkey parts provide the flavor we regard so highly in soups, stocks, and bean dishes, without the fat of the more traditional smoked pork products.

And we have finally, five centuries later, discovered again the turkey dishes of the ancient Mexican hearth—the *moles*, the enchiladas, the spiced chile dishes. The turkey was the first and the only domesticated meat of the aboriginal American homeland, and it returns today to take its proper place.

Leftover Turkey Stock

Once the Thanksgiving bird has served its festive purpose and been plundered on many days thereafter for sandwiches, casseroles, and croquettes, the time inevitably comes to dispose of the final remains. There the carcass sits, taking up most of the refrigerator, accusing one by its very presence of not having efficiently utilized every lingering scrap. But let's face it—by this time everyone is heartily sick of turkey and wishes it would disappear without a trace. Here's how to do it without experiencing a single pang of guilt. Throw all the remains of the bird, including any congealed pan juices, fat, leftover vegetables, bits of stuffing, into a large pot with a lot of water. Cook it for half a day, by which time every ounce of virtue will have been extracted. You now throw away all the solids and keep the liquid; it is one of the finest soup stocks you will ever make, rich with flavor and body. Once the stock has been strained, chilled, and skimmed of fat, it can be frozen, to be used on some later day when the flavor of turkey is once again welcome.

Makes 2½–3 quarts

Carcass of 1 roasted turkey, including all bits of meat, vegetables,
stuffing, pan juices, gravy, and so on
1 large onion, coarsely chopped
2 large carrots, sliced
3–4 stalks celery, with leaves, coarsely chopped
1–2 parsnips, sliced
12 whole peppercorns
5–6 quarts cold water
Salt

1. In a large soup or stockpot put the turkey carcass, broken into large pieces, the turkey remains, the vegetables, peppercorns, and cold water. Bring to the simmer, then cook, uncovered, over low to moderate heat for 3–4 hours until the liquid is reduced by about half. Skim off any scum that may rise to the top during cooking.

2. Strain the stock, discarding all the solid matter. For every quart of liquid, season with about 1 teaspoon salt.

3. Chill the stock, then skim off and discard all the fat that has congealed at the top.

4. Use the stock for soup or sauce, or freeze for later use.

Turkey Soup with Wild Rice and Dried Corn

Homemade turkey stock can be the basis for any number of wonderful soups. This one provides a somewhat unusual but wholly American selection of ingredients. The rich turkey stock is a marvelous foil for the nutty flavor of wild rice and the sweet chewiness of dried corn. It is a very hearty and full flavored combination, although it contains no meat and very little fat.

Serves 8–10

2 Tb. vegetable oil
1 medium onion, finely chopped
2 carrots, diced
2 quarts Turkey Stock (see preceding page)
½ cup wild rice
½ cup dried sweet corn
1 Tb. lemon juice
3–4 Tb. chopped fresh coriander leaf (cilantro)

1. In a large pot heat the oil over moderate heat. Add the chopped onion and the carrots and sauté, stirring, until the onion just begins to turn golden.

2. Add the turkey stock, the wild rice, and the dried corn. Bring to the simmer, then cook, uncovered, over low heat for 1½–2 hours until the rice and the corn are tender.

3. Stir in the lemon juice and the chopped coriander. Serve very hot.

Smoked Turkey Stock

More delicate than stocks made with the more traditional smoked pork products, this is easy to do and makes a beautifully flavored base for soups and casseroles.

Makes about 2 quarts

2 large onions, coarsely chopped
2 large carrots, sliced
2 Tb. oil
2–3 lbs. smoked turkey parts
12 cups (3 quarts) water
12 peppercorns
5 whole allspice berries

1. In a large pot sauté the onions and carrots in the oil over low to moderate heat, stirring occasionally, until the onions are a deep golden brown and very soft.

2. Add the turkey parts, water, and seasonings. Bring to a simmer, then cook, uncovered, over moderate heat for about 2–3 hours or until the liquid is reduced by about one-third.

3. Cool slightly, then strain. Chill the strained stock overnight, then skim off all of the fat that has congealed at the top.

The American idealization of the roast turkey dinner. Norman Rockwell's *Freedom from Want.*

Vermont Smoked Turkey and Creamy Cheddar Soup

Once you've made smoked turkey stock, here's a lovely soup to make from it. It is a good choice for a cold winter's night, rich, smooth, and filled with the flavor of New England.

Serves 4–6

1 small onion, minced
1 carrot, diced
2 Tb. butter
½ tsp. sweet paprika
4 Tb. flour
4 cups Smoked Turkey Stock (see preceding page)
2 Tb. sweet (cream) sherry
½ tsp. dried sage
⅛ tsp. nutmeg
Several good grinds black pepper
Good dash cayenne pepper
½ cup light cream or half-and-half
1 cup grated mild Cheddar cheese

1. In a medium saucepan sauté the onion and carrot in the butter over moderate heat until the onion wilts and just begins to turn golden.

2. Stir in the paprika and mix well. Add the flour and mix well to form a *roux*. Cook, stirring, until the *roux* turns a light golden color.

3. Add the stock, sherry, and seasonings and whisk to blend well. Bring to a simmer, stirring occasionally, until the mixture is slightly thickened and smooth. Simmer a few more minutes.

4. Stir in the cream and bring just to a simmer.

5. Remove from heat and stir in the cheese until blended and smooth. Serve hot. Garnish with herbed croutons or dry stuffing mix, if desired.

Herbed Turkey Breast with Chestnut Risotto Stuffing

The French and the Italians are the ones who must be acknowledged for making the felicitous match between turkey and chestnuts. In this recipe an Italian-style risotto, with nutty sweet dried chestnuts, is a rich and flavorful foil for a simple herb-scented turkey breast. The mixture may also be used to stuff a whole small turkey.

Serves 4–6

1 Tb. olive oil
2 Tb. butter
1 large onion, finely chopped
1 cup dried Italian chestnuts, soaked overnight in water
1 cup Arborio rice
2½ cups chicken stock
⅛ tsp. freshly ground black pepper
1 tsp. dried sage
2 Tb. freshly grated Parmesan cheese
1 3- to 4-lb. turkey breast (whole, bone in)
4–6 sprigs fresh rosemary
4–6 fresh sage leaves
2 cloves garlic, slivered
Olive oil
Salt and pepper

1. In a medium saucepan heat the oil and the butter over moderate heat. Add the onion and sauté until it begins to turn golden.

2. Drain the chestnuts and chop coarsely.

3. Add the rice and the chestnuts to the sautéed onion.

4. Add the stock, the pepper, and the dried sage and bring to a simmer. Cover and cook over low heat about 30 minutes until all the liquid is absorbed. Remove from the heat and stir in the Parmesan. Let the stuffing cool slightly.

5. Generously butter a small roasting pan or baking dish large enough to hold the turkey breast. Place the stuffing in the pan, then place the turkey breast on top. Try to get as much of the stuffing underneath the breast as possible. Preheat the oven to 325°F.

6. With your fingers, carefully separate the turkey skin from the meat. Insert the rosemary sprigs, the sage leaves, and the garlic slivers under the skin. Brush the breast lightly but thoroughly with olive oil, then salt and pepper generously.

7. Roast the turkey for 19 minutes per pound. Let stand 10 minutes before carving.

THE TURKEYS' REVOLT AGAINST THANKSGIVING.—[Drawn by F. S. Church.]

"We are Bitterly Opposed to the Enforcement of President Grant's Thanksgiving Proclamation, and will Leave the Country rather than Submit."

Two early and divergent views of the Thanksgiving dinner. Top: the turkey's point of view. Bottom, from Dutchess County, New York: killing, scalding, picking, and plumping turkeys for the market.

Turkey Talk

As the unique bird of our national table, the turkey has become a part of our national argot, appearing in slang expressions that are, like ourselves, irreverent and down to earth. To "talk turkey" means to get down to business, to deal with the real issues, to get straight to the heart of things without evasion, distraction, or hyperbole. To go "cold turkey" means to quit a behavior or an indulgence suddenly and completely, with no recourse to a gradual or temporary withdrawal. Presumably the expression has its roots in a deep-seated reluctance to eat cold leftovers without any intermediary reheating or regarnishing. And finally there is the term "turkey," a more recent linguistic development, that can be applied to things, events, or people. To call something a "turkey" means that it doesn't work, doesn't come off, is a mistake or a flop. To call someone a "turkey" is to characterize that person as a jerk, someone who behaves stupidly or inappropriately. This use of the term "turkey" reflects our widely held belief that the bird we love to eat is stupid and incompetent, good for nothing but to offer itself, with no more than an outraged gobble, into the hands of its executioners. Unlike the eagle, the bird that has become our national political symbol, the turkey is earthbound and it is perhaps for this that we hold it in such contempt.

Braised Turkey Provençal

The French took enthusiastically to the turkey, adapting it to many traditional recipes. This one, a classic Provençal treatment, is best done with dark meat parts because of the relatively long cooking. Fortunately, we no longer have to hack up a whole turkey to get the parts we want, as they are routinely available in the supermarket.

Serves 4

2 Tb. olive oil
2½–3 lbs. dark meat turkey parts (thighs, legs, or wings)
1 large onion, chopped
2 carrots, sliced
3 cloves garlic, crushed
3–4 plum tomatoes, coarsely chopped
½ tsp. salt
⅛ tsp. freshly ground black pepper
½ cup dry white wine
1 Tb. fresh rosemary leaves, or 1 tsp. dried rosemary
1 medium white turnip, cut in small cubes
2 Tb. butter
2 Tb. flour
2–3 Tb. finely chopped flat-leaf Italian parsley
Additional salt and pepper, if necessary

1. In a large heavy skillet or Dutch oven heat the olive oil over moderately high heat. Add the turkey parts and brown slowly, turning the parts to brown evenly. Remove the turkey from the pot and set aside.

2. To the skillet add the onion, carrots, and garlic and sauté until the onion just begins to turn golden.

3. Stir in the tomatoes and sauté another few minutes.

4. Return the turkey to the pot, then add the salt, pepper, wine, and rosemary. Cover and cook over low heat for about 2 hours or until the turkey is very tender. Add the turnip and cook another 10–15 minutes until it is tender.

5. Remove the turkey from the pot and set aside. In a small skillet heat the butter, swirling constantly, until it is a rich brown. Stir in the flour and cook, stirring, until it is smooth. Slowly add the mixture to the liquid in the pot; whisk until smooth and thickened. Stir in the parsley, and taste for salt and pepper. Return the turkey to the pot and heat through.

Spicy Turkey Sausage Patties

Sausage has always been an important part of the American table, and although it is traditionally made from pork, it can be done very successfully with turkey, which produces a leaner, less fatty product. These spicy patties are very good as is, served with a mess of sautéed onions and peppers, but they are also excellent in casserole dishes (see p. 265) or in spaghetti sauce. The chipotle chile gives them a subtle smoky undertone.

Makes about 12 patties
Serves 4

*1 dried chipotle pepper (smoked jalapeño), seeded, or 1 fresh jalapeño or
    serrano pepper, seeded, or ¼ tsp. crushed dried hot peppers*
1 medium onion, coarsely chopped
3 large cloves garlic
1 lb. ground turkey
1 tsp. salt
1 tsp. paprika
1 tsp. ground ancho chile
1 tsp. crumbled dried sage
Vegetable oil

1. Soak the chipotle pepper in enough warm water to cover for about 20 minutes. Drain.

2. Grind together (or process to a coarse puree in the food processor) the onion, the garlic, and the drained chipotle (or other chile).

3. In a large bowl combine the puree, the turkey, and all the other seasonings. Mix very thoroughly, then form into small 2½–3-inch patties.

4. Pour enough oil into a skillet to just lightly film the bottom of the pan. Fry the sausage patties over moderate heat, turning once, until they are richly browned on both sides. Drain the patties on paper towels.

Aztec drawing of a turkey, the only domesticated food animal of the New World, highly regarded in both ancient and modern Mexican cuisine.

Turkey in Red Chile Sauce (Turkey Mole)

This is a typical and versatile Mexican turkey dish. The fowl, cooked in a spicy red sauce, can be eaten as is with rice or tortillas, or, in more traditional fashion, cut off the bone, shredded, and returned to the sauce to be used as a filling for tacos or enchiladas. Note the use of the chipotle chile. The chipotle is a smoked dried jalapeño, very pungent, but its heat is not so intense if it is cooked whole in the sauce. Used in this way, it provides a pleasant piquancy and a lovely smoky undertone to the sauce's flavor.

Serves 4–6

2 Tb. vegetable oil or lard
1 medium onion, chopped
2 cloves garlic, crushed
1 Tb. ground ancho chile
1 Tb. ground pasilla chile
2 large red tomatoes, coarsely chopped
1 tsp. ground achiote
1 tsp. cumin seeds
½ tsp. cinnamon
½ tsp. oregano
1 whole chipotle chile
½ tsp. salt
1 Tb. cider vinegar
2–3 lbs. turkey parts (dark meat preferred)

1. In a large heavy pot or Dutch oven heat the oil or lard over moderate heat. Add the onion and garlic and sauté until the onion is beginning to brown.

2. Add the ancho and pasilla powders and stir briefly with the onion.

3. Add the tomatoes, all the seasonings, and the vinegar and mix well.

4. Remove as much skin as possible from the turkey parts. Add the turkey to the sauce, bring to the simmer, then cook, covered, over low heat for 2–3 hours until the turkey is very tender. Turn the turkey parts in the sauce occasionally.

5. Taste the sauce for salt; remove the chipotle and discard. Serve the turkey as is, or let it cool, then remove the meat from the bone, shred or chop coarsely, and return to the sauce. Serve the turkey garnished with fresh chopped coriander leaf, shredded lettuce, and guacamole.

Turkey Cutlets with Onion-Dijon Puree

Turkey cutlets, or tenders, thin slices of boneless breast meat now routinely available in most markets, are a nice alternative to veal or chicken. The trick is to cook them as quickly as possible to keep them tender and moist. Here they get all dressed up with a rich onion puree and melted cheese.

Serves 3–4

2 Tb. butter
1 Tb. olive oil
4 cups chopped onions (about 3–4 large onions)
1/4 tsp. salt
2 Tb. Dijon mustard
1–1 1/2 lbs. turkey tenders or cutlets (about 1/4-inch thick)
Flour for dredging
3–4 Tb. vegetable oil
Salt and pepper
Thin slices of good Swiss-type cheese (Emmenthal, Jarlsberg, and so on)

1. In a heavy skillet melt the butter and the olive oil over low to moderate heat. Add the onions and sauté, stirring occasionally, until the onions are very soft and a deep rich brown. (This will take 30–40 minutes and should not be hurried. The onions should cook very slowly in the fat until they are soft and caramelized.)

2. Remove from the heat and cool slightly. Puree the onions in a food processor, then stir in the salt and the mustard and mix well.

3. Lightly dredge the turkey cutlets in flour.

4. In a large skillet heat the vegetable oil over moderate to high heat. Sauté the cutlets quickly, turning once, until they are lightly browned on each side. As the cutlets are browned, remove them to a baking tray or shallow casserole. Lightly salt and pepper the sautéed cutlets.

5. Spread the onion puree generously over the cutlets. Top with thin slices of the cheese.

6. Broil the cutlets just until the cheese is melted and bubbly.

Note: Any leftover onion puree can be refrigerated in a covered jar and used for flavoring soups or stews.

Turkey Gumbo

Not as common as chicken or seafood are in gumbo, turkey nonetheless makes a splendid one, its rich meat complemented by the intense flavors of this traditional Creole preparation.

Serves 4–6

½–¾ lb. smoked spicy or garlic sausage, cut in small chunks
2–3 lbs. dark meat turkey parts
2 Tb. lard or oil
1 large onion, chopped
1 large sweet green pepper, seeded and chopped
3 stalks celery, chopped
4 cloves garlic, crushed
2 Tb. flour
2 large ripe tomatoes, coarsely chopped
1 cup stock (chicken, turkey, or ham)
1 bay leaf
1 tsp. dried thyme
½ tsp. ground allspice
½ tsp. Tabasco sauce
½ lb. okra, sliced
Good handful chopped flat-leaf Italian parsley
Salt and pepper and Tabasco to taste
2–3 cups hot cooked rice

1. Brown the sausage chunks lightly; remove from the pan and set aside.

2. In a large heavy pot or Dutch oven brown the turkey parts lightly in the lard or oil. Remove the turkey from the pot, salt and pepper lightly, and set aside.

3. To the oil in the pot add the onion, pepper, celery, and garlic, and sauté over moderate heat until lightly browned.

4. Stir in the flour and cook, stirring, to make a lightly browned *roux,* about 3–4 minutes.

5. Return the turkey and sausage to the pot; add the tomatoes, stock, and seasonings. Stir, then cover and cook over low heat for about 2 hours.

6. Add the sliced okra and continue cooking for another hour, or until the turkey is very tender and coming off the bone. Stir in the parsley, salt, pepper, and Tabasco to taste. Serve with the hot cooked rice.

Taverna Turkey

The Greek way of preparing beef stew, *stifado*, works wonderfully with dark, meaty turkey thighs. This is a hearty, richly flavored dish, best served with Greek home-fried potatoes or rice cooked in chicken stock.

Serves 6–8

1 large onion, chopped
2 Tb. good fruity olive oil
3 cloves garlic, crushed
2 carrots, sliced
3–4 lbs. turkey thighs
1 cup tomato sauce
½ cup dry red wine
2 bay leaves
1 tsp. cinnamon
¼ tsp. ground allspice
½ tsp. salt
¼ tsp. crushed dried hot peppers
Several good grinds black pepper
1 Tb. olive oil
12–16 small boiling onions, peeled

1. In a heavy pot or Dutch oven sauté the onion in the fruity olive oil until it just begins to brown. Add the garlic and carrots and sauté a few minutes more.

2. Add the turkey and all the other ingredients except the additional Tb. of olive oil and the boiling onions. Mix thoroughly, then cover and cook over low heat for 2–2½ hours, or until the turkey is very tender and coming away from the bone.

3. While the stew is cooking, heat the remaining olive oil in a skillet over moderate heat. Add the boiling onions and sauté slowly, shaking the pan frequently, until the onions are glazed and a rich brown color. Add the glazed onions to the stew for the last 15–20 minutes of cooking.

Hickory Grilled Breast of Turkey

Grilling is an ancient technique that has stood the test of time because it produces flavorful succulent food that requires no fats or oils for the process. Marinated turkey works wonderfully on the grill, provided it is not overcooked. I use breast halves in this recipe because it is easier to gauge more accurately the proper cooking time. To do this dish you will need a grill with a cover.

Serves 4–6

¼ cup soy sauce
2 Tb. honey
1 2½- to 3-lb. turkey breast half (bone in) (if you want more and
    your grill can accommodate them, prepare 2 halves)

1. Combine the soy sauce and the honey and rub thoroughly all over the turkey breast. Marinate the turkey for 4–6 hours or overnight, turning the meat once or twice in the marinade.

2. Heat the coals on the grill. When they are red hot, throw on a good handful of hickory chips. Place the turkey breast on a rack about 5 inches from the coals. Let the flames sear the skin side of the breast, then cover the grill and cook the turkey breast for about 30 minutes, turning it once or twice as it cooks and basting it with the marinade.

3. Let the turkey stand for 5–10 minutes before slicing.

Early photo of a turkey market in Athens, Greece

The Ultimate Leftover

There are many Americans, and I must confess to being one of them, who regard the Thanksgiving feast as but a pleasant preamble to the real treat, leftover turkey sandwiches. Indeed, we sandwich connoisseurs deliberately plan to hold the big dinner early enough in the day so that there is time for the turkey and fixings to cool down adequately and for the appetite to return so that one can indulge in the ultimate leftover. Here's how it's done: Take two slices of your favorite bread (this is a matter of choice—mine is a freshly sliced, moist Jewish rye). Slather one slice with good mayonnaise, pile on thin slices of cold turkey, salt and pepper generously. Now spoon on a layer of cold stuffing. Lettuce and tomato are optional but very good. Some folks add a bit of cranberry relish or even a few dabs of cold gravy to moisten. This is a real sandwich, a whole meal between two slices of bread, and not to be cut in dainty quarters. Grasp the whole firmly with both hands, open wide, and have plenty of napkins ready. This is turkey at its best.

While on the subject of leftover turkey sandwiches, one must take note of that other traditional American favorite—the hot open-face turkey sandwich. Long a staple of the roadside diner, it consists of slices of fluffy white American "store-bought" bread, piled with warmed leftover turkey, the whole drenched in brown gravy. The open-face sandwich is traditionally eaten with a scoop of mashed potatoes, also puddled in brown gravy. The dish is a study in white, brown, and smooth. Because it is eaten with a knife and fork, it is not considered by purists to be a true sandwich, but it is a genuine and well-loved part of the American turkey repertoire.

Curried Turkey Hash

Hash is another old-time American favorite, combining as it does our beloved potato with any leftover meat. Its origin is probably French, from the verb *hacher,* to hash or cut up fine. Although hash is usually panfried, this recipe calls for baking, a better way to treat leftover turkey, which has a tendency to become a little dry. Serve this delicately curry-flavored hash with a good fruit chutney or a zippy homemade ketchup.

Serves 4–6

1 large onion, finely chopped
2 Tb. butter or oil
2 tsp. ground cumin
1 tsp. turmeric
1 tsp. fenugreek
½ tsp. ginger
½ tsp. ground coriander
3 cups finely chopped cooked turkey
3–4 cups diced cooked potato
2 large stalks celery, finely diced
1 egg
½ cup light cream
1 cup chicken or Turkey Stock (see p. 172)
1 tsp. salt
Several good dashes Tabasco sauce
Several good grinds black pepper

1. In a small skillet sauté the onion in the butter or oil until just wilted. Add the cumin, turmeric, fenugreek, ginger, and coriander and sauté, stirring, another few minutes.

2. In a large bowl combine the diced turkey, potato, and celery. Scrape the spiced onion mixture from the pan into the turkey mixture and mix to blend thoroughly.

3. In a small bowl whisk the egg lightly. Stir in the cream, stock, and the rest of the seasonings. Blend thoroughly. Preheat the oven to 350°F.

4. Generously butter a large shallow casserole or baking dish, approximately 9 x 13-inches or 10 x 12-inches. Spoon the turkey mixture into the casserole, pressing down and smoothing with a spatula into an even layer. Pour the egg mixture carefully over the turkey.

5. Bake for 30–35 minutes or until set and lightly browned.

Turkey in Double Mushroom Sauce

A nice and rather elegant way to use up leftover turkey. Fresh and dried mushrooms contribute to a richly flavored sauce that goes well with the turkey. This can be served over rice, noodles, or fettuccine, but for a more unusual presentation, spoon the hot mixture over Pecan Polenta Rounds (see p. 22).

Serves 4

¼ cup dried porcini mushrooms (or other dried mushrooms)
2 Tb. butter
1 small onion, finely chopped
1 small sweet red pepper, seeded and finely chopped
½ lb. fresh mushrooms, sliced or coarsely chopped
3 Tb. flour
1¼ cups chicken stock
¼ tsp. mace
⅛ tsp. black pepper
2½–3 cups diced cooked turkey
¼ cup light cream

1. Soak the dried mushrooms in warm water to cover for about 20 minutes. Drain and chop coarsely.

2. In a medium saucepan heat the butter over moderate heat. Add the onion and the pepper and sauté, stirring, until the onion wilts and begins to turn golden.

3. Add the fresh mushrooms and sauté, stirring, until the mushrooms are just lightly browned.

4. Add the flour, mix well, and cook, stirring, for another 2–3 minutes.

5. Add the stock, the mace, and the pepper and cook, stirring or whisking, until the sauce comes to the simmer and thickens. Add the reserved drained mushrooms and the diced turkey, mix well, and bring to the simmer.

6. Stir in the cream, mix well, and heat until very hot. Serve the turkey over rice, noodles, or the polenta rounds.

Turkey Bobotie

Minced or ground meat loaves, pies, and croquettes are a traditional part of northern European cuisine, and this South African dish is a blend of Dutch and Oriental influences. It is usually made with beef or lamb, but probably originally used a game meat, such as venison. In this recipe ground turkey does the honors. The mixture can be baked in a loaf pan like a conventional meat loaf, but it is also very nice for individual servings baked in small molds, muffin tins, or corn-stick pans.

Serves 4

1 cup stale white bread cubes
½ cup milk
1 Tb. butter
1 large onion, finely chopped
1 egg, lightly beaten
1 lb. ground turkey
1 tsp. salt
¼ tsp. black pepper
1 Tb. curry powder
3 Tb. good fruit chutney
¼ cup raisins
3 Tb. finely chopped blanched almonds

1. In a large mixing bowl combine the bread cubes and the milk and mix well.

2. In a small skillet melt the butter over moderate heat. Add the onion and sauté until the onion begins to turn golden.

3. Add the onion to the bread cubes, then stir in the egg.

4. Add the turkey, the seasonings, the chutney, the raisins, and the almonds. Mix thoroughly, kneading the mixture with your hands or a heavy spoon. Preheat the oven to 350°F.

5. Pack the mixture into a well-buttered 9 x 5 x 3-inch loaf pan or individual molds. Press down and smooth the mixture with your fingers or the back of a spoon.

6. Bake about 40 minutes for the loaf; 25 minutes for small molds. Remove from the oven and carefully pour off any accumulated fat.

7. Slice or unmold and serve with rice and chutney.

Cincinnati Hot Shots

The city of Cincinnati offers many things, but to those of us who are always looking for something new to eat, Cincinnati offers its own unique chili. Served in chili parlors throughout the city, it is a ground beef mixture spiced with cumin, oregano, unsweetened chocolate, and cinnamon. Beans, chopped raw onion, and cheese garnish the chili, which is eaten with—of all things—spaghetti. A genuine American melange. These little meatballs, made of ground turkey rather than beef, take their inspiration from the flavor of Cincinnati chili. They are a nice addition to the buffet table.

Makes 25–30 meatballs

1 egg
¼ cup tomato sauce
1 medium onion, finely minced
1 tsp. salt
1 tsp. ground chile ancho
1½ tsp. ground cumin
½ tsp. oregano
2 Tb. unsweetened cocoa
¼ tsp. crushed dried hot peppers
1 lb. ground turkey
2 Tb. masa harina (corn tortilla flour)
2 Tb. vegetable oil
¼ cup red jalapeño jelly

1. In a large mixing bowl beat the egg lightly, then add the tomato sauce and mix well.

2. Add the onion and the seasonings and mix well.

3. Add the ground turkey and the masa harina to the seasoning mix. With a heavy spoon or, preferably, your hands, knead the mixture thoroughly until it is smooth and very well blended.

4. Roll the mixture into small balls, each about the size of a small walnut.

5. In a large heavy skillet heat the oil over moderate heat. Place the meatballs in the pan and brown them slowly, turning them so that they brown evenly on all sides. Remove the browned meatballs from the pan with a slotted spoon and set aside.

6. Pour off the oil remaining in the pan and discard. With a paper towel wipe the pan out so that no oil remains.

7. Over low heat melt the jalapeño jelly, breaking it up and spreading it with a spoon or spatula. When the jelly is melted, return the meatballs to the pan and stir them around in the jelly until they are all evenly coated. Continue cooking and stirring until the meatballs are glazed and thoroughly heated through.

Early engraving of a Thanksgiving hunter bringing home the wild turkey

Turkey Pibil

Earth-pit cooking is one of humankind's most ancient techniques, surviving to this day in the Hawaiian luau, the New England clambake, and the *pib* of Mexico's Yucatan peninsula. A pit is dug in the earth or sand and lined with stones; a large fire is built over the stones and allowed to burn completely out, heating the stones red-hot in the process. The ashes are shoveled out and the food, wrapped in protective vegetation— corn husks, banana leaves, seaweed—is placed on the stones, covered, and slowly cooked. The resulting food is moist and succulent, with every bit of flavor and natural juices retained. Earth-pit cooking is still a delicious way to deal with our native bird. If you don't want to dig a pit in your backyard, and you're fresh out of banana leaves, you can do it with great success in your oven. A clay-pot cooker is ideal; or you can use an earthenware casserole with a tight-fitting cover; or you can wrap the turkey parts, with the marinade, in heavy-duty aluminum foil.

Serves 6–8

3–3½ lbs. turkey thighs
¼ cup orange juice
¼ cup lemon juice
6 cloves garlic, crushed
1 tsp. salt
1 tsp. ground chile ancho
1 Tb. ground achiote (annatto seed)*
1 tsp. oregano
1 tsp. ground cumin

1. With a sharp knife remove the skin from the turkey thighs and discard; place the thighs in a glass, enamel, or stainless steel container.

2. In a small bowl combine all the remaining ingredients and mix thoroughly. Spoon the marinade over the turkey thighs; cover the container and refrigerate for at least 6 hours or overnight.

3. Preheat the oven to 300°F. Place the turkey thighs, with the marinade, in a water-soaked clay-pot cooker, or an earthenware casserole; or wrap them securely in aluminum foil and place in a casserole or baking dish.

4. Bake for 2½–3 hours until the turkey is very tender and falling off the bone. Serve the turkey, with the juices, with corn tortillas, black beans, and fried bananas.

*Annatto seeds (achiote) are available whole in Mexican and Latin American grocery stores. They are sometimes ground or you can grind them yourself in an electric spice (coffee) grinder.

Smoked Turkey Salad with Chutney

The delicate flavor of smoked turkey goes very well with tart-sweet fruits and fruit chutney, and is further enhanced by some of the aromatic spices of traditional curries. If you buy an already prepared piece of smoked turkey, there is no cooking involved, making this a quick and easy dish for hot weather.

Serves 4–6

⅔ cup mayonnaise
¼ cup good fruit chutney (mango, peach, melon, and so on)
1 Tb. lime juice
½ tsp. cinnamon
½ tsp. ground ginger
½ tsp. ground coriander
¼ tsp. ground cumin
Good dash cayenne pepper
1½–2 lbs. boneless smoked turkey breast, diced
1 medium crisp tart apple, peeled, cored, and diced
⅓ cup raisins
1 cup seedless grapes

1. In a small bowl combine the mayonnaise, chutney, lime juice, and seasonings. Mix thoroughly.

2. In a large bowl combine the diced turkey, apple, raisins, and grapes. Pour the dressing over the turkey mixture and mix gently but thoroughly. Chill.

3. Serve the turkey salad chilled on a bed of mixed greens.

Chocolate Chili
Braised Beef with Spices and Chocolate
New World Pfeffernüsse
Mexican Chocolate Cheesecake
Triple Chocolate Bean Cake
Mocha Walnut Torte
Raspberry-Chocolate Truffle Pie
Chocolate Chunk Bread Pudding
Chocolate Chip Cookie Ice Cream Cake
Hot Fudge Sauce
Praline Brownies
Crème Brûlée au Chocolat
Mississippi Mud Cake
Black and White Chocolate Roll
White Chocolate–Three Ways
1. White Chocolate Sauce
2. White Chocolate Whipped Cream
3. White Chocolate Ice Cream
Vanilla Pear and Apple Puree
Fresh Fruit Trifle

CHOCOLATE AND VANILLA

When Linnaeus, the eighteenth-century Swedish naturalist, devised his system of classification for plants, he named chocolate *Cacao theobroma,* Cacao, food of the gods. Chocoholics from that time on have credited him with a fine poetic sensibility for so designating their favorite indulgence, but in fact chocolate was regarded as the food of the gods long before Europe discovered the New World. In an ancient Toltec myth it was Quetzalcoatl, the feathered serpent god, who was credited with the planting of cacao trees in the tropics of southern Mexico, and he was called "the god of light, the giver of the drink of the gods, chocolate."

No other food gained such exalted status in both the New and the Old Worlds, and one must ask what it is about chocolate that provides its very special panache. Both the Mayas and the Aztecs regarded it as a potent aphrodisiac, a reputation that traveled with cacao to Europe where, in its first few centuries, it was widely believed to provoke lust. Accordingly, it was condemned by those who didn't approve of lust and embraced by those who did. The proponents of lust appear to have won out, because chocolate was widely and enthusiastically received.

Unlike other foods for which aphrodisiac qualities have been claimed, chocolate does in fact contain several pharmocologically active substances, the alkaloids theobromine and caffeine. Caffeine, which occurs in much higher concentrations in coffee, is a known stimulant, while the role of theobromine is not entirely clear. In addition, some modern researchers have claimed, though not conclusively, that chocolate contains phenylethylamine, a chemical implicated in mood alteration and the alleviation of depression. So who knows? It may very well be that chocolate, as a mild stimulant and mood elevator, has the ability to put its consumers in the right frame of mind!

Chocolate was clearly held in very high regard by pre-Columbian Americans. Native to the tropical lowlands of southern Mexico and central America, cacao beans were imported by the Aztecs into central Mexico, where they were so valued that they were used as a form of currency. "Cacao" is an Aztec word, meaning the tree and the seeds of the tree from which chocolate is made. (Our word "cocoa" is simply an anglicization of the original "cacao.") "Chocolate," also an Aztec word, refers to the product made from cacao beans, and is said to be derived from the terms for "bitter water."

And bitter indeed it was, for most of the evidence indicates that chocolate was consumed unsweetened. The early accounts describe Mexican chocolate as a compound of roasted ground cacao beans mixed with long red pepper (chile), a cinnamon-like spice (very likely allspice), achiote (a red seed used as a coloring agent), and sometimes vanilla. No sweetening agent seems to have been added, making clear that the flavor of chocolate as it was originally used was very different from what it became when it reached Europe. An early Italian voyager to the New World described its flavor as "somewhat bitter" and thought it "more suited to pigs than men."

But the same writer grudgingly admitted that "it satisfies and refreshes the body without intoxicating," and Cortez himself reported that "One cup of this precious drink permits one to walk for a whole day without eating." These two early European accounts provide the key to the aboriginal American use of chocolate: It was consumed as a mild stimulant and energy-providing beverage. Unlike coffee, which contains no significant nutrients, chocolate has some protein and a high percentage of fat, in the form of cocoa butter. So it was a valuable energy-rich food, as well as a quick picker-upper. Montezuma often drank this precious liquid, whipped to a thick froth and served in golden goblets, before visiting one of his numerous wives.

From the court of Montezuma to the court of Spain—so began the odyssey of chocolate, for of all the foods discovered in the New World it was chocolate that underwent the most dramatic transformation. It left its home a bitter stimulant drink and returned as a sweet confection, a food of pleasure, a food of fun. Whatever its original use and value to the people of the New World, chocolate did not realize its full potential until it was refashioned in the culinary traditions of Europe.

The first thing Spain did to chocolate was to sweeten it with sugar, altering forever the path of its flavor from bitter to sweet. (The Spanish would continue, in limited areas, to use unsweetened chocolate as a seasoning ingredient in meat dishes, a trick they had picked up in Mexico.) For the allspice and chile that the Mexicans had used to flavor their chocolate, the Spanish substituted cinnamon. And they added ground almonds as a thickener, where Mexicans had used ground toasted cornmeal, *atole,* to make a thick gruel-like beverage.

Although Spain kept the secret of cacao and chocolate to herself for about one hundred years after its discovery, the knowledge (and the beans) eventually leaked out, and chocolate drinking became the rage of Europe. Chocolate joined the other stimulant beverages, coffee and tea, recently introduced from the East, and coffee and chocolate houses became prestigious centers for social exchange. But it was still as a hot beverage, in the tradition of its origin, that chocolate was consumed, and it would not be for another two hundred years that chocolate would undergo its final apotheosis.

Except for the sweetening, all the innovations in the development of chocolate occurred in the nineteenth century. First was the discovery by a Dutchman, Conrad van Houten, of a way to remove some of the cocoa butter that occurs naturally in chocolate. Pure chocolate, as processed from cacao beans, contains about 55 percent fat. Van Houten found that, by removing about half of that, the resulting product, cocoa powder, dissolved much more easily in water, and produced a much lighter and more digestible beverage than the high-fat pure chocolate.

Second of the great chocolate innovations was developed by Rudolph Lindt, a Swiss chocolate manufacturer, who discovered that when subjected to an extended process of rolling and kneading, chocolate achieved a smooth, unctuous, melt-in-the-mouth texture; the process, known as "conching" because of the shell-like shape of the rollers, produced a smooth chocolate fondant that became the basis of most of the eating and confectionary chocolate we enjoy today. Lindt also found that adding more cocoa butter to the mixture resulted in an even richer eating chocolate. These two techniques, conching and the addition of extra cocoa butter, were the real impetus for the explosion of the chocolate industry, for where solid chocolate had previously been grainy and gritty and not particularly suitable for eating, it now became a melting, luxurious, mouth-pleasing experience.

The third innovation also came from the Swiss, who, with their great tradition of dairying, invented "milk chocolate"; by adding milk they produced a lighter, sweeter eating chocolate that was rich and smooth but with a less intense chocolate flavor. It is milk chocolate that forms the basis of most of the popular American confections and candy bars, appealing particularly to the sweet tooths of the young.

In the end it is hard to say absolutely why chocolate is and has always been so highly valued. Is it the flavor?—for that changed profoundly from its initial bitter, peppery profile to its current sweet one. Is it because chocolate is a stimulant or a quick source of energy in a wonderfully flavored package? Is it chocolate's high fat content, providing (because it melts at body temperature) that special melting texture we call mouth-feel? Or is it a combination of all these attributes, and the fact that we eat chocolate purely for pleasure and not for nourishment? For in that sense chocolate has not changed at all; through all its transformations it remains for us what it was for Montezuma—a voluptuous, pleasurable, and luxurious food.

It would be difficult to talk about chocolate without acknowledging vanilla, for, from ancient times vanilla has been chocolate's handmaiden. The fruit of a twining orchid plant, native to the tropics of central America, vanilla had been used to flavor chocolate long before Europe enthusiastically seized upon the sweet alliance. Vanilla contains no sugar, but has a sweetening effect, and it may well be because of this that it was so early combined with chocolate.

The characteristic flavor and aroma of vanilla are not evident in the green pods or beans, and it is tantalizing to speculate how ancient people discovered the processes necessary to produce the vanilla we know. The harvested beans are sweated and fermented for a period of days, then dried and cured in the sun. The total curing process, which may last for months, results in the production of a crystalline substance called vanillin that is the source of vanilla's fragrance and flavor. Cured vanilla beans are highly aromatic and were used in ancient Mexico as a perfume and as home aromatizers, much as we use potpourris today.

When vanilla left the New World it was enthusiastically received by the Old, not just for its heightening effect on chocolate, but as a delicate flavor in its own right. It has become the world's most popular flavoring for sweet foods, used, unlike chocolate, in Asia and the Middle East, as well as Europe. In America it remains as it has always been a well-loved, familiar taste, an indispensable seasoning for puddings, custards, cakes, cookies, candies, soda pop, and, of course, ice cream. Despite the forays of such upstarts as jamocha almond fudge and peanut butter and jelly and bubble gum chip, vanilla ice cream stands triumphant as America's all-time favorite.

Chocolate Chili

This isn't really the name of the dish—I just made it up to get your attention. It is a New Mexican recipe, interesting because it shows the use of chocolate as a seasoning ingredient rather than as a sweetened confection. That tradition originated in pre-Columbian Mexico, traveled to Spain, and then came back to America in an area that has blended Mexican, Hispanic, Anglo, and Native American elements into a distinctive cuisine. In New Mexico the mixture is used as a stuffing for roast poultry, but for my taste it is too rich for that and works better served with plain rice, or layered into a spoon bread (see p. 23), or stuffed into scooped-out shells of green or yellow summer squash. Try this recipe for a different taste experience. The chocolate is not evident as such but provides a depth and richness to the flavor that is unusual and very good.

Serves 3–4

1 lb. lean ground beef
1½ cups tomato sauce
1 tsp. salt
1 Tb. unsweetened cocoa
½ tsp. allspice
½ tsp. ground coriander
1 tsp. ground ancho chile
½ cup pine nuts
½ cup raisins

1. In a medium skillet brown the ground beef thoroughly. Pour off and discard all the fat and liquid from the meat.

2. Add all the remaining ingredients to the browned beef, mix well, then simmer, uncovered, over low heat for about 30 minutes until it is quite thick.

Early American chocolate pot and stirrer. The stirrer, with its moveable parts, originated in the Mexican *molinillo*, a wooden whisk that whipped the liquid chocolate to a froth.

Braised Beef with Spices and Chocolate

The use of unsweetened chocolate as a seasoning ingredient has a long history in Mexico, one that seems to involve festive or ceremonial cooking—not surprising, as cacao was an expensive luxury not to be used on a daily basis. This use of chocolate in spiced sauces continues today, particularly in the region of Oaxaca, and traveled to Spain with the conquistadores where it persists today in a few areas, most notably in the northeast corner of Aragon and the Basque country. This braised beef reflects the traditions of both Mexico and Spain; it has a rich and complex sauce that also works well with pork or lamb.

Serves 6–8

2 Tb. olive oil
2½–3½ lbs. lean boneless bottom round of beef (in 1 piece)
2 large onions, thinly sliced
½ tsp. salt
1 tsp. paprika
Several good grinds black pepper
½ cup tomato sauce
3 oz. orange juice concentrate
2 Tb. sherry wine vinegar
½ cup beef stock
1 oz. (1 square) unsweetened baking chocolate
Sliced orange and chopped parsley for garnish

1. In a large heavy pot or Dutch oven heat the olive oil over moderate heat.

2. Dry the beef with paper towels, then brown it slowly in the oil, turning it frequently, until it is thoroughly browned on all sides.

3. When the beef is completely browned, remove it from the pot and set aside. Add the onions to the pot and sauté slowly, stirring, until they are soft and richly browned.

4. Return the beef to the pot; sprinkle it with salt, paprika, and pepper. Add the tomato sauce, orange juice, vinegar, and stock. Bring to a simmer, then cover and cook over low heat for about 2½–3 hours or until the beef is tender when pierced with a fork.

5. Remove the beef from the sauce and let stand for about 10–15 minutes. Keeping the sauce on very low heat, add the chocolate and stir until the chocolate is melted and thoroughly incorporated.

6. Cut the meat into thin slices and arrange on a heated platter. Spoon the hot sauce over the meat, garnish with the orange slices and chopped parsley. Serve with saffron rice or steamed potatoes.

New World Pfeffernüsse

From Roman times to the Renaissance, Europe craved the spices of the exotic East and frequently combined them in recipes for both sweet and savory dishes. German *Pfeffernüsse*—literally, pepper nut—is a traditional Christmas cookie that uses the aromatic spices cinnamon, nutmeg, ginger, and cloves, along with black pepper, for a sweet and spicy holiday treat. Here is the *Pfeffernüsse* reinterpreted with a New World cast of seasonings. The ancient Aztec tradition of flavoring chocolate with allspice, chile, and vanilla reappears in a thin, crisp, chocolate-y cookie with a sweet, spicy glaze.

Makes 48 cookies

½ cup (1 stick) plus 2 Tb. butter, softened
⅔ cup sugar
2 Tb. red jalapeño pepper jelly
1 egg
½ tsp. vanilla
¼ cup unsweetened cocoa
½ tsp. allspice
¼ tsp. cayenne pepper
1½ cups flour
1 cup quick oats

GLAZE

3 oz. semisweet chocolate
3 Tb. red jalapeño pepper jelly

1. In a mixing bowl cream the butter and the sugar; when they are thoroughly creamed beat in the 2 Tb. jalapeño jelly.

2. Add the egg and beat in thoroughly, then stir in the vanilla.

3. Add the remaining dry ingredients and mix until completely blended in. Preheat the oven to 350°F.

continued

New World Pfeffernüsse continued

4. Butter a 10 x 15-inch rimmed cookie sheet. With a spatula or broad knife spread the cookie dough in an even layer over the pan. Make the layer as even as possible or some parts will brown too quickly.

5. Bake for about 20 minutes until just lightly browned.

6. While the cookies are baking, make the glaze: Combine the chocolate and jalapeño jelly in a small saucepan. Heat over low heat, stirring, until melted and smooth.

7. Remove the cookie sheet from the oven and immediately spread the chocolate glaze evenly over the surface. Cut the cookies while still hot into small squares or rectangles. Let them cool completely in the pan before removing.

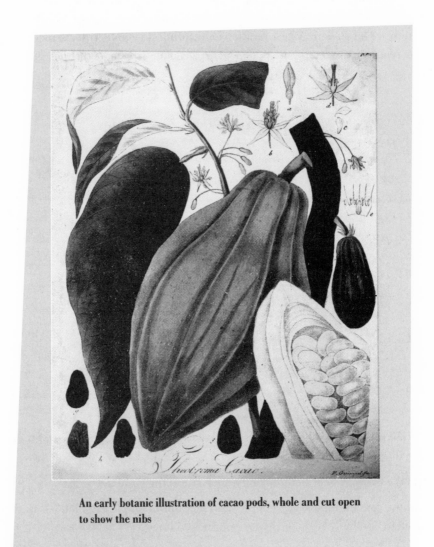

An early botanic illustration of cacao pods, whole and cut open to show the nibs

Mexican Chocolate Cheesecake

This cake is Mexican not by virtue of its origin but because of its unique flavor. Since Spanish colonial times, chocolate in Mexico has almost always been compounded with sugar, cinnamon, and ground almonds. Individual cooks and chocolate makers all have their own special blends. It is a combination that works well in cheesecake, a dessert that America has brought to its most elaborated form. This is a rich luscious cake that needs no additional garnish, but you may wish to glaze it with a thin layer of chocolate, as suggested at the end of the recipe.

Serves 10–12

16 square cinnamon graham crackers
3 Tb. butter
½ cup finely chopped almonds
3 8-oz. squares cream cheese (1½ lbs.), softened
1½ cups sugar
6 eggs
1 cup heavy cream
6 ozs. semisweet chocolate
2 Tb. coffee
1 tsp. vanilla
1 tsp. almond extract
2 tsp. cinnamon

1. Crush or pulverize the graham crackers into fine crumbs.

2. In a small saucepan melt the butter, then stir in the cracker crumbs and the almonds and mix thoroughly.

3. Butter the bottom and sides of a 9-inch springform pan. Pat the crumb mixture in an even layer over the bottom of the pan.

4. In a food processor or blender combine the cream cheese, the sugar, the eggs, and the heavy cream. Blend until smooth. (Process in several batches if necessary.) Pour the mixture into a large bowl. Preheat the oven to 350°F.

5. Melt the chocolate with the coffee over low heat, stirring, until it is smooth and well blended. Cool slightly.

6. Stir the chocolate, the vanilla and almond extracts, and the cinnamon into the cheese mixture. Mix thoroughly. Pour the mixture over the crumb crust.

7. Bake for about 1 hour until the cake is set and the center is no longer liquid. Cool, then chill thoroughly before unmolding. Glaze, if desired, with 2–4 ozs. melted semisweet chocolate and garnish with 2 Tb. finely chopped almonds.

Triple Chocolate Bean Cake

What, one wonders, would Montezuma's cooks have made of this confection, which combines two ancient foods, black beans and chocolate, in a brand new way? The pureed beans provide a moist, dense texture that is a perfect complement to the rich flavor of chocolate and *crème de cacao*. The finished cake can be glazed with a simple chocolate glaze, but I like it best chilled, cut into thin slices, and served with ice cream and/or hot fudge sauce. A triple whammy!

Serves 10–12

1 cup (2 sticks) unsalted butter
2 ozs. (2 squares) unsweetened chocolate
6 ozs. (6 squares) semisweet chocolate
1 1-lb. can black beans (2 cups), drained, rinsed thoroughly in cold water,
   and drained again
¼ cup crème de cacao
5 eggs
1 cup sugar
1 tsp. vanilla
1 cup flour

OPTIONAL GLAZE

4 ozs. semisweet chocolate
2 Tb. butter

1. In a small heavy saucepan melt the butter and the unsweetened and semisweet chocolates over low heat, stirring, until the mixture is smooth and well blended. Remove from heat and set aside.

2. In a blender or food processor puree the drained beans with the *crème de cacao* until smooth.

3. In a large mixing bowl beat the eggs until they are light and fluffy. Add the sugar gradually and continue to beat until the mixture is thick and pale. Preheat the oven to 325°F.

4. With the mixer at low speed stir in the melted chocolate, then the pureed beans and the vanilla.

5. Stir in the flour and mix until just thoroughly blended.

6. Spoon the batter into a well-buttered 9- or 10-inch Bundt pan. Bake for about 45 minutes until a straw inserted into the middle comes out clean.

7. Cool the cake in the pan for 30 minutes, then unmold onto a serving plate. If you want a glaze, melt the chocolate and butter together and spread on top of the cake. Chill and serve with ice cream.

From the Bean to the Bar

Although the machinery has changed, the basic process for making chocolate from cacao beans remains the same as it was in pre-Columbian Mexico. The harvested pods containing the cacao beans are split open and the beans are allowed to ferment for a short period. Then they are cleaned and dried and shipped to chocolate manufacturers, who roast them; it is at this point that the characteristic aroma and flavor of chocolate first become apparent. The outer shells of the beans are cracked open and discarded, and the inner "nibs," the heart of the cacao bean, are ground. Grinding produces heat, which liquifies the natural cocoa butter in the nibs, resulting in a thick paste that is called chocolate "liquor." The chocolate liquor, when cooled, is formed into bars or squares, and this is chocolate in its purest form, a product we know as unsweetened baking chocolate. From this point chocolate can go in several directions. A good portion of the cocoa butter can be removed, resulting in cocoa powder. Or more cocoa butter can be added in, to produce a richer fondant chocolate. Sugar and other flavor enhancers like vanilla are added, and milk solids if milk chocolate is desired. These mixtures are then conched to produce smooth eating chocolate. Several factors are critical in the production of high-quality chocolate: the blending of different varieties of cacao beans, the roasting, the amount of the cocoa butter that is added, the ratio of cocoa butter to sugar, and the length of the conching process. All chocolate manufacturers have their own jealously guarded secret formulas, and it is the consumer's sweet obligation to decide which is the fairest of them all.

Mocha Walnut Torte

In spite of their disparate origins, coffee and chocolate have always had an affinity for one another. The two, which met as stimulant beverages in the chocolate and coffee houses of sixteenth-century Europe, intensified their relationship through the centuries, producing in their union of flavors a brand new flavor—mocha.

Serves 8

CRUST

½ cup (1 stick) unsalted butter, slightly softened
⅓ cup firmly packed light brown sugar
¾ cup flour
½ cup finely chopped walnuts

CHOCOLATE LAYER

6 eggs
⅔ cup sugar
6 oz. semisweet chocolate
¼ cup strong coffee
⅓ cup flour

BUTTERCREAM

4 oz. semisweet chocolate
4 oz. (½ stick) unsalted butter
½ tsp. instant coffee powder
1 Tb. Kahlúa or other coffee liqueur
1 egg yolk

2 Tb. finely chopped walnuts

1. Make the crust: In a medium bowl combine the butter, the light brown sugar, the flour, and the walnuts. Mix with the fingertips until the mixture is uniformly crumbly, the butter distributed evenly in small pea-sized pieces.

2. Butter the bottom and sides of a 9-inch springform pan. Spread and press the crumb mixture into an even layer over the bottom (not the sides) of the pan.

3. Make the chocolate layer: In a large bowl beat the eggs until light and foamy. Gradually add the sugar and continue to beat until the mixture is thick and pale and tripled in volume. Preheat the oven to 350°F.

4. In a small saucepan melt the chocolate with the coffee over low heat until smooth. Remove from the heat and set aside.

5. With the mixer at low speed mix the cooled melted chocolate into the eggs until it is thoroughly blended in.

6. Sift the flour into the batter and mix just until it is well blended.

7. Pour the chocolate batter over the crust. Bake for about 40–45 minutes until the top is firm. Remove the cake from the oven and let it cool in the pan.

8. Make the buttercream: In a small saucepan melt the chocolate with the butter over low heat, stirring, until smooth.

9. Remove from the heat and stir in the instant coffee and the coffee liqueur.

10. Whisk in the egg yolk and beat the mixture until it is very smooth. Chill until a good spreading consistency is achieved.

11. Run a sharp knife around the edge of the cooled cake and unmold from the springform. Spread the buttercream in a thin even layer over the top and sides of the cake. Sprinkle the walnuts in a rim around the edge.

Two illustrations form a 1685 French treatise on coffee, tea, and chocolate. On the left, an American native with his chocolate stirrer and pot; below him, a cacao tree and vanilla pods. On the right, the meeting of coffee, tea, and chocolate. Coffee is represented by an Arab, tea by a Chinaman, and chocolate by an American native.

Heaven and Hell

Although chocolate seems to be held in unequivocal esteem by our culture, a closer look reveals that the American ethos is somewhat ambivalent about this very unique food. From our European heritage comes a fundamental belief in the superiority of white or light over dark or black. And the Puritan ethic, so much a part of our tradition, equates indulgence, fun and luxury, with sin. Certainly in our own times dieters, and particularly young women, are subject to an almost obsessive love-hate relationship with chocolate, which represents all that is both desired and dangerous. The names we give to our most elaborate chocolate concoctions indicate our ambivalence about this dark and voluptuous substance that we crave and fear at the same time: "Chocolate Death," "Chocolate Sin," "Chocolate Temptation," "Killer Chocolate Cake," and the most obvious of all, "Devil's Food Cake," a name designed to differentiate a dark, dense cake from the sweet, fluffy, pallid, white "Angel's Food Cake." Is it that by giving a name to our fear we liberate ourselves from it? Or do the names simply reinforce our not-so-deeply hidden belief in wickedness and our inability to resist it? It is certainly ironic that chocolate, which grows in tropical climates, is a cash crop that is harvested by people of color who can almost never afford to eat it; 90 percent of the world's supply is produced for white-skinned consumers in northern Europe and America. At least as far as chocolate is concerned, the devil seems to have triumphed.

Raspberry-Chocolate Truffle Pie

The chocolate truffle was presumably so named because of similarities in size, color, and expense to its fungal counterpart. It is the most luxurious of chocolate confections, a melting mixture of quality chocolate, butter or cream, and liqueur. In this pie a rich dark chocolate truffle layer is swirled with a tart-sweet raspberry puree, then garnished with whipped cream and raspberries. Serve the pie in very small slices, as it is extraordinarily rich.

Serves 8–10

1 baked shallow 9-inch pastry shell
1 pint fresh raspberries
½ cup sugar
¾ cup heavy cream
8 oz. high-quality semisweet or bittersweet chocolate, broken into chunks
2 Tb. Chambord or other raspberry liqueur
1 cup heavy cream, whipped and lightly sweetened, for garnish

1. Reserve a small handful of the raspberries for garnish. Combine the remaining raspberries and the sugar in a blender or food processor and puree until the sugar is completely dissolved.

2. Strain the puree to remove the seeds.

3. In a small heavy saucepan heat the cream and the chocolate over low heat. Do not simmer or scald, but stir the mixture constantly until it is thick and smooth and the chocolate is completely melted and blended into the cream.

4. Remove from the heat and stir in the liqueur. Cool slightly.

5. Spoon 3–4 tablespoons of the chocolate mixture evenly over the bottom of the pastry shell. Chill for about 30 minutes.

6. Spoon ¼ cup of the raspberry puree evenly over the chilled chocolate layer. Pour the remaining chocolate mixture over the raspberry puree.

7. Spoon 2–3 tablespoons of additional raspberry puree over the top of the chocolate. (Any remaining puree can be frozen for later use.) With a table knife carefully swirl the raspberry puree through the chocolate. Swirl just enough to make an attractive pattern, but don't overdo it. Chill the pie thoroughly, at least 3 hours.

8. Spoon the whipped cream around the edge of the pie, leaving the center open to show the swirl design. Garnish the pie with the reserved raspberries.

Chocolate Chunk Bread Pudding

Bread pudding, like stuffing, is one of those wonderfully soul-satisfying dishes that resulted from the frugal housewife's need to use up stale bread. Imported to America from England and the continent, these puddings were simple mixtures of stale bread cubes baked in a custard, frequently embellished with dried or cooked fruits. This one is more typically American, with its rum- and vanilla-flavored custard and chunks of dark chocolate. Make the pudding a day ahead, as it really needs an overnight in the refrigerator to achieve its proper dense texture.

Serves 6

2 cups milk
1 cup light cream
2 Tb. butter
4–5 slices firm-textured stale white bread, cut in small cubes
        (no need to trim the crusts)
2 eggs
½ cup sugar
1 tsp. vanilla
¼ cup golden rum
¾ cup coarsely chopped semisweet or bittersweet chocolate
        (or prepackaged chocolate "chunks")
Heavy cream or lightly sweetened whipped cream for garnish, if desired

1. In a medium saucepan scald the milk and the light cream. Remove from the heat and stir in the butter until it is melted.

2. Place the bread cubes in a large bowl. Pour the hot milk mixture over the cubes and let stand for 30 minutes.

3. Whisk the eggs thoroughly, then add them with the sugar to the bread mixture. Stir in the vanilla and the rum and mix thoroughly. Preheat the oven to 325°F.

4. Turn the mixture into a well-buttered 2-quart deep casserole. Sprinkle the chocolate chunks over the top.

5. Bake for 50–60 minutes until the top is puffed, set, and browned. (The center will sink as the pudding cools.)

6. Chill the pudding thoroughly, preferably overnight, then serve with heavy cream or whipped cream for garnish, if desired.

Chocolate Chip Cookie Ice Cream Cake

Of the hundreds of chocolate products available, none is so fundamentally American as the chocolate chip, first used in 1930 by Ruth Wakefield in her famous Toll House cookie. She used a chopped-up chocolate bar, and the cookie was such a success that the Nestlé company came out with commercial chips in 1939. In this recipe a giant chocolate chip cookie is topped with another American classic, vanilla ice cream, and garnished with mini-chips. It can be made ahead of time, frozen, and kept in the freezer for a quick and festive dessert.

Serves 6–8

½ cup (1 stick) butter, softened
½ cup granulated sugar
¼ cup firmly packed dark brown sugar
1 egg
1 tsp. vanilla
1 cup flour
½ cup oats (quick or regular)
1 cup chocolate chips
1 pint vanilla ice cream, softened
3–4 Tb. mini-chocolate chips

1. In a medium bowl cream the butter with the granulated and brown sugars. When the mixture is smooth, beat in the egg and the vanilla. Preheat the oven to 375°F.

2. Add the flour and the oats and mix until well blended. Stir in the chocolate chips and mix well.

3. Spread the dough evenly in a lightly buttered 9-inch square or round cake pan, or deep 9-inch pie plate. Bake for 20 minutes until the top is lightly browned. Cool completely.

4. Spread the softened ice cream evenly over the cooled cake. Sprinkle the mini chips over the ice cream.

5. Cover the cake with plastic wrap and freeze. Remove the cake from the freezer 10–15 minutes before serving.

A Chocolate Bar in Every Pocket

The use of chocolate in America paralleled that in Europe; well into the nineteenth century it was used primarily as a hot sweetened beverage. The first chocolate factory in America was opened in 1765 in Massachusetts by Dr. James Baker, and "Baker's" remains to this day a respected name in the chocolate industry. But it was not until 1900, soon after the European innovations in chocolate confectionary, that eating chocolate became available to the mass American market. That fortunate development was due to the vision of an enterprising young candy manufacturer named Milton Hershey. He sold a million-dollar caramel business because he believed that the future lay in chocolate, and more specifically, in milk chocolate. The first Hershey's bar was produced in 1894, and Hershey's Kisses began rolling off the line in 1907. These inexpensive, highly sweetened milk-enriched confections were an instant success and the chocolate candy bar became the right of every American, rich or poor. During World War II the American government asked the Hershey Company to produce Hershey's bars for the K rations for GIs abroad, and by the time of the Japanese attack on Pearl Harbor, the bars were being produced at the rate of 500,000 a day. Chocolate had finally come full circle back to the New World. It was forever transformed from what it had been when the Spanish discovered it at the court of Montezuma, but it was functioning once again as Cortez himself had described it—as an energy-rich nutritious meal-on-the-hoof for soldiers on the move.

As this book went to press, the Hershey Company came out with yet another chocolate confection for troops in the field—the Desert Bar, designed to withstand the desert heat of the Middle East, where America was defending its way of life in the oilfields of Kuwait.

Hot Fudge Sauce

The origin of the term "fudge" is unclear, but it is an American confection that developed around the turn of the century and was popularized in a wave of competitive fudge-making at a number of eastern women's colleges. "Wellesley fudge" and "Vassar fudge" are still popular variations on the rich, smooth, dense chocolate candies that bear ample witness to America's sweet tooth. Fudge has come to mean not only the candy, but any product—cake, pie, frosting, sauce—that is deep and darkly chocolate, rich and smooth. Hot fudge sauce is a genuine classic. Traditionally served over vanilla ice cream, it softens the ice cream while the ice cream cools and solidifies the hot sauce. It is an indulgence that deserves only the finest ingredients—no corn syrup, water, or cocoa powder—just high-quality chocolate and cream.

Makes about 1¾ cups

1 cup light cream
8 oz. high-quality semisweet or bittersweet chocolate,
*   broken into chunks or squares*
½ tsp. vanilla

1. In a small heavy saucepan heat the cream and the chocolate over low heat. When the chocolate starts to melt, stir the mixture constantly until it is hot, smooth, and glossy. Do not simmer or scald. Keep stirring the mixture until thick and smooth.

2. Remove the sauce from the heat and stir in the vanilla. Serve the sauce hot over vanilla ice cream.

Note: The sauce can be stored in a covered jar in the refrigerator for several weeks. To reheat, stir over low heat until it is hot and smooth.

Hershey's Kisses rolling off the line in the 1920s

Praline Brownies

The brownie is an American invention; the name referred originally to a kind of cookie, but came ultimately to designate a rich chocolate cake cut into squares or bars. There are by tradition two kinds of brownie—the chewy fudge type and the cake type. In my book a REAL brownie is the fudgy kind—dense, moist, incredibly chocolatey, and not too sweet, a profound and serious chocolate experience. These brownies can certainly get by on their own without any adornment, but the praline topping is a pleasant extra.

Makes 32 brownies

1 cup (2 sticks) unsalted butter
5 oz. (5 squares) unsweetened chocolate
3 oz. semisweet chocolate
4 eggs
2 cups sugar
1¼ cups flour
2 tsp. vanilla
¾ cup coarsely chopped pecans

PRALINE TOPPING

3 Tb. unsalted butter, softened
½ cup firmly packed brown sugar
¾ cup light cream
½ tsp. vanilla
1 cup coarsely chopped pecans

1. In a small heavy saucepan melt the butter and chocolate over low heat, stirring, until melted and smooth. Cool slightly.

2. In a mixing bowl beat the eggs until light and frothy. Slowly add the sugar, beating until the mixture is thick and pale.

3. Stir in the chocolate mixture and mix until well blended. Preheat the oven to 350°F.

4. Stir in the flour and mix until thoroughly blended. Stir in the vanilla and the ¾ cup nuts.

5. Spread the mixture evenly in a buttered 13 x 9-inch baking pan. Bake about 20 minutes or until just firm. Do not overbake.

6. While the brownies are baking, make the topping: Combine the butter and the brown sugar in a small saucepan. Heat, stirring, until melted and smooth.

7. Stir in the cream and cook, stirring, until the mixture is hot, smooth, and thick. Remove from the heat and stir in the vanilla and the 1 cup nuts.

8. When the brownies are done, remove from the oven and let stand 5 minutes. Heat broiler.

9. Spread the topping evenly over the brownies; place under the broiler for a few minutes until the topping bubbles all over. Watch carefully; you want the topping to bubble but not burn.

10. Let the brownies cool completely in the pan before cutting them into squares.

Liquid Delight

Chocolate began its odyssey as a beverage and continues to this day to provide pleasure in liquid form. Hot cocoa remains a traditional favorite, sweet and heartwarming, but twentieth-century America gave rise to a raft of cold chocolate beverages that the first consumers of chocolatl could not have dreamed of. The inspiration for these concoctions came from the American dependence on dairy products, primarily milk and ice cream, and the marvelous invention of carbonated water in bottles. From chocolate milk to ice cream sodas to malteds and frosteds and phosphates, we spoon and slurp through straws gallons of rich frothy bubbly chocolate beverages that have become standards of the corner candy store and the drugstore soda fountain. Perhaps the most eccentric of these drinks is a native of New York; it is called an "egg cream," though it contains neither eggs nor cream. It consists quite simply of a couple of good squirts of chocolate syrup mixed with a little milk; the glass is then filled with carbonated water. Simple, unassuming, and the stuff of which childhood memories are made—but don't ask for one in Detroit or Des Moines!

Crème Brûlée au Chocolat

I once made this for a friend who had never had it before. She took a spoonful and said, "This is the best chocolate pudding I ever ate!" I'll say! For Americans, nurtured on a tradition of bland cornstarch puddings, *crème brûlée* (broiled cream) is an insane luxury, a prime example of the French genius for cooking with eggs and cream. No thickeners, fillers, or starches here—just the finest chocolate, heavy cream, and eggs. It is not a dish for the calorie-conscious. The *crème* should be thoroughly chilled and eaten shortly after it is cooked, as the crackly broiled sugar topping tends to soften if the dish sits around too long.

Serves 8–10

3 cups heavy cream
⅓ cup sugar
6 oz. high-quality semisweet or bittersweet chocolate, broken into chunks
6 egg yolks
1 tsp. vanilla
½ cup lightly packed light brown sugar

1. In a heavy saucepan heat the cream over low heat until it is hot, but do not scald or simmer. Add the sugar and the chocolate to the hot cream and stir until they are completely melted and the mixture is smooth and well blended. Remove from the heat and set aside.

2. In a large mixing bowl beat the egg yolks until they are thick. Slowly pour the chocolate mixture into the beaten yolks, mixing until it is very well blended. Stir in the vanilla and mix well. Preheat the oven to 350°F.

3. Strain the mixture into a shallow 8- or 9-inch casserole or baking dish. Set this casserole into a larger container or baking tin, then carefully pour boiling water into the larger container so that the water comes about halfway up the sides of the smaller casserole.

4. Place the double casserole onto the middle rack of the oven. Bake for about 40–45 minutes until the *crème* is just lightly set.

5. Remove the *crème* from the hot water bath and let it cool for at least 1 hour.

6. After the *crème* has cooled, fill the larger container with ice cubes or cracked ice. Place the *crème* dish on the ice, making sure that the ice comes part way up the sides of the dish. (The ice bath ensures that the *crème* will not cook further while the topping broils.)

7. Sprinkle the brown sugar evenly over the top of the *crème*. Place the double dish under the broiler and watch it like a hawk. Broil just long enough for the sugar to melt and bubble; do not let it burn. It should take only a minute or so.

8. Cool the *crème,* then chill it thoroughly.

Mississippi Mud Cake

An aptly descriptive name for a cake as dark and moist as delta mud. This is a dense fudge-type cake best served in small pieces.

Serves 10–12

1 cup (2 sticks) butter
4 squares (4 oz.) unsweetened chocolate
4 eggs
2 cups sugar
2 tsp. vanilla
1 cup flour

THE FROSTING

6 oz. semisweet chocolate
2 Tb. butter
3 Tb. strong coffee

½ cup coarsely chopped pecans
½ cup shredded sweet coconut

1. In a small heavy saucepan melt the 1 cup butter and the unsweetened chocolate over low heat, stirring, until the mixture is smooth and well blended. Remove from the heat and set aside.

2. In a large mixing bowl beat the eggs until they are foamy. Slowly stir in the sugar, beating constantly, until the mixture is thick and pale.

3. Slowly pour in the chocolate mixture, mixing on low speed until it is completely blended in. Stir in the vanilla. Preheat the oven to 350° F.

4. Sift the flour into the batter, mixing only until it is thoroughly blended in.

5. Spoon the batter into a well-buttered 9- or 10-inch springform pan. Carefully spread the batter to form an even layer.

6. Bake the cake for about 30 minutes until the top is just beginning to crack and is firm to the touch. Cool the cake in the pan.

7. Make the frosting: In a small saucepan combine the semisweet chocolate, the butter, and the coffee. Cook over low heat, stirring constantly, until the mixture is smooth and well blended.

8. When the cake is thoroughly cool, run a sharp knife around the edge and unmold onto a serving plate. Spread the semisweet frosting over the top.

9. Combine the pecans and the coconut, then sprinkle the mixture evenly over the frosting.

Black and White Chocolate Roll

A dark chocolate roll filled with white chocolate cream, both set off by fresh strawberries. In our house this concoction is known as the "giant Ho-Ho," an affectionate tribute to the packaged little cream-filled chocolate rolls that my children adored when they were small. This one appeals to all ages.

Serves 8–10

$1\frac{1}{2}$ cups heavy cream
6 oz. white chocolate
6 oz. semisweet chocolate
3 Tb. strong coffee
6 eggs, separated
$\frac{1}{2}$ cup sugar
1 tsp. vanilla
Confectioner's sugar
1 cup sliced fresh strawberries, plus additional whole strawberries for garnish

1. In a small heavy saucepan heat the cream over low heat until it is very warm. Do not allow it to come to the simmer. Add the white chocolate and stir until it is melted and the mixture is smooth. Chill thoroughly.

2. In another small saucepan combine the semisweet chocolate and the coffee. Cook over low heat, stirring, until the chocolate is melted and the mixture is smooth. Remove from heat and set aside.

3. In a large mixing bowl beat the egg yolks until they are foamy. Gradually beat in the $\frac{1}{2}$ cup sugar and continue to beat until the mixture is thick and pale.

4. Beat the egg whites until they are stiff.

5. Stir the melted semisweet chocolate into the egg yolks. Mix until it is thoroughly blended. Stir in the vanilla.

6. Carefully fold the beaten egg whites into the chocolate mixture. Preheat the oven to 350°F.

7. Butter a 17 x 11 x 1-inch jelly-roll pan. Line the pan with waxed paper and butter the paper.

8. Pour the batter carefully into the pan, spreading it in an even layer. Bake for 15 minutes. Remove the pan from the oven and cover it loosely with a clean damp cloth. Let stand for 15 minutes.

continued

Black and White Chocolate Roll continued

9. On a table place two 20-inch-long sheets of waxed paper, the long sides facing you and the front sheet overlapping the back sheet. Sift confectioner's sugar all over the sheets. Unmold the cake onto the sugared paper, then carefully peel off the waxed paper.

10. Whip the chilled white chocolate cream until thick and stiff.

11. Spread the whipped white chocolate over the chocolate cake, spreading it evenly to within ½ inch of the edges. Place the sliced strawberries evenly over the white chocolate cream.

12. Carefully roll the cake up from the long side nearest you by lifting the waxed paper underneath and guiding it with your hands. Slide the rolled cake onto a serving plate. Chill for several hours before serving. Garnish with whole strawberries.

White Chocolate

White chocolate is currently very fashionable, a fact that true chocolate lovers find difficult to understand. White chocolate is the fat component of chocolate, cocoa butter, sweetened with sugar and flavored with vanilla. Cocoa solids, which are responsible for the dark color and the characteristic flavor and aroma of true chocolate, are removed or separated from the cocoa butter in the production of white chocolate, leaving only a faint residue of the fragrance and flavor of chocolate. Because it lacks the unique and intense flavor of chocolate, white chocolate is at its best in creams, coatings, and sauces where a more delicate flavor is desirable.

White Chocolate—Three Ways

For true chocolate lovers white chocolate isn't really chocolate at all, but it does have its aficionados, among whom is my son Lex. These three simple recipes were designed for him, using white chocolate as a sauce, a whipped cream, and an ice cream.

1. White Chocolate Sauce

1 cup heavy cream
3 oz. white chocolate, broken into chunks

1. In a small heavy saucepan heat the cream over low heat. Add the white chocolate and stir constantly until the mixture is melted and smooth.

2. Chill the sauce, then serve with fresh strawberries or raspberries or Pears Poached in Spiced Red Wine (see p. 268).

2. White Chocolate Whipped Cream

Make the above sauce, then chill overnight. Whip until stiff. Use as you would ordinary whipped cream.

3. White Chocolate Ice Cream

1. Double the recipe for white chocolate sauce. Chill thoroughly.

2. Beat 2 egg yolks into the chilled sauce. Blend the mixture according to the directions of your ice cream maker. Chocolate chips can be added if desired.

Flavor in Many Forms

The aromatic and delicate flavor of vanilla can be delivered in a variety of forms. The best known and most commonly available is vanilla extract, a flavoring liquid produced by soaking chopped cured vanilla beans in an alcohol solution until the maximum flavor has been extracted; the liquid is then strained and aged. "Imitation" vanilla is made from synthetic compounds, much cheaper than vanilla pods; it is very similar in flavor and aroma but lacks the delicacy and complexity of true vanilla. Vanilla powder is made from ground cured vanilla beans; it is useful when vanilla flavor in a dry form is required, as in a sugar coating for cookies. Vanilla sugar is simply confectioner's sugar to which the flavor and aroma of vanilla have been added. Both vanilla extract and vanilla sugar can easily be made at home. All you need are five or six cured vanilla beans; they are expensive but they go a long way and last a long time. To make the extract, soak 2 or 3 vanilla beans in 6 ounces of brandy or cognac for six weeks or more. As you use the extract replace it with additional brandy. To make vanilla sugar, embed 2 or 3 beans in a jar with 1 pound of confectioner's sugar. Cover tightly and let stand for 3 weeks before using.

Vanilla Pear and Apple Puree

One of our most beloved myths is that of Johnny Appleseed, the eighteenth-century New England gentleman who walked about the country planting apple trees. Johnny, it seems, was a mild eccentric who took it upon himself to plant all sorts of things that he regarded as "health" foods, some of which turned out to be of no nutritional value whatsoever. Not so the apple, of course, which was brought to America from England and which became a backbone of the colonial diet. Apples had a long traditional alliance with cinnamon and nutmeg, but the New World's vanilla provided a beautiful new flavor, one that enhanced all sorts of fruits. This pear and apple puree, brightened with vanilla, is a delicious elaboration of our traditional applesauce.

Makes 5–6 cups puree
Serves 8–10

6 large Bartlett pears, fully ripe, peeled, quartered, and cored
6 large tart-sweet apples (Granny Smith, Winesap, Mackintosh),
        peeled, cored, and cut in chunks
½ cup water
½ cup orange juice
2 Tb. lemon juice
⅓ cup sugar
1½ tsp. vanilla

1. In a large pot combine the pears, the apples, the water, and the orange and lemon juices. Cook, uncovered, over moderate heat for 20–30 minutes or until the fruit is quite soft. Stir in the sugar for the last 5–10 minutes of cooking.

2. Cool slightly, then in the food processor puree the mixture thoroughly. Stir in the vanilla and mix well. Serve chilled.

Fresh Fruit Trifle

Custards—baked or boiled mixtures of milk and eggs—were made in Europe in the Middle Ages, although they may in fact be much older than that. Sweetened custards were flavored with a variety of fruits, cinnamon, and almonds; when vanilla arrived on the scene it was quickly incorporated as a flavoring for custards and custard sauces. The English, who have always been extremely fond of custard, use it as a component in the trifle, a traditional concoction of sherry-soaked spongecake, jam, and custard. The dish was later appropriated by the Italians, who substituted rum and macerated fruit and renamed it *zuppa Inglese,* English soup. Here is the trifle with its vanilla-flavored custard, redone with a variety of fresh summer fruits. It is a spectacular dessert, most attractive if served in a clear glass bowl so the many layers can be seen.

Serves 8

2 cups peeled, sliced ripe peaches
3 Tb. peach or apricot liqueur
2 cups fresh blueberries
2 cups milk
2 Tb. butter
½ cup sugar
3 Tb. cornstarch
2 eggs
1 tsp. vanilla
1½ cups heavy cream
1 Tb. sugar
12 ladyfingers, split
½ cup fresh raspberries, or sliced fresh strawberries

1. Combine the peaches and the liqueur, mix well, and set aside.

2. Wash the blueberries, drain thoroughly, and set aside.

3. In a medium saucepan scald the milk with the butter. Set aside.

4. In a small bowl combine the sugar and the cornstarch, mix well, and set aside.

5. In a small bowl beat the eggs and set aside.

6. Stir a small amount of the hot scalded milk into the sugar-cornstarch mixture, blend thoroughly, and return to the saucepan. Cook over low heat, stirring constantly, until the mixture is smooth and thick.

7. Gradually beat a small amount of the hot mixture into the beaten eggs, then return this mixture to the pot. Cook over low heat, stirring constantly, until it is thick and smooth. Remove from the heat, stir in the vanilla, then cool.

8. Beat the cream with the 1 Tb. of sugar until stiff.

9. To assemble the trifle: Line the bottom of a 2- to 2½-quart bowl (preferably glass) with half of the split ladyfingers, cut sides up. Sprinkle the ladyfingers with half of the liquid from the peaches.

10. Spread half of the cooled custard over the ladyfingers. With a slotted spoon, place the sliced peaches over the custard, reserving the peach liquid.

11. Place the rest of the ladyfingers, cut sides up, in a layer over the peaches. Sprinkle the ladyfingers with the remaining peach liquid.

12. Spread the rest of the custard over the ladyfingers, then spread the blueberries in a layer over the custard.

13. Spoon the whipped cream in a layer over the blueberries. Garnish the whipped cream with the raspberries or strawberries.

14. Cover the bowl with plastic wrap and chill for several hours.

Native woman from the tropics of Mexico gathering pods from the vanilla orchid plant

Country Ham and Peanut Soup

African Peanut Chicken Soup

Peanut Raisin Sauce

Peanut Sauce with Greens

Peanut Shrimp Salad

Peanut Beef Kabobs with Spicy Peanut Dipping Sauce

Chicken in Peanut Coconut Curry

Spicy Peanut Chicken Wings

Peanut Vegetable Harvest Casserole

Spiced Peanut Croquettes

Peanut Sesame Noodles

Peanut Slaw

Apple Peanut Bread

Peanut Shortbread Cookies

Frozen Peanut Chip Pie

PEANUTS

Take me out to the ball game;
Take me out with the crowd:
Buy me some peanuts and Cracker Jack;
I don't care if I never get back!

It is no accident that the peanut is commemorated in a song about baseball, for America's favorite nut has long functioned on the popular level, a cheap and tasty snack food at sports events, amusement parks, country fairs, and, of course, zoos, where it satisfies the visitors as well as the residents. Annually we munch tons of salted roasted peanuts; they are as commonplace in our homes as they are on the street, in airplanes, and in taverns, bars, and cocktail lounges. It is curious, then, that although we clearly love peanuts, we don't take them very seriously. Because they were first popularized as an inexpensive snack for the common folk, they carry a connotation of lower class, almost, at times, of vulgarity; in the hierarchy of salted cocktail nuts, the peanut clearly ranks lowest.

The peanut's unfortunate lack of prestige as compared with, say, the cashew or the almond, has very little to do with its intrinsic nature and everything to do with the social circumstances in which it became a part of the American scene. A native of South America, it was a valuable food for pre-Columbian Andean people, who immortalized its distinctive shape in pottery. It had traveled to Mexico long before the Spanish arrived and was valued for its rich oil and protein content, as well as the unique flavor and texture it contributed to ancient spiced *moles*. And by the time the first colonists arrived in Virginia, the peanut was being cultivated by native tribes here in North America.

The earliest European settlers seem to have thoroughly ignored this strange new nut, perhaps because, unlike the nuts with which they were familiar—almonds, walnuts, hazelnuts—this one didn't grow on trees but rather underground. The fact is, of course, that the peanut isn't really a nut at all, but a legume, more closely related to peas and beans than to hickories or pecans. But as its shell and its texture were nut-like, it was called the pea-nut.

While early America, and indeed, all of Europe, were giving the peanut the cold shoulder, the peanut was getting a much warmer reception in other parts of the world. Trundled about the trade routes by Spanish and Portuguese navigators, it was taken enthusiastically into many of the cuisines of sub-Saharan Africa, a vast area sorely in need of protein-rich foods. Along with a number of other New World foods—corn, peppers, and potatoes—the peanut was quickly absorbed as a tasty and nutritious component of savory soups and stews. Renamed the groundnut, it became a valuable staple of African cuisine, and it was from Africa that the peanut would return to make its first major impact on America.

At the same time that the peanut was conquering Africa, it was making rapid inroads into much of the Orient. Brought to the Philippines by the Spanish and to India by the Portuguese, it traveled both by sea and over land throughout the Far East; it came to China by one of these routes and was reported there as early as 1538. As that date was less than fifty years after the discovery of America, it is a telling index of just how rapid the peanut's progress was. Surely one of the reasons for its acceptance in so much of the Orient was its ease of cultivation; it grew well in warm coastal sandy soils and, typical of leguminous plants, enriched poor soils by fixing the nitrogen in them.

But it takes more than easy cultivation and nutritional benefits to make people accept a new food; as a general rule a new food has somehow to fit into already existing culinary patterns, complementing traditional cooking practices and enhancing traditional taste preferences. This the peanut seems to have done with ease, adding new flavor and texture variations to a number of savory Asian sauces, enlarging the gustatory experience at the same time that it enhanced the nutritional content by providing an inexpensive source of vegetable protein.

So while a large part of the world's population was cheerfully gobbling up this unpretentious little legume, grinding it into flavorful pastes and sauces, roasting and salting it for a nutritious snack, tossing it into salads and stir-fried dishes to provide a delicious crunch, colonial America was still resistant to the peanut as anything except food for livestock. When the slave trade began, the peanut returned to America with African blacks, who continued to use it as they had used it in their homeland, as a valuable food to implement their meagre diet. While plantation owners filled their protein needs with meat and dairy products, their slaves ate beans and greens and cornmeal, dressed with spicy peanut sauces, and whole peanuts roasted on the hearth fire. Through the Civil War the peanut remained a food for animals and for slaves, although it did also serve as a cheap coffee substitute for the Confederate troops.

But after the war, in the last decades of the nineteenth century, the peanut began to venture beyond the South, probably carried by Union soldiers who had acquired during the long, hard years of the war an acquaintance and a liking for the roasted peanut. Young men who could not find other employment began vending bags of freshly roasted peanuts on the streets of large northern cities; inexpensive, tasty, and filling, peanuts provided a value-packed "fun" experience for anyone with a nickel in his pocket. And at the turn of the century in Tuskegee, Alabama, a black scientist named George Washington Carver undertook as his life's mission the education of the public about the South's most underrated and potentially most valuable crop.

So the peanut, from its inauspicious beginnings as animal and slave food, became the province of the masses. Its final popularization occurred when a St. Louis doctor introduced peanut butter—nothing but ground roasted peanuts—as a health food for the elderly at the 1904 World's Fair. Within twenty years or so, through the efforts of an aggressive food industry, peanut butter became *the* favored food of American children; spread on bread, with or without jelly or jam, eaten with a glass of milk, it provided an inexpensive and nutritious meal that has stocked school lunch boxes ever since.

From animals to slaves, from the common man to kids—the peanut's fate was sealed. With such a history, who could take it seriously? Could the peanut ever rise above its status as a cheap, plebeian, juvenile food?

Well, it took awhile, but it is happening. And it's happening through the same cuisines that embraced the peanut on its very first go-around. From black Americans has come a revival of the old "soul" food, the spicy peanut stews and sauces, no longer the denigrated food of slaves, but an esteemed tradition in its own right that is making a valuable impact on the American mainstream. And with the newly awakened interest in regional cuisine, many old Southern recipes for breads, soups, salads, and confections are rekindling interest in the peanut's long, if bumpy, history.

Even Europe, which has continued steadfastly to ignore the peanut, has been heavily influenced by the little legume, whose oil has become one of the most highly prized cooking oils in the world. The French may look askance at peanut butter and peanut pie, but they favor peanut oil above all for its delicate flavor and its ability to cook at high temperatures.

And finally, the peanut has returned triumphant from Asia, where so many centuries ago it was enfolded with such a delicious ease into the cuisines of Malaysia, Indonesia, China, India, Thailand, and Vietnam. These traditions, becoming today so fundamentally a part of our own, have elevated the peanut to a more appropriate status—homely and small, perhaps, but a giant among nuts.

Country Ham and Peanut Soup

In the South, peanuts were thought for many long years to be food fit only for slaves and for animals; as peanuts nourished the domestic pig, so too did they form an enduring culinary alliance with many traditional Southern pork products. In this recipe the distinctive flavors of cured country ham and peanuts combine for a rich and creamy soup.

Serves 4–6

1 medium onion, finely chopped
1 carrot, finely diced
2 Tb. butter
2–3 oz. cured country ham, finely chopped (about ½ cup chopped)
3 Tb. flour
4 cups hot chicken stock
Good dash cayenne pepper
¼ tsp. mace
¼ cup unsalted peanut butter
½ cup light cream
½ cup chopped roasted unsalted peanuts for garnish

1. In a medium saucepan sauté the onion and the carrot in the butter over moderate heat until the onion begins to wilt. Add the chopped ham and sauté a few minutes more.

2. Stir in the flour to make a *roux;* cook, stirring over low heat for about 3 minutes.

3. Whisk in the hot stock, stirring, until the liquid is smoothly blended into the *roux.* Bring to a simmer, add the pepper and the mace, then cook, uncovered, over low heat for about 20 minutes.

4. Add the peanut butter and stir until it is smoothly blended into the soup.

5. Stir in the cream and heat until very hot, but do not boil.

6. Pass the chopped peanuts to garnish individual servings.

African Peanut Chicken Soup

Some years ago I developed recipes for a restaurant specializing in soup. Of the more than one hundred soups that we served, this one was, and remains, the all-time favorite. It is a heart-warming, mouth-pleasing, nurturant soup that illustrates how cooks in Africa and the American South used peanuts for a variety of savory and nourishing dishes.

Serves 8–10

2 medium onions, chopped
2 large sweet red and/or green peppers, seeded and chopped
3–4 cloves garlic, crushed
2 Tb. vegetable oil or peanut oil
1 28-oz. can Italian-style tomatoes, with juice, coarsely chopped
8 cups chicken stock
¼ tsp. black pepper
¼ tsp. crushed dried hot peppers
½ cup long-grain rice
1–1½ cups diced cooked chicken
⅔ cup unsalted peanut butter

1. In a large heavy pot sauté the onions, the peppers, and the garlic in the oil over moderate heat until the onions are just beginning to brown.

2. Add the tomatoes, the stock, the black and dried hot peppers. Simmer, uncovered, over low heat for about 1 hour.

3. Add the rice and the chicken and simmer for another 10–15 minutes until the rice is tender. Stir in the peanut butter and whisk it until it is completely dissolved and smooth. Taste for salt and chile pepper, adding more if necessary. Serve hot.

Planting peanuts in Georgia

Peanut Raisin Sauce

Tangy sweet/sour fruit sauces and glazes have long been an American favorite with smoked ham and pork, a tradition that has its origins in English cooking. This sauce, with its addition of ground and chopped peanuts, is an interesting variation on the theme. It is easy to make and easy to use: just spoon some hot over baked, broiled, or panfried ham steaks or smoked pork chops.

Makes about 1 cup

½ cup raisins
¼ cup cider vinegar
¼ cup water
2 Tb. dark brown sugar
⅛ tsp. ground allspice
2 Tb. peanut butter
⅓ cup finely chopped salted dry-roasted peanuts

1. In a small saucepan combine the raisins, vinegar, water, sugar, and allspice. Bring to the simmer, then cook, stirring, over low heat for about 5 minutes until the sauce is well blended and the raisins are soft.

2. Add the peanut butter and stir until it is well blended and smooth.

3. Remove the sauce from the heat and stir in the chopped peanuts. Serve hot.

Note: This sauce can be stored almost indefinitely in the refrigerator. It will thicken considerably as it cools. Reheat, stirring, over low heat.

Common Peanut (*Arachis hypogœa*).
a, a, flowers; *b, b,* ovaries on lengthened stipes; *c, c,* forming fruit; *d,* ripe pod, *e,* pod opened, showing seeds.

Peanut Sauce with Greens

This spicy peanut sauce, of African origin, makes a tasty and nutritious meatless meal when served with rice or corn foo foo (cornmeal mush).

Serves 4–6

½ lb. fresh greens (kale, collard, mustard greens, broccoli rabe)
1 medium onion, coarsely chopped
2 large cloves garlic, crushed
2 Tb. peanut oil
1½ tsp. curry powder
2 cups canned crushed tomatoes or tomato sauce
½ tsp. salt
2 Tb. peanut butter
¼–½ tsp. crushed dried hot peppers
½ cup unsalted roasted peanuts, coarsely chopped
1 recipe Cornmeal Mush I (see p. 16) or 2–3 cups hot cooked rice

1. Wash the greens and drain thoroughly; chop coarsely.

2. In a large skillet sauté the onion and garlic in the oil over moderate heat until the onion is just beginning to wilt. Stir in the curry powder and sauté a few minutes more.

3. Add the tomatoes and the salt, mix well, and cook over low heat for about 15 minutes. Stir in the chopped greens and cook for 10 minutes.

4. Stir in the peanut butter until it is smooth and well blended, then add the hot peppers. Taste for salt and hotness, adding a bit more salt and hot peppers if necessary. Stir in the chopped peanuts.

5. Serve hot over the cornmeal mush or rice.

American Crunch

Crispy, crunchy, and salted—that's how Americans like their between-meal nibbles. A large and flourishing snack-food industry has taken good advantage of many foods that had their origin here in the New World, for, with the sole exception of the pretzel, which came from Europe, the crunchy snacks we so much enjoy today have a long and venerable history on these shores. Popcorn was probably the first, developed many thousands of years ago by the ancient corn-eaters of Mexico. The potato chip is a more recent development, invented at the turn of the century by a hotel chef in Saratoga, New York, who tired of hearing a customer's complaints that his French fries weren't crispy enough. And the roasted salted peanut is an age-old snack, as much fun to munch today as it was in its original South American home. Did you ever wonder how they salt peanuts inside the shell? The peanuts are soaked in a salty brine which permeates the shell to the nuts inside. The peanuts are then thoroughly dried and roasted, leaving behind a light salty coating. Next time you open one of those little sacks of peanuts or popcorn or potato chips or corn chips, remember that you are participating in a long and popular tradition—untold generations of crackle and crunch!

Peanut Shrimp Salad

Always a hit on the buffet table, this delightful shrimp salad is a nice change from the predictable mayo and celery combination. This recipe shows again the Asian talent for peanut sauces, this one with a hint of Indonesia.

Serves 4–6

2 lbs. cooked shrimp, peeled and deveined (about 3 lbs. raw)
2 cups canned pineapple chunks, packed in juice not syrup, and drained
*   (reserve juice for sauce)*
1 medium sweet red pepper, seeded and diced
1 medium sweet green pepper, seeded and diced
1 8-oz. can water chestnuts, rinsed in cold water, drained thoroughly, and sliced
⅓ cup black soy sauce
⅓ cup reserved pineapple juice
1 Tb. brown sugar
4 cloves garlic, crushed
¼ tsp. crushed dried hot peppers
½ Tb. lemon juice
⅓ cup peanut butter
¼ cup salted roasted peanuts, coarsely chopped
Cucumber slices, tomato wedges, hard-boiled egg wedges for garnish

1. Combine the shrimp, the pineapple chunks, the diced peppers, and the water chestnuts in a bowl.

2. In a small saucepan combine the soy sauce, pineapple juice, brown sugar, garlic, hot peppers, and lemon juice. Bring to a simmer, then cook, stirring, over low heat for about 5 minutes.

3. Stir in the peanut butter and mix until the sauce is smooth and thoroughly blended. Remove from heat.

4. Pour about three quarters of the sauce over the shrimp mixture. Mix gently but thoroughly. Taste, and add more sauce if necessary. Gently mix in the chopped peanuts.

5. Serve the shrimp salad on a bed of greens and garnish with the cucumber slices, tomato wedges, and egg wedges.

Peanut Beef Kabobs with Spicy Peanut Dipping Sauce

The Vietnamese are extremely fond of beef and, like Americans, use it ground in a variety of tasty meatballs and kabobs that have become very popular in Vietnamese restaurants here in America. These little cigar-shaped kabobs, crunchy with chopped peanuts and enhanced with a sweet and tangy peanut sauce, are equally at home on the buffet table or at the backyard barbecue. They can be threaded on skewers and grilled over hot coals, or dredged in cornstarch and fried until crisp.

Makes 12–14 kabobs

Serves 3–4

1 lb. medium lean ground beef

1 Tb. nuoc mam *(Vietnamese fish sauce)*

1 tsp. powdered lemongrass

1 tsp. finely minced gingerroot

1 large clove garlic, crushed

⅛ tsp. black pepper

⅓ cup finely chopped salted dry-roasted peanuts

1 head Boston lettuce, sliced cucumber and carrot,

    sprigs of fresh mint and coriander leaf for garnish

1. In a medium bowl combine the meat, the seasonings, and the chopped peanuts. Mix with a large spoon, or better yet, knead with your hands until the mixture is smooth and very well blended.

2. Pinch off pieces of the mixture about the size of a small plum. For grilling, stick a water-soaked bamboo skewer through the meat. Squeeze and mold the meat around the skewer to form a 2-inch cigar-shaped kabob. Grill the kabobs over hot coals, turning once; they should be slightly rare in the center. For frying, omit the skewers; form the meat into 2-inch cigar-shaped kabobs. Dredge the kabobs in cornstarch, then fry over moderate heat in 3–4 Tb. peanut or vegetable oil. Turn once or twice with a spatula until they are browned and crisp on all sides.

3. Serve the kabobs on a platter of Boston lettuce leaves, with sliced carrot and cucumber, and sprigs of fresh coriander leaf and fresh mint. Provide each diner with a small dish of peanut dipping sauce.

Note: To eat the kabobs, place a kabob on a lettuce leaf, then garnish with a few sprigs of mint and coriander. Roll up the kabob in the lettuce leaf, then dip into the peanut sauce.

Peanut Dipping Sauce

Makes 1 cup sauce

1 Tb. peanut or vegetable oil
1 tsp. finely minced gingerroot
2 large cloves garlic, finely minced
¼ tsp. crushed dried hot peppers
2 Tb. bottled chili sauce (the American tomato variety)
2 Tb. soy sauce
2 Tb. hoisin sauce
2 Tb. peanut butter
½ cup water

1. In a small saucepan heat the oil over moderate heat. Add the gingerroot, garlic, and hot peppers, and cook, stirring, until the mixture is just starting to turn golden and is very aromatic.

2. Stir in the chili sauce and cook, stirring, a few more minutes.

3. Add the soy sauce, the hoisin, the peanut butter, and the water. Cook, stirring, over low heat, until the mixture is smooth and well blended. Simmer gently for a few minutes. Serve the peanut sauce at room temperature. Additional sauce can be stored in a covered container in the refrigerator. Bring to room temperature before serving.

Pre-Columbian bottle from Peru in the form of a peanut woman

Chicken in Peanut Coconut Curry

Throughout its travels the peanut underwent some stunning transformations, and nowhere so dramatically as in the cuisines of Asia. Indeed, the most exotic treatment of the peanut I have come across occurs in Laos, where the bodies of headless grasshoppers are stuffed with whole peanuts and then roasted over charcoal for a crunchy street snack. The cooking of Malaysia, where the peanut was first introduced to the Orient, is a blend of many elements—the curry seasonings of India, the soy sauce of China, the coconut of the Pacific Islands. The peanut joined these traditions to form a whole new set of rich and complex sauces. This is a mild curry with a full and appealing flavor. Serve it with cooked rice or Chinese noodles.

Serves 4–6

2 Tb. peanut oil
1 medium onion, finely chopped
3 cloves garlic, crushed
1 tsp. cumin
1 tsp. turmeric
1 tsp. ground ginger
½ tsp. ground coriander
Good pinch crushed dried hot peppers
1 cup unsweetened coconut milk*
2 Tb. soy sauce
3 Tb. peanut butter
3–4 lb. chicken, skinned and cut in serving pieces
¼ cup dry-roasted salted peanuts, finely chopped
3–4 Tb. fresh coriander leaf (cilantro; optional, but good)
2–2½ cups hot cooked rice or 10–12 oz. Chinese-style noodles, cooked and drained

1. In a large heavy skillet heat the oil over moderate heat. Add the onion and the garlic and sauté, stirring, until the onion begins to turn golden.

2. Add the cumin, turmeric, ginger, coriander, and hot peppers. Stir the mixture over low heat for a few minutes.

3. Stir the coconut milk, soy sauce, and peanut butter into the skillet. Stir until smooth and well blended.

4. Place the chicken parts in the sauce; cover and cook over low heat for about 40 minutes or until the chicken is tender. Remove the cover and cook a little longer to thicken the sauce.

5. Garnish the curry with the chopped peanuts and coriander leaf. Serve with hot cooked rice or noodles.

Unsweetened coconut milk is available in cans in most Oriental and Indian groceries. To make your own, combine 2 cups unsweetened dried shredded coconut with 2¼ cups very hot water. Let stand for 1 hour. Blend or process the mixture for a few seconds, then strain through cheesecloth into a jar. Makes about 2 cups.

Peanut harvest in the American South

Spicy Peanut Chicken Wings

In the cuisines of Southeast Asia, so profoundly influenced by the focal culinary traditions of China, the unique flavor and texture of peanuts are exploited in a number of savory sauces that are very appealing to contemporary American taste. These spicy Chinese-inspired wings make a terrific cocktail nibble or buffet item; the flavor is best when the wings are still slightly warm or at room temperature.

Makes about 12 wings

2–2½ lbs. chicken wings (about 12)
Salt and pepper
2 Tb. peanut butter
2 Tb. dark (black) soy sauce
1½ Tb. honey
1 clove garlic, crushed
¼–½ tsp. crushed dried hot peppers
⅓ cup finely chopped salted roasted peanuts
Good handful fresh coriander leaf (cilantro), chopped

1. Chop the tips off the chicken wings; discard or save for stock. Preheat the oven to 400°F.

2. Line a baking pan with foil (this will save clean-up later). Place the wings in a single layer on the tray; salt and pepper them lightly.

3. Bake the wings for about 30 minutes until they are just beginning to brown and get crisp.

4. While the wings are baking, combine the peanut butter, soy sauce, honey, garlic, and the hot peppers in a small saucepan. Heat the mixture over low heat, stirring, until it is well blended and spreadable.

5. Spoon or brush the peanut sauce generously over the wings. Return the wings to the oven for 10–15 minutes until the sauce is set. Do not allow the sauce to burn.

6. Remove the wings from the oven and sprinkle immediately with the chopped peanuts and the coriander. Let cool slightly before serving.

Peanut Vegetable Harvest Casserole

Inspired by West African ground-nut stews, this hearty casserole shows how profoundly African cuisines were influenced by New World foods, particularly the peanut, which provided a valuable source of plant protein. It makes a splendid vegetarian meal, and although many combinations of vegetables are good, you should always include onions, peppers, some starchy root, greens, and corn. Okra is a frequent addition and cubed squash or pumpkin can also be used.

Serves 6–8

2 Tb. peanut oil

1 large onion, coarsely chopped

3 large cloves garlic, crushed

1 large sweet green pepper, seeded and cut in chunks

1 large sweet red pepper, seeded and cut in chunks

2 carrots, cut in chunks

2 medium potatoes, cubed

1 28-oz. can Italian-style tomatoes, with juice

*1 cup cooked, canned, or frozen blackeye peas (kidney or pinto beans
   can also be used)*

*2–3 cups chopped fresh greens (spinach, kale, or collard),
   or 1 10-oz. package frozen chopped spinach*

1 cup corn kernels (fresh is best, but frozen or canned can be used)

1 tsp. salt

2 heaping Tb. peanut butter

¼–1 tsp. Mombasa ground hot red pepper, or crushed dried hot peppers

⅓ cup unsalted roasted peanuts, coarsely chopped

3 cups hot cooked rice

1. In a large heavy pot or Dutch oven heat the oil over moderate heat. Add the onion and garlic and sauté, stirring occasionally, until the onion is golden.

2. Add the pepper chunks and sauté a few more minutes.

3. Stir in the carrots, potatoes, and tomatoes. Simmer, uncovered, over low heat until the carrots and potatoes are just tender

4. Add the blackeye peas or beans, the chopped greens, and the corn and cook for about 10 minutes.

5. Stir in the salt and the peanut butter and mix thoroughly. Add the hot pepper, going slowly at first, mixing well and tasting until the desired hotness is achieved. The flavor should be moderately pungent but not searing.

6. Stir in the chopped peanuts and mix well. Serve the casserole with hot cooked rice.

Spiced Peanut Croquettes

India is now one of the world's largest producers of peanuts, and in a culture that is so heavily dependent on vegetable foods, the peanut has proved an invaluable source of plant protein. And it fits easily into a cuisine whose genius lies in the use of aromatic herbs and spices. These tasty little croquettes are crunchy and spicy, and show not only India's use of peanuts, but of potatoes and chile peppers as well.

Makes 12 croquettes
Serves 4

2 medium all-purpose potatoes
2 Tb. butter
1 medium onion, finely chopped
1 tsp. cumin
½ tsp. turmeric
¼ tsp. ground ginger
¼ tsp. ground coriander
¼ tsp. crushed dried hot peppers
½ tsp. salt
1 cup unsalted roasted peanuts, finely chopped
Flour for dredging
5–6 Tb. peanut oil or vegetable oil
Chopped fresh coriander leaf (cilantro) for garnish

1. Cook the potatoes in boiling water until they are very tender. Drain, then peel, and set aside.

2. In a medium saucepan or skillet melt the butter over moderate heat, then add the onion and sauté until it is just wilted. Stir in the cumin, turmeric, ginger, coriander, and hot peppers and sauté a few minutes more.

3. Mash the potatoes into the spice mixture, then mix thoroughly with a heavy spoon. Add the salt and the peanuts and mix well. Chill the mixture for an hour or two.

4. Form heaping tablespoons of the chilled mixture into flat oval croquettes, about 2½ to 3-inches. Dredge the croquettes lightly in flour.

5. In a heavy skillet heat 3–4 Tb. of the oil over moderately high heat. Fry the croquettes in the hot oil, turning once, until they are well browned on each side. Drain the croquettes on paper towels. Continue frying the croquettes, adding more oil to the pan if necessary.

6. Sprinkle the hot croquettes with a little salt and garnish with the chopped coriander. They are very good served with Tomato Chutney (see p. 117).

Note: The croquettes can be made ahead of time and reheated in a 350°F. oven for about 15 minutes.

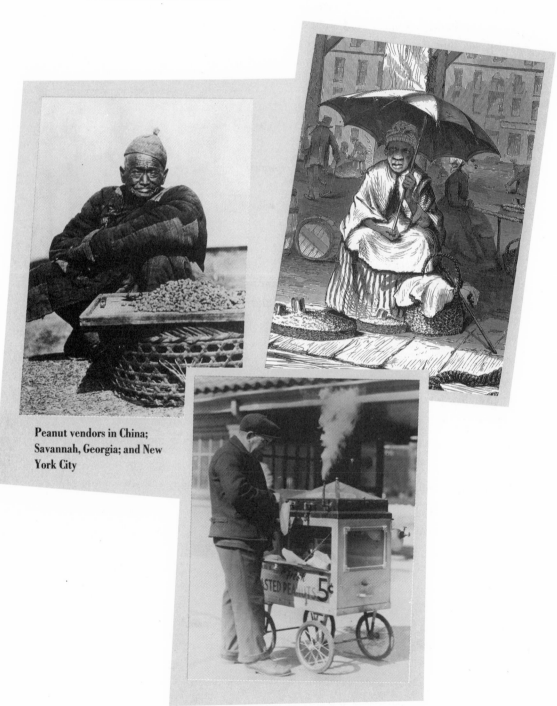

Peanut vendors in China; Savannah, Georgia; and New York City

Peanut Sesame Noodles

This has become a very popular dish in recent years, testifying to the growing Asian influence on American cuisine. These noodles are easy and delicious and demonstrate, once again, the peanut's affinity for the savory sauces of the Orient. The dish can be served either hot or cold; indeed, the clever cook will make a whole batch of it, eat it hot, then dress up the cold leftovers the next day with bean sprouts, shredded cucumber and carrot, cold cooked chicken or seafood. The recipe can be doubled.

Serves 2–4

½ lb. spaghetti
3–4 Tb. sesame oil
1 bunch (about 6) scallions, finely chopped
2 cloves garlic, crushed
¼ tsp. crushed dried hot peppers
1 Tb. rice vinegar
1 tsp. sugar
1 Tb. soy sauce
½ cup finely chopped salted dry-roasted peanuts
Good handful fresh coriander leaf (cilantro), chopped

1. Cook the spaghetti in boiling salted water for 9–10 minutes until it is tender but still firm. Do not overcook. Drain the spaghetti, rinse in cold water, then drain again thoroughly. Mix the spaghetti lightly but thoroughly with 1–2 Tb. of the sesame oil and set aside.

2. In a large pot sauté the scallions, garlic, and hot peppers in the remaining oil over moderate heat, stirring, until the scallions are just wilted.

3. Add the spaghetti to the pot, then add the vinegar, sugar, and soy sauce. Stir to blend well, then cook until the noodles are heated through.

4. Stir in the peanuts and the chopped coriander. Taste for salt.

Peanut Slaw

Tart-sweet and tangy, this is a nice variation on usual cole slaw, with peanuts adding their special flavor and crunch.

Serves 4–6

3 cups shredded cabbage
1 large carrot, shredded
1 tart-sweet apple (Granny Smith or Winesap), cored and shredded
    (no need to peel)
¼ cup mayonnaise
3 Tb. cider vinegar
1 tsp. sugar
⅛ tsp. black pepper
½ cup salted dry-roasted peanuts, finely chopped

1. In a medium bowl combine the cabbage, the carrot, and the apple.

2. In a small bowl combine the mayonnaise, vinegar, sugar, and pepper. Blend thoroughly.

3. Add one half of the salad dressing to the shredded vegetables and mix thoroughly. Taste and add more dressing if necessary. Stir in the chopped peanuts and mix well. Chill before serving.

A variety of popular peanut confections, including Goobers, a name using the old Southern black term for peanuts

Apple Peanut Bread

One of the oldest names for the peanut in the American South was "goober," a word that derived from the African *nguba*. The Americanized "goober" has been retained in a number of popular confections and candy bars, though few people are aware of its African origin. In this recipe the goober plays three roles. Ground peanuts, chopped peanuts, and peanut oil combine with apples and cinnamon in a moist not-too-sweet loaf that is very good with coffee or tea.

Makes 1 loaf

½ cup firmly packed dark brown sugar
½ cup sugar
½ cup peanut oil
¼ cup peanut butter
2 eggs
2 cups grated apple (about 3 medium apples, cored and peeled)
2 Tb. orange juice
2 tsp. cinnamon
2 cups flour
1 tsp. baking soda
½ tsp. salt
1 cup coarsely chopped unsalted roasted peanuts

1. In a large mixing bowl combine the sugars and the peanut oil; beat until well blended, then stir in the peanut butter and blend thoroughly. Preheat the oven to 350°F.

2. Add the eggs one at a time, beating well after each addition.

3. Combine the grated apples, orange juice, and cinnamon, and mix well.

4. Combine the flour, baking soda, and salt; mix dry ingredients thoroughly into the sugar–peanut butter batter.

5. Stir the grated apple mixture and the chopped peanuts into the batter and mix well.

6. Turn the batter into a well-buttered 9 x 5 x 3-inch loaf pan. Bake for 40–50 minutes until nicely browned and firm to the touch, or until a straw inserted in the middle comes out clean.

7. Cool the loaf in the pan for about 30 minutes, then turn it out onto a serving plate.

Small Talk

The American idiom clearly reflects our traditional view of the peanut, as something small, cheap, and of no great worth. To call someone a "peanut" is to comment on a lack of physical size or stature, and whether the term is used affectionately or sarcastically, it calls attention to a person who is undersized, unduly small, not very important. To refer to some thing as "peanuts" is a derogatory comment, implying that the subject is puny, trivial, and not worthy of serious consideration. The "peanut gallery" referred originally to the higher, cheaper seats in a theater, where the masses who didn't have much money bought inexpensive seats and munched on peanuts as a cheap snack. The people who sat in the peanut gallery, then, were regarded as lacking in class or significance. All these expressions of our national slang use the peanut's small size as a key to something much deeper—status, class, money—and developed as a way of distinguishing the common folk from the privileged, the haves from the have-nots.

Peanut Shortbread Cookies

Rich and crisp, with a double dose of peanut flavor, these little cookies are extremely good and easy to make. They freeze well, which is probably irrelevant, as I have found that they get eaten up before I can stash them away!

Makes 40 cookies

1 cup (2 sticks) butter, softened
½ cup peanut butter, at room temperature
1 cup sugar
1 egg, separated
1 tsp. vanilla
1⅓ cups flour
1 cup quick or regular oats
1 cup salted dry-roasted peanuts, finely chopped

1. In a medium mixing bowl combine the softened butter and peanut butter and mix thoroughly.

2. Add the sugar and cream it thoroughly into the butter.

3. Stir in the egg yolk and vanilla and blend them into the mixture.

4. Add the flour and the oats and mix them thoroughly into the butter mixture. Preheat the oven to 300°F.

5. Spread the dough evenly in a buttered 10 x 15-inch rimmed baking pan. Smooth the top with a broad knife or spatula.

6. Beat the egg white lightly with a fork; pour it over the top of the dough and with a pastry brush spread it all over the surface.

7. Sprinkle the chopped nuts evenly over the egg white.

8. Bake for 25–35 minutes until the top is very lightly browned. Remove from the oven and cut into small squares or rectangles while still hot. Cool completely in the pan before removing.

Frozen Peanut Chip Pie

Sweet and salty, crunchy and smooth, rich and chewy—this is how Americans like their peanuts and chocolate. It is a long way from ancient Mexico, where unsweetened chocolate and peanuts combined in the sauces of spiced *moles*. This pie is very rich— almost like a frozen candy bar—so serve it in very small wedges.

Serves 8–10

Pastry for a 9-inch pie shell
½ cup smooth peanut butter, at room temperature
½ cup firmly packed light brown sugar
½ cup light corn syrup
3 eggs
½ cup light cream or half-and-half
1 tsp. vanilla
1½ cups semisweet chocolate chips
2 Tb. butter
⅓ cup salted dry-roasted peanuts, finely chopped

1. In a large mixing bowl cream the peanut butter with the brown sugar until smooth and fluffy. Stir in the corn syrup and blend until smooth.

2. Add the eggs one at a time, beating well after each addition. Stir in the cream and the vanilla and blend thoroughly. Preheat the oven to 350°F.

3. Sprinkle 1 cup of the chocolate chips evenly over the bottom of the pie shell. (Reserve ½ cup of the chips for the glaze.) Pour the peanut filling over the chips.

4. Bake the pie for 30 minutes until the filling is puffed, firm, and lightly browned.

5. In a small saucepan melt the remaining ½ cup chocolate chips with the butter over low heat. Blend the glaze until smooth.

6. Carefully spread the melted chocolate glaze evenly over the top of the warm pie. Sprinkle the chopped peanuts over the chocolate.

7. Cool the pie completely, then wrap carefully with plastic wrap and freeze. Remove the pie from the freezer 5 minutes before cutting and serving. Serve with vanilla ice cream, if desired.

Chicken and Pineapple Soup Vietnamese Style
Sweet and Pungent Meatballs with Pineapple
Avocado, Tomato, and Orange Salad with Achiote Dressing
Guacamole
Cashew Pilaf
Cashew Coconut Dipping Sauce
Sunflower Seed Cocktail Biscuits
Oven-Roasted Jerusalem Artichokes
Fruited Wild Rice and Sausage Casserole
Maple Mustard Sauce
Grilled Shrimp Jamaican Style
Pears Poached in Spiced Red Wine
Praline Pound Cake
Pecan Pie Squares
New World Golden Fruitcake
Brazil Nut Banana Cake

ODDS AND ENDS

After Columbus first opened the door to the New World, he was followed in short order by Cortez in Mexico, Pizarro in Peru, and a tidal wave of conquistadores on the mainland of America—Narváez, Ponce de León, Cabeza de Vaca, De Soto, Coronado. Their names roll off the tongue like marching drums, reverberating through our history with the clanking of armor and the clashing of cultures. After them came the English, the French, the Dutch, all emissaries of a world centered in Europe, all bent on plucking the riches of this vast New World for their God, their kings, their inheritors. And riches they found, not El Dorado or the Seven Cities of Gold, but a treasury of virgin forests and rolling prairies and mighty rivers, brimming with a variety of unfamiliar plants and animals.

Of the many exotic new foods encountered here, some were to have a profound impact on the cuisines of the Old World and the subsequent cuisine of a multiethnic America. But there were others that had somewhat different histories: some traveled abroad to become important in but a few limited areas; some went and never came back; others simply stayed where they had always been, of continuing interest here in their homeland but nowhere else. These are the odds and ends of the New World cornucopia, a variety of fruits and vegetables, nuts and seeds, tubers, grains and seasonings, that form the supporting cast in the ongoing drama of the American table.

The New World's most impressive fruit was surely the pineapple, instantly appreciated and admired by the very earliest Spanish explorers. Its original name in some West Indian languages was "anani," a name the French appropriated as *ananas*. The Spanish called it *piña* and the English pine-apple because it resembled a giant pine cone. Whatever its name, this highly aromatic, juicy, tart-sweet tropical fruit was embraced by Europe as a delightful luxury and accepted into a number of Oriental cuisines as a novel addition to a sweet-sour-savory tradition. The pineapple found an ideal adoptive home in the Hawaiian Islands; it returned to America in a variety of canned chunks, slices, and tidbits. Indeed, canned pineapple remains a mainstay of the American pantry, functioning as a quick dessert, salad component, and a tart-sweet garnish for smoked and spiced meat dishes.

Not nearly so well known or so widely traveled as the pineapple, the avocado received a more limited acceptance as an exotic fruit. Because of its high oil content and subtle flavor, it functions more as a texture food; and because it requires a warm climate and is highly perishable, it plays a somewhat limited culinary role. It is esteemed by the French, who serve it quite simply in pitted halves with a spoonful or two of vinaigrette, or filled with crab or shrimp. And it has been warmly welcomed in the Middle East and North Africa, where it joined an enduring tradition of mixed vegetable salads. The avocado's name has not changed from the original Nahuatl; in the language of the Aztecs *aguacate* meant "tree testicle," an appropriate name for the pear-shaped fruits. Some call it the "alligator pear" because of its scaly green or blackish skin.

Of the many indigenous New World nuts, the peanut, as we have seen, had the most profound impact on a number of Old World cuisines, both as an inexpensive source of vegetable protein and as a novel flavor and texture food. Other nuts, like the cashew and the Brazil, both natives of the South American tropics, found a limited acceptance in some Asian cuisines; they function in America primarily as a salted cocktail snack. The one nut that seems never to have succeeded beyond its native shores is our beloved pecan, a true American nut native to the southern United States. Its sweet delicate flavor is as familiar to Americans as it is unfamiliar to the rest of the world, and it has become an enduring part of the American tradition in pies, confections, and ice cream, frequently paired with the flavor of that other American original, maple.

Cane sugar was unknown in the New World before 1492; it was one of the first crops to be planted here by Europeans, who early on established a sugar industry in the West Indies. Before that time, honey and a variety of fruits were used for sweetening, but in the northeast corner of the country, from New York State through New England into southern Canada, there existed in abundance the sugar maple tree and an ancient native technology for collecting and refining its sweet sap. Maple syrup and crystallized maple sugar soon became a popular flavor in colonial times, a unique sweetener that never ventured outside its North American homeland.

In addition to vanilla and the sweet and pungent capsicum peppers, the New World contributed only a few other significant seasoning ingredients. One was allspice, the little black berry of a West Indian evergreen tree, which has many of the aromatic and flavoring characteristics of cinnamon, nutmeg, and cloves. Named "pimienta de Jamaica" or Jamaican pepper by the Spanish because of its resemblance to the black peppercorns of the Spice Islands, it has become a widely used spice throughout the world; it is available either ground or whole as a flavoring for sweets, marinades, pickles, sausages, and spiced syrups and wines.

Achiote, the tiny red seeds of another tropical American tree, the annatto tree, would probably not be recognized by most of the world outside of Mexico and the Caribbean, where it is a commonly used coloring agent. In West Indian cookery the seeds are heated in cooking oil until they release their characteristic deep yellow or orange color, and in the Yucatan peninsula of Mexico the seeds are ground with garlic, chile, and other ingredients into dark red seasoning pastes called *adobos,* used to color and flavor meat and poultry dishes. Although the world is not very familiar with achiote as such, it is in fact one of the most widely used coloring agents in commercial and processed food, accounting most notably for the orange or yellow color in a variety of Cheddar-like cheeses.

If yellow and orange were colors that were valued on the micro level, just imagine how impressed early settlers must have been with the American sunflower, its tremendous height and huge golden flowers emblematic of the immense richness and breadth of this New World. Native Americans had long utilized both the seeds and the roots of the sunflower in their diet, but these foods did not play any part in the mainstream until many years later. A plant of northern and temperate climates, the sunflower was well received in eastern and northern Europe, an area that had no ready source of vegetable oil; the nutty little sunflower seeds were to prove a valuable source of cooking oil, as well as a flavorful nutritious snack.

Another native harvest that early settlers did accept was wild rice, the rice-like seeds of a wild grass that grew in the lake country of northern Minnesota and southern Canada. Dark and chewy, with a unique flavor and texture, wild rice remained an exclusively American food, closely tied in culinary tradition with other classics of the American harvest—turkey, squash, and corn.

And last, mention must be made of a New World food that was to play a crucial role in other parts of the world, but not in America itself. That food was manioc, or cassava, a tropical tuber native to South America that was a staple in the West Indies when Columbus arrived. The people of the New World had an ancient traditional technology for treating manioc, which can contain lethal amounts of Prussic acid, or cyanide. The tuber is grated, then soaked in water so that the dangerous substance is leached out; the grated washed material is then dried and ground into flour to make a kind of bread. Easily grown in hot humid environments and requiring little cultivation, manioc provided a valuable source of calories (mainly from carbohydrate) for people who had difficulty raising other crops. After the discovery of the New World, manioc traveled to Africa and parts of Asia, where it has become an essential food staple. The only way it returned to America was in the form of tapioca, a starch used for puddings and thickeners. Tapioca pudding remains one of the less pleasant memories of my childhood; we called the gluey little starch globules "fish eyes," and vowed that never, in the name of dessert, would we ever inflict such indignity on *our* children!

So ends the account of the foods of the New World, though in fact the reckoning is not yet over. For even now new foods are still being discovered in the tropical forests of South America and the high country of the Andes. A variety of medicinal and food plants—seeds, grains, roots and tubers, leaves and bark—long familiar to native people but unknown to the rest of the world are being uncovered and investigated. Who knows what their future impact may be?

For now we have in our kitchens and on our tables the still astounding evidence of our past, the food so amply given us by a New World that was old when we came upon it. Its harvest is our history, its foods an ever-changing yet unalterable part of who we were, what we are, and may yet become.

Chicken and Pineapple Soup Vietnamese Style

It is not at all surprising that the pineapple was so easily taken into Southeast Asian cooking. Its unique tart-sweet flavor fits perfectly into a seasoning tradition that favors sweet and sour, pungent and savory. This is an unusual soup, very light, but with a fine mouth-filling flavor. The combination of ingredients may seem odd but they really work very well together.

Serves 6

1 medium onion, thinly sliced
2 Tb. vegetable oil
1 medium ripe tomato, coarsely chopped
2 cups fresh pineapple, peeled, cored, and coarsely chopped (about 3–4 slices)
4 cups chicken stock
1 tsp. powdered lemongrass
Good pinch crushed dried hot peppers
1 Tb. fish sauce (Vietnamese nuoc mam *or Thai* nam pla*)*
1 cup cooked white meat chicken, shredded
Good handful fresh coriander leaf (cilantro), chopped

1. In a medium saucepan sauté the onion in the oil over moderate heat until it wilts.

2. Add the tomato, pineapple, stock, lemongrass, hot peppers, and fish sauce. Simmer, uncovered, over low heat for about ½ hour.

3. Stir in the chicken, then the coriander. Bring to a simmer. Serve hot.

Sweet and Pungent Meatballs with Pineapple

In the first book about America written in Spanish, published in Seville in 1519, the author wrote of the pineapple: "When there is one of these in a room it fills the whole house with its smell." That observation is as valid today as it was nearly 500 years ago; to my mind the pineapple is at its most glorious as a fresh fruit, perfectly ripened and eaten out of hand, filling the nose and mouth with its perfumed aroma and tart-sweet flavor. But the pineapple also performs well in cooked dishes, particularly those of Hawaiian or Polynesian influence, areas where the pineapple so flourishes that one might almost believe it has always been there.

Serves 4

THE MEATBALLS

1 lb. lean ground beef
1 small onion, grated
1 egg, lightly beaten
1/3 cup bread crumbs
1 tsp. salt
1 tsp. ground ginger
1/4 tsp. crushed dried hot peppers
2 Tb. vegetable oil

1 medium onion, coarsely chopped
3 cloves garlic, crushed
1 Tb. finely minced gingerroot
1/4 tsp. crushed dried hot peppers
1 small sweet green pepper, seeded and cut in chunks
1 small sweet red pepper, seeded and cut in chunks
2 cups canned pineapple chunks, packed in juice, not syrup, drained,
       with 1/2 cup of the juice reserved
2 Tb. soy sauce
1 Tb. rice vinegar
1/2 tsp. sugar
1 1/2 Tb. cornstarch

2 cups hot cooked rice

1. Make the meatballs: In a bowl combine the beef, grated onion, egg, bread crumbs, salt, ginger, and hot peppers. Mix thoroughly, then form into small balls, each about the size of a small walnut.

2. Film the bottom of a large skillet with the oil. Add the meatballs, turn heat to moderate, and brown the meatballs slowly, turning them so that they brown evenly on all sides. As the meatballs brown, remove them from the pan with a slotted spoon and set aside.

3. When all the meatballs have been browned, pour off and discard the fat in the pan, leaving just enough to film the bottom. Add the chopped onion, garlic, gingerroot, and hot peppers. Sauté, stirring, over moderate heat until the onion begins to turn gold.

4. Add the chopped peppers and sauté a few minutes. Add the meatballs and the drained pineapple chunks to the pan.

5. In a small bowl combine the pineapple juice, soy sauce, vinegar, sugar, and cornstarch. Mix until thoroughly blended.

6. Turn the heat up to moderately high, and stir the meatballs, pineapple, and peppers until they are very hot. Pour in the sauce mixture and cook, stirring, until the sauce is thickened and the meatballs, pineapple, and peppers are evenly glazed and hot. Serve with plain hot cooked rice.

From its original homeland in the tropics of the New World, the pineapple has become a popular and profitable crop in much of Asia and the South Pacific.

Color It Red

Although flavor and texture are critical qualities of the food we eat, color and appearance are also very important, and it is interesting to note how much color the New World contributed to the world's food. It is hard to imagine what our food would be like without red ripe tomatoes and ruddy tomato sauces, without the color provided by sweet and pungent red peppers and their derivative products, chili powder, cayenne, and paprika. Much of the processed food we eat is heavily colored with the tiny red achiote seeds that the Aztecs used to color their chocolate. There seems to be something widely appealing and attractive about redness or ruddiness in food that made these ingredients particularly valuable to a wide variety of cuisines. Flavor aside, they provide zest and enhancement to the visual experience, making traditional familiar ingredients more appealing and more desirable. The people of Central and South America were using tomatoes, red peppers, and achiote for color and flavor long before Columbus set sail; these ancient traditions continue here today while the rest of the world sees its food in new and exciting ways, colored New World red.

Avocado, Tomato, and Orange Salad with Achiote Dressing

With its subtle flavor and luscious creamy texture, the avocado performs beautifully in any number of salads. Here it teams up with its ancient comrade, the tomato, and a new friend, the orange, brought to the New World by the Spanish. This is a very pretty combination, the colors of the fruits enhanced by the deep yellow achiote-colored oil.

Serves 4

½ cup vegetable oil
1 Tb. achiote (annatto) seeds
2 Tb. lemon juice
2 Tb. orange juice
1 clove garlic, crushed
¼ tsp. salt
¼ tsp. oregano
¼ tsp. Tabasco sauce
2 small ripe avocados, peeled, pitted, and sliced
2 medium ripe tomatoes, cut in small wedges
1 navel orange, peeled and separated into sections
2–3 Tb. fresh coriander leaf (cilantro), chopped, for garnish, if desired

1. In a small saucepan or frying pan combine the oil and the achiote seeds. Cook over low to moderate heat, stirring, until the seeds color the oil a deep yellow-orange. Cool, then strain the oil and discard the seeds.

2. In a small bowl or a jar with a tightly fitting cover combine the oil, the lemon and orange juices, the garlic, salt, oregano, and Tabasco. Whisk or shake until the sauce is thoroughly blended.

3. Place the avocados, the tomatoes, and the orange sections in a shallow bowl. Pour on some of the dressing and mix thoroughly. Let stand for a little while, then taste and add more sauce if necessary. Garnish the salad with the fresh coriander, if desired.

Note: For an interesting Greek-style variation on this salad, omit the orange and add 1 cucumber, peeled and diced. Toss in a couple of tablespoons of crumbled feta cheese, a handful of black olives, and an additional ¼ teaspoon or so of oregano. Omit the chopped coriander and top the salad with a couple of good grinds of black pepper and some chopped parsley.

Guacamole

The avocado remains one of the most unique foods of the New World, a marvelous adventure in texture. The Aztecs combined mashed avocado with chile peppers and called it *guacamole*—the name means "avocado mixture"—and it is still, to my mind, one of the best ways to use the avocado. The Spanish contributed the citrus and the coriander leaf to make a dip or sauce with a creamy texture and wonderful zesty flavor.

Makes about 2 cups

2 medium fully ripe avocados
1 Tb. fresh lime juice
1 Tb. fresh lemon juice
1 clove garlic, crushed
2 scallions, finely chopped
1 jalapeño, serrano, or other fresh hot green chile pepper, seeded and minced,
        or ½–1 tsp. Tabasco sauce
¼ tsp. salt
3–4 Tb. fresh coriander leaf (cilantro), finely chopped
1 small ripe tomato, coarsely chopped (optional)

1. Cut the avocados in half and remove the pits. Spoon the avocado from the skins into a bowl. Mash the avocado with a fork (do not puree).

2. Stir the lime and lemon juices, the garlic, scallions, chile pepper, and salt into the mashed avocados and mix thoroughly.

3. Stir in the coriander leaf and the chopped tomato, if desired. Cover the surface of the guacamole closely with plastic wrap until serving time. Serve at room temperature as a dip with corn chips, or as an accompaniment to chili, tacos, or enchiladas.

Cashew Pilaf

Cashew nuts are native to Brazil, but are today more widely grown in India. Like the Hawaiian macadamia, the cashew is a luxury nut, eaten for the most part as a roasted salted snack. It has a wonderful subtle flavor that should not be overlooked in creative cooking with nuts. In this delicate rice pilaf, buttery cashews provide an unusual taste and texture.

Serves 4–5

1 cup roasted unsalted cashew nuts, in pieces or coarsely chopped
2 Tb. butter
1 medium onion, minced
1 cup converted long-grain rice
2 cups chicken stock
⅛ tsp. white pepper
⅛ tsp. ground mace
½ tsp. grated orange rind

1. In a medium saucepan sauté the cashews in 1 Tb. of the butter over moderate heat, stirring, until the nuts are just beginning to brown. Remove the nuts from the pan and set aside.

2. In the same pan sauté the onion in the remaining 1 Tb. butter until it wilts and is just beginning to turn golden.

3. Add the rice to the onion and sauté, stirring, a few minutes.

4. Add the stock, pepper, mace, and orange rind to the rice, mix well, then bring to the simmer. Cover and cook over low heat for about 20 minutes until the rice is tender and all the liquid has been absorbed. Remove the pan from the heat and let stand covered for a few minutes.

5. Fluff up with a fork and stir the reserved cashews into the pilaf. Serve immediately.

Cashew Coconut Dipping Sauce

Did you ever wonder why you never see cashew nuts in the shell? The reason is that the cashew is a relative of poison ivy and the shells contain some of the same irritants found in that noxious weed. Although most of the offending chemicals are removed in processing, cashew exporters take no chances and discard the shells before the nuts reach the consumer.

The cashew is more delicately flavored than the peanut, but lends itself equally well to a variety of Oriental savory sauces. This Thai-style dipping sauce is best at room temperature, served with cucumber and carrot sticks, slices of tart apple, and cooked, peeled shrimp. It can also be used as a sauce for hot or cold cooked noodles.

Makes about 1½ cups

2 Tb. peanut oil

1 Tb. finely minced gingerroot

2 large scallions, mostly white parts, finely minced

¼ tsp. crushed dried hot peppers

¾ cup unsweetened coconut milk (see p. 239)

½ cup cashew butter*

1 Tb. soy sauce

½ tsp. sugar

1 Tb. lime juice

½ tsp. powdered lemongrass

3 Tb. finely chopped fresh coriander leaf (cilantro)

¼ cup finely chopped roasted cashews

1. In a small heavy saucepan heat the oil over moderate heat. Add the gingerroot, scallions, and hot peppers and sauté, stirring, until the scallions begin to wilt and the mixture is aromatic.

2. Stir in the coconut milk, the cashew butter, the soy sauce, the sugar, the lime juice, and the lemongrass. Cook, stirring, over low heat, until the sauce is smooth and well blended.

3. Remove from the heat and stir in the chopped coriander and the chopped cashews. Serve at room temperature.

*Available in health food stores and sometimes at supermarkets.

Sunflower Seed Cocktail Biscuits

Many varieties of sunflower were indigenous to North America, and, although they were widely used by native people, they do not seem to have been much admired by early colonists. When the sunflower traveled abroad, however, it received an enthusiastic welcome by eastern Europe, which valued the seeds as a source of cooking oil and as a tasty inexpensive snack. When Russians or Poles get together, they spend lots of time noisily cracking sunflower shells with their teeth to get at the flavorful little seeds. Sunflower seeds are tiny, but they have a delicate nutty flavor and a pleasant crunch.

Makes about 30 biscuits

½ cup (1 stick) butter, softened
¼ lb. cream cheese, softened
1 cup flour
About 1 cup roasted salted sunflower seeds (hulled)
¼ tsp. cayenne pepper
Paprika

1. Cream the butter and the cream cheese together, then stir in the flour.

2. Stir in ½ cup sunflower seeds and the cayenne pepper and mix thoroughly.

3. Form the dough into 2 rolls, 1 inch in diameter. Wrap in waxed paper and chill in the refrigerator for 1–2 hours. (For a quicker chilling, place the rolls in the freezer for about 20 minutes.)

4. Preheat the oven to 350°F. Cut the chilled dough into thin slices, about ¼ inch thick.

5. Spread the remaining sunflower seeds in a shallow dish. Press one side of the dough slices in the seeds. Place the slices, seed side up, on an ungreased baking pan. Sprinkle the slices lightly with paprika.

6. Bake the biscuits for 12–15 minutes or until lightly browned. Remove the biscuits from the baking pan with a spatula while they are still hot and let them cool on wire racks.

Oven-Roasted Jerusalem Artichokes

Jerusalem artichokes do not come from Jerusalem and bear no relation whatsoever to the artichoke. They are the root portion of one variety of the American sunflower; hence, the other more appropriate name by which they are known—sunchokes. They can be eaten either raw or cooked; raw, their texture is much like that of the water chestnut, so that sliced or julienned they add a pleasant crunch to salads or stir-fried dishes. The texture of cooked chokes is similar to that of potatoes, but the flavor is slightly sweet and nutty. They may be peeled or not, according to personal taste (I don't), but note that, like the potato, the cut flesh oxidizes and darkens when exposed to air, so either cook the sliced chokes immediately or cover them with cold water.

Serves 4

1 lb. Jerusalem artichokes
2–3 Tb. vegetable oil
Paprika
Salt

1. Scrub the artichokes well and peel, if desired. Slice them thinly, about ⅛″ thick. Preheat the oven to 350°F.

2. Mix the sliced artichokes thoroughly with the oil, making sure that all the surfaces are oiled. Spread the slices in a single layer in a large baking pan. Sprinkle lightly with paprika.

3. Bake the sliced chokes for 40–45 minutes, turning them once or twice with a spatula, until they are crisp and nicely browned.

4. Remove them from the oven and sprinkle lightly with salt.

An 1884 engraving of natives gathering wild rice in the lake country of Minnesota

Fruited Wild Rice and Sausage Casserole

Native to Canada and Minnesota, wild rice is a grain that is in no way related to culti-vated rice, although it is cooked in much the same way. Wild rice is unique among grains for its dark, almost blackish color and its distinctive nutty flavor and chewy texture. It never really traveled beyond its native shores; it is gathered in small har-vests and is a good deal more expensive than the other more common cultivated grains. Wild rice is at its best in soups, pilafs, and casseroles that show off its unique appearance, flavor, and texture.

Serves 6–8

2 Tb. butter
1 medium onion, finely chopped
2 carrots, diced
2 stalks celery, diced
1 cup wild rice
3 cups chicken stock
1/8 tsp. freshly ground black pepper
1/2 cup converted white rice
1/2 cup raisins
1/2 cup dried apricots, diced
1 tsp. crumbled dried sage
1 lb. fresh sausage, cooked and coarsely crumbled*

1. In a Dutch oven or stove-to-oven casserole melt the butter over moderate heat. Add the onion, carrots, and celery, and sauté, stirring, until the onion just begins to turn golden.

2. Stir in the wild rice, stock, and pepper; bring to the simmer, then cover and cook over low heat for about 45 minutes.

3. Stir in the white rice, the raisins, and the apricots, cover, and cook for about 15–20 minutes. Preheat the oven to 350°F.

4. Stir in the sage and the cooked crumbled sausage. Mix thoroughly, then cover and bake for 20–30 minutes. Fluff up the rice with a fork and serve.

Note: Spicy Turkey Sausage Patties, coarsely crumbled (see p. 180), are also particularly good in this casserole.

Maple Mustard Sauce

Maple sugar is chemically identical to ordinary sugar. Only impurities in the tree bark provide its unique flavor and color. In this recipe, the characteristic sweetness of maple syrup is balanced by the tang of sharp mustard and a little rich saltiness from soy sauce. The flavors combine for a wonderful glaze and sauce for grilled chicken or ribs. It is also excellent as a glazing sauce for cooked onions, carrots, apples, sweet potatoes, and turnips.

Makes ¾ cup

½ cup maple syrup
¼ cup good sharp mustard
1 Tb. soy sauce

Combine all the ingredients in a small bowl and mix thoroughly.

An early photo from New England of the collection of syrup from sugar maples

Grilled Shrimp Jamaican Style

The Spanish expedition, led by Columbus, was so intent on acquiring the black pepper of the East Indies that they named the chile "pepper," and the allspice berry "Jamaican pepper." Neither, of course, has any relation to black pepper. The allspice tree was native to Jamaica and was so named because its spicy little fruit had many of the flavor characteristics of the other more widely known aromatic spices, cinnamon, ginger, nutmeg, and cloves. It is not surprising that allspice turns up as a primary flavoring ingredient in Jamaican barbecue sauces. This sauce should be fiery hot, but can be toned down by decreasing the amount of chile pepper.

Serves 4–6

⅓ cup lime juice
⅓ cup soy sauce
1 Tb. dark rum
1 medium onion, coarsely chopped
2 cloves garlic
1–2 fresh habanero peppers (Scotch Bonnets), seeded
1 bay leaf
½ tsp. dried thyme
1 tsp. ground allspice
2 lbs. large shrimp or prawns, peeled and deveined

1. In a blender or food processor combine all the ingredients except the shrimp. Puree until smooth.

2. Pour about ½ cup of the marinade over the shrimp and mix well. (Any remaining marinade can be stored in the refrigerator; it improves with age.) Marinate the shrimp for 1–2 hours.

3. Thread the shrimp on water-soaked bamboo skewers and grill over hot coals, turning once, about 2 minutes on each side. Do not overcook.

4. Serve the shrimp hot or cold, with fresh lime wedges.

Note: This sauce is also excellent with chicken or pork. Marinate the meat for at least 4–6 hours or overnight, then roast or barbecue.

Pears Poached in Spiced Red Wine

Jamaican allspice flavors these simple but delicious poached pears, which can be served as is or dressed up with vanilla ice cream or white chocolate sauce. For a really spectacular dessert place 4 drained poached pear quarters on a plate in a petal design. Spoon some white chocolate sauce over them, then drizzle raspberry puree around the edges. Garnish with a mint sprig.

Serves 6

10–12 small to medium firm ripe pears
1½ cups dry red wine
¼ cup sugar
Juice ½ lemon (about 2 Tb.)
1 cinnamon stick
10–12 whole allspice berries

1. Cut the pears in quarters; core and peel.

2. In a large skillet combine the wine, sugar, lemon juice, and spices. Bring to a simmer and cook over low heat about 10 minutes until slightly reduced.

3. Add the pear quarters to the liquid and cook over low to moderate heat for about 5–7 minutes, or until just tender, turning the pears occasionally.

4. Remove from heat and cool. Let the pears marinate in the sauce for at least 6–8 hours before serving. Serve chilled.

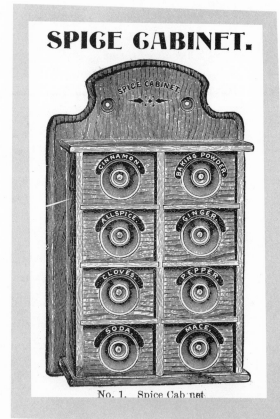

SPICE CABINET.

No. 1.   Spice Cabinet

Praline Pound Cake

The praline was originally a French confection of sugared almonds. It was reinvented in New Orleans by French nuns who made it what it is today by using the New World's delicious sweet pecan. The praline is a marvelous concoction of sugar, cream, vanilla, and pecans; these ingredients appear here in a rich but delicate pound cake.

Makes one 9- or 10-inch Bundt cake

Serves 12

1 cup (2 sticks) unsalted butter, softened
½ cup firmly packed brown sugar
½ cup light cream
2 cups finely chopped pecans
2 tsp. vanilla
5 eggs
¾ cup granulated sugar
2 cups sifted all-purpose flour
Confectioner's sugar for dusting

1. In a saucepan combine the butter and brown sugar. Heat, stirring, until the mixture is melted and smooth.

2. Stir in the cream and cook, stirring, until the mixture just begins to bubble. Remove from heat, stir in the nuts and vanilla, and set aside to cool slightly.

3. In a large mixing bowl beat the eggs until frothy.

4. Slowly add the granulated sugar and continue beating until the mixture is thick and pale.

5. Stir the nut mixture into the egg mixture and mix thoroughly. Preheat the oven to 350°F.

6. Stir in the flour and mix thoroughly.

7. Pour the batter into a well buttered 9- or 10-inch Bundt pan. Bake for 35–45 minutes, or until a straw inserted in the center comes out clean.

8. Cool in the pan for 20–30 minutes, then unmold. When thoroughly cool, dust the cake with confectioner's sugar.

Pecan Pie Squares

The pecan is a Southern nut and pecan pie is a Southern confection—surely, along with the praline, a glorious high point in the pecan's history. In this recipe the pie is translated into pick-uppable squares with a shortbread crust. Small portions are appropriate for such an incredibly rich and sweet dessert.

Makes 32 squares

1½ cups (3 sticks) unsalted butter, softened
1½ cups sugar
1½ cups flour
1 cup quick oats
½ cup firmly packed dark brown sugar
3 eggs
¼ cup maple syrup
½ cup half-and-half
2 cups coarsely chopped pecans
1 tsp. vanilla

1. In a large bowl combine 1 cup of the butter (2 sticks), ¾ cup of the sugar, the flour, and the oats. Mix with the fingers until the mixture has the consistency of coarse meal.

2. Lightly butter the bottom and sides of a 13 x 9 x 2-inch baking pan. Pat the shortbread mixture evenly into the bottom of the pan.

3. In the top of a double boiler over hot water cream the remaining ½ cup butter (1 stick) and the brown sugar until smooth. Stir in the remaining ¾ cup sugar, the eggs, the maple syrup, and the half-and-half.

4. Cook the mixture in the double boiler, stirring constantly, for about 5–7 minutes, or until smooth and thoroughly blended. Remove from the heat and stir in the nuts and the vanilla. Preheat the oven to 350°F.

5. Pour the nut mixture over the unbaked crust. Bake for 45–50 minutes until it is set and lightly browned.

6. Cool completely in the pan, then cut into squares with a sharp knife.

New World Golden Fruitcake

Fruitcake, which comes from our English heritage, is very much a traditional and festive winter holiday food. This version is characterized by pineapple and pecans, two New World foods, and a liberal dousing of rum, a spirit that was an offshoot of the West Indies sugar industry.

Makes two 10-inch Bundt cakes or four 8 x 5-inch loaf cakes

Serves 24–30

3 cups diced dried pineapple

1 cup dried apricots, cut in quarters

1 cup golden raisins

1 cup glacé cherries, halved

3 cups pecan meats, coarsely broken

½ cup dark (golden) rum, plus additional rum for soaking

¼ cup Amaretto or other almond liqueur

2 cups (4 sticks) unsalted butter

2 cups sugar

10 eggs

4 cups flour

1 tsp. vanilla

1. In a large bowl combine the fruits, nuts, rum, and Amaretto. Mix well and let stand several hours, stirring occasionally.

2. In a large bowl cream the butter and sugar until light.

3. Add the eggs one at a time, beating well after each addition.

4. Stir in the flour, and mix well. Preheat the oven to 325°F.

5. Add the vanilla and the fruit mixture. Blend thoroughly (this will take a lot of muscle, as the batter is thick).

6. Spoon the batter into well-buttered molds or pans.* Bake about 70 minutes for large molds; 45–50 minutes for smaller ones.

7. Soak some cheesecloth in rum; wrap the cake(s) in the cheesecloth, then in plastic wrap. Store in a cool place or refrigerator for at least 1 month before serving.

*This recipe can be cut in half, if desired.

Brazil Nut Banana Cake

The Brazil nut has come into prominence recently as a factor in the attempt to save the rapidly disappearing rain forests of South America. Since the tree has resisted cultivation anywhere else in the world, an increased demand for the nuts, it is assumed, would help to preserve the trees and the tropical ecology of which they are an ancient part. That is a goal worth working for and easy to help with, as Brazil nuts are truly delicious, large and meaty, with a unique sweet, nutty flavor. Try them sliced and sautéed in a little butter until lightly browned as a garnish for green beans or sugar snap peas. They are an unusual alternative to almonds or walnuts in cakes and cookies, as in this simple but rich banana cake.

Makes one 9- or 10-inch Bundt cake

Serves 10–12

1 cup (2 sticks) butter, softened

1 cup sugar

2 eggs

4 medium very ripe bananas, mashed

1 tsp. vanilla

2 cups flour

1½ tsp. baking soda

1 tsp. cinnamon

1 cup coarsely chopped or sliced Brazil nuts

1 cup flaked sweet coconut

Vanilla confectioner's sugar for garnish (see p. 222)

1. In a large bowl cream the butter with the sugar until smooth.

2. Add the eggs one at a time, beating well after each addition.

3. Add the mashed bananas and the vanilla and mix until thoroughly blended.

4. Combine the flour, the baking soda, and the cinnamon; add to the banana mixture and mix until just thoroughly blended in.

5. Stir in the chopped nuts and the coconut. Preheat the oven to 350°F.

6. Generously butter a 9- or 10-inch Bundt pan. Spoon the batter into the pan, then bake for 45–50 minutes until the top is browned and firm and a straw inserted in the middle comes out clean.

7. Cool the cake in the pan for 20–30 minutes, then unmold onto a serving plate. Cool completely, then dust with the vanilla confectioner's sugar.

Selected Bibliography
Index
Photographic Acknowledgments

Selected Bibliography

Anderson, E. N. *The Food of China.* New Haven: Yale University Press, 1988.

Andrews, Jean. *Peppers: The Domesticated Capsicums.* Austin: University of Texas Press, 1984.

Asher, Sandra P. *The Great Peanut Book.* New York: Grosset & Dunlap, Inc., 1977.

Bakeless, John. *The Eyes of Discovery.* New York: Dover Publications, 1950.

Benitez, Ana M. *Pre-Hispanic Cooking.* Mexico: Euroamericanas, 1974.

Brillat-Savarin, Jean Anthelme. *The Physiology of Taste.* New York: Liveright, 1970.

Brothwell, Don and Patricia. *Food in Antiquity.* New York: Frederick A. Praeger, 1969.

Chang, K. C., ed. *Food in Chinese Culture.* New Haven: Yale University Press, 1977.

Codex Mendoza (Aztec Manuscript). Miller Graphics. Productions Liber S.A. CH-Fribourg. 1978.

Coe, Michael D. *The Maya.* New York: Frederick A. Praeger, 1966.

Columbus, Christopher. *The Journal of Christopher Columbus.* Translated by Cecil Jane. New York: Bonanza Books, 1989.

Crosby, Alfred W., Jr. *The Columbian Exchange.* Westport, Connecticut: Greenwood Press, 1972.

Cushing, Frank Hamilton. *Zuñi Breadstuff.* New York: Museum of the American Indian, 1974.

David, Elizabeth. *Spices, Salt and Aromatics in the English Kitchen.* Harmondsworth, Middlesex: Penguin Books, 1970.

Diaz del Castillo, Bernal. *The Discovery and Conquest of Mexico.* New York: Farrar, Straus and Giroux, 1956.

Franklin, Wayne. *Discoverers, Explorers, Settlers.* Chicago: University of Chicago Press, 1979.

Gerard, J. *The Herball.* London, 1633.

Gerbi, Antonello. *Nature in the New World.* Pittsburgh: University of Pittsburgh Press, 1985.

Guy, Christian. *An Illustrated History of French Cuisine.* New York: Bramhall House, 1962.

Hardeman, Nicholas P. *Shucks, Shocks, and Hominy Blocks.* Baton Rouge, Louisiana: Louisiana State University Press, 1981.

Heiser, Charles B., Jr. *Nightshades: The Paradoxical Plants.* San Francisco: W.H. Freeman & Co., 1969.

Historicus. *Cocoa: All about It.* London: Sampson Low, Marston & Co., 1892.

Hughes, Meredith S., and Hughes, E. Thomas. *The Great Potato Book.* New York: Macmillan, 1986.

Laubin, Reginald and Gladys. *The Indian Tipi.* New York: Ballantine Books, 1957.

McGee, Harold. *On Food and Cooking.* New York: Charles Scribner's Sons, 1984.

Parry, J. H. *The Age of Reconnaissance.* New York: Mentor Books, 1963.

Poma de Ayala, Felipe Guamán. *Nueva Corónica y Buen Gobierno.* Edited by P. Rivet. Paris: Institut d'Ethnologie, 1936.

Prescott, William H. *History of the Conquest of Mexico and History of the Conquest of Peru.* New York: Modern Library, 1979.

Roe, Daphne A., M.D. *A Plague of Corn: The Social History of Pellagra.* Ithaca, New York: Cornell University Press, 1973.

Root, Waverley, and Richard de Rochemont. *Eating in America: A History.* New York: William Morrow & Co., 1976.

Rosengarten, Frederic, Jr. *The Book of Spices.* New York: Jove Publications, Inc., 1981.

Salaman, Redcliffe, *The History and Social Influence of the Potato.* Cambridge: Cambridge University Press, 1949.

Sale, Kirkpatrick. *The Conquest of Paradise.* New York: Alfred A. Knopf, 1990.

Sanders, W. T. and B. J. Price. *Mesoamerica: The Evolution of a Civilization.* New York: Random House, 1968.

Shapiro, Laura. *Perfection Salad.* New York: Farrar, Straus and Giroux, 1986.

Soustelle, Jacques. *Daily Life of the Aztecs.* Stanford, California: Stanford University Press, 1961.

Sowell, Thomas. *Ethnic America.* New York: Basic Books, 1981.

Struever, Stuart, ed. *Prehistoric Agriculture.* Garden City, New York: The Natural History Press, 1971.

Ucko, P. J. and G. W. Dimbleby, eds. *The Domestication and Exploitation of Plants and Animals.* Chicago: Aldine-Atherton, Inc., 1969.

Vaillant, G. *The Aztecs of Mexico.* New York: Doubleday, 1941.

Von Hagen, Victor. *The Ancient Sun Kingdoms of the Americas.* New York: World Publishing Co., 1957.

Walden, Howard T. *Native Inheritance.* New York: Harper and Row, 1966.

Weatherford, Jack. *Indian Givers.* New York: Fawcett Columbine, 1988.

Weatherwax, Paul. *Indian Corn in Old America.* New York: Macmillan, 1954.

Woodham-Smith, Cecil. *The Great Hunger.* New York: Harper and Row, 1962.

Yturbide, Teresa Castello. *Presencia de la Comida Prehispanica.* Mexico: Banamex Fomento Cultural, 1986.

Index

Note: page numbers in **boldface** refer to recipes; page numbers in *italics* refer to illustrations.

achiote, 253, 258
  in turkey pibil, **192**
achiote dressing: avocado, tomato, and
    orange salad with, **259**
African influences and dishes, 73, **79**,
    139
  peanut(s), 228, 246
    chicken soup, **231**
    sauce with greens, **233**
    vegetable harvest casserole, **241**
  tomatoes, 115
all-American potato salad, **66**
all-American stuffed peppers, **90**
allspice, 252–3, 267
  in grilled shrimp Jamaican style, **267**
  pears poached in spiced red wine
    with, **268**
almond(s)
  to roast, 94
  in roast pepper Romesco sauce, **94**
amino acids, pellagra and, 24
Andean cuisine, *see* Peruvian influ-
    ences and dishes
apple(s)
  beer-baked beans with sausage and,
    160

apple(s) *(cont.)*
  peanut bread, **246**
  and pear puree, vanilla, **223**
  tomatoes compared to, 113
  and tomato pie, **137**
ashes for processing corn, 10
Asian influences and dishes, *see*
    Oriental influences and dishes
aspic, spicy tomato, **131**
avgolemono, fresh tomato, **112**
avocado(s)
  guacamole, **260**
  history of, 252
  salad of tomato, orange, and, with
    achiote dressing, **259**
Aztec cuisine and influences
  chile peppers in, 74, 78, 82
    medicinal and other non-culinary
      uses of, 98, *99*
  chocolate (cacao), 195–6, 197
    Pfeffernüsse, New World, **201**
  guacamole, **260**
  tomatoes, 113
  turkey, 170–1
  see also Mexican influences and
    dishes, pre-Columbian

Baker, James, 212
Balkan style cornmeal mush with feta
    cheese and dill, **17**

banana Brazil nut cake, **272**
Barbados, 89
barbecue, 119
  butter beans, **155**
  pork, **119**
  sauce, bourbon, grilled chicken in,
    35
barley: gingered pilaf of beans, bulgur,
  and, **150**
bean(s), 139–61
  baked, 140
  black
    chocolate cake, triple, **204**
    quiche, **156**
    and rice, Cuban, **148**
  canned, 145
  corn and, 24, **29**, 141
  flatulence and, 154
  grains and, 140–1
  lima (butter), 146
    barbecue, **155**
    chowder, curried, **146**
    in super succotash, **29**
  New World varieties of, 139, 140
  pasta fazool, **151**
  red (kidney)
    gingered pilaf of barley, bulgur,
      and, **150**
    and rice, Creole, **149**
  soaking and cooking directions,
    144–5
  soup
    chili, **145**
    smoky, **143**
  white (cannellini)
    pasta fazool, **151**
    pasta shells primavera stuffed
      with, **152**
beef
  braised, with spices and chocolate,
    200
  chili, chocolate, **199**

beef *(cont.)*
  meatballs with pineapple, sweet and
    pungent, **256**
  peanut kabobs with spicy peanut
    dipping sauce, **236**
  peppers stuffed with, all-American, **90**
  pepper steak, **102**
  in potato moussaka, **54**
  rolls stuffed with polenta, **18**
  Texas red, **84**
beer-baked beans with apples and
  sausage, **160**
Benét, Stephen Vincent, 3
biscuits, sunflower seed cocktail, **263**
black Americans, peanuts and, 228,
  229, *245*
black bean(s)
  chocolate cake, triple, **204**
  quiche, **156**
  and rice, Cuban, **148**
bobotie, turkey, **189**
Boston, as "bean town," 140
bourbon, 35
  balls, Christmas, **38**
  barbecue sauce, grilled chicken in,
    35
  eggnog, **36**
  history of, 36
Brazil nut(s), 252
  banana cake, **272**
bread
  apple peanut, **246**
  focaccia, sweet pepper, **104**
  potatoes in, 62
  pudding, chocolate chunk, **210**
  spoon, chili-cheese, **23**
  tomato herb, **135**
  tortilla, yeast-raised, **11**
  see also saffron potato rolls
Brillat-Savarin, Jean Anthelme, 169
brownies, 214
  praline, **214**

bulgur: gingered pilaf of barley, beans and, **150**
burgers, Lisbon, **124**
butter beans
  barbecue, **155**
  see also lima beans

cabbage, in colcannon, **49**
cacao
  origin of the word, 196
  pods, *202*
  process for making, 205
cake
  Brazil nut banana, **272**
  chocolate
    bean, triple, **204**
    cheesecake, Mexican, **203**
    Mississippi mud, **218**
  coffee, maple-corn, **39**
  pound, praline, **269**
  sweet potato, with toffee–cream cheese frosting, **70**
calves' liver with green chile sauce, **88**
Campbell's tomato soup, 112
capsaicin, 98
capsicum peppers, *see* chile pepper(s); pepper(s), sweet bell
Caribbean influences and dishes, 73, 89
  black beans and rice, Cuban, **148**
  pumpkin soup, West Indian, **147**
  seafood pie in sweet potato crust, **67**
  sweet pepper sofrito, Puerto Rican, **99**
Carver, George Washington, 229
cashew nut(s), 252
  coconut dipping sauce, **262**
  pilaf, **261**
cassava (manioc), 253–4
casserole
  fruited wild rice and sausage, **265**

casserole *(cont.)*
  peanut vegetable harvest, **241**
  spiced tomato eggplant, **122**
  vegetable, Tex-Mex, **164**
"caviar": pepper, eggplant, and walnut, **100**
Chanukah, 63
cheddar cheese soup, Vermont smoked turkey and creamy, **175**
cheese
  cheddar, creamy: and smoked turkey soup, Vermont, **175**
  -chili spoon bread, **23**
  cream: –toffee frosting, sweet potato cake with, **70**
  feta: cornmeal mush, Balkan style, with dill and, **17**
cheesecake, Mexican chocolate, **203**
chicken
  in bourbon barbecue sauce, grilled, **35**
  corn chowder, **6**
  in double tomato sauce, **125**
  paprika, **92**
  in peanut coconut curry, **238**
  pimiento loaf, **96**
  roast, with tortilla stuffing, **12**
  soup
    peanut, African, **231**
    pineapple and, Vietnamese style, **255**
    Southern-style tomato, vegetable, and, **115**
chick-peas, tomato salad with tuna and, **133**
Child, Julia, 157
chile (pepper[s]), 105
  capsaicin in, 98
  culinary possibilities of, 74
  fish fillets with, **97**
  -ginger dessert sauce, **105**
  in grilled shrimp Jamaican style, **267**
  history of, 73–4

chile (pepper[s]) *(cont.)*
   Indian spiced lamb with, **86**
   medicinal and other non-culinary
      uses, 98
   names of, 78
   potatoes with tomatoes and, **51**
   sauce(s)
      green, calves' liver with, **88**
      pastes and relishes based on, 89
   sexual associations of, 82
chili, 78
   bean soup, **145**
   -cheese spoon bread, **23**
   chocolate, **199**
   lamb, Southwest, **83**
   powder, 78, 84
   sauce, commercial, 78
   Texas red, **84**
Chinese influences and dishes
   crab and corn soup, 7
   dim-sum stuffed peppers, **91**
   peanut(s), 228
      spicy peanut chicken wings, **240**
   pepper steak, **102**
   string beans stir-fried with elephant
      garlic, **158**
chocolate, *207*
   ambivalence about, 208
   beverages, 215, *217*
   braised beef with spices and, **200**
   bread pudding, chunk, **210**
   cake
      bean, triple, **204**
      cheesecake, Mexican, **203**
      Mississippi mud, **218**
   candy, 212, *213*
   chili, **199**
   chip cookie ice cream cake, **211**
   crème brûlée au, **216**
   egg cream, 215
   history of, 195–7, 212
   hot fudge sauce, **213**
   milk, 197

chocolate *(cont.)*
   mud cake, Mississippi, **218**
   origin of the word, 196
   Pfeffernüsse, New World, **201**
   pharmacologically active substances
      in, 195, 196
   pot and stirrer, *199, 207*
   in pre-Columbian America, 195–6
   processing of, 197, 205
   -raspberry truffle pie, **209**
   roll, black and white, **219**
   vanilla and, 198
   white, 220
      ice cream, **221**
      sauce, **221**
      whipped cream, **221**
chowder
   chicken corn, **6**
   curried lima bean, **146**
   potato, with roasted garlic and pep-
      per puree, **47**
Christmas bourbon balls, **38**
chutney
   smoked turkey salad with, **193**
   tomato, **117**
Cincinnati hot shots, **190**
clams, potatoes with tomatoes and, **56**
cocoa, hot, 215
coconut
   cashew dipping sauce, **262**
   milk, 239
   peanut curry, chicken in, **238**
coffee, *207*
coffee cake, maple-corn, **39**
colcannon, **49**
colonial era dishes, 80
   spoon bread, 23
Columbus, Christopher, xi, 73
confetti corn custard, **25**
consommé, bloody Mary's, **48**
cookie(s)
   chocolate chip, ice cream cake, **211**
   peanut shortbread, **248**

corn, 3–39, *105*
  baby, 30
    marinated peppers and, with black
      bean–garlic vinaigrette, **30**
  and beans, 24, 29, 141
  on the cob
    cooking methods for, 34
    to cut kernels off, 6
  creamed (canned cream-style), 7
    and crab soup, fresh, **7**
    in Navajo triple corn muffins, **33**
    and shrimp fritters Thai style, **26**
  dairy products and, 5
  dried sweet, 28
    and smoked salmon casserole, **28**
    turkey soup with wild rice and, **173**
  early innovations affecting, 4–5
  fresh
    and chicken chowder, **6**
    custard confetti, **25**
    succotash, super, 29
    see also on the cob, *above*
  history of, 3–5
  hominy (grits), 10
    in American South, 14
    Milanese, **14**
    posole, New Mexican, **8**
    posole, vegetable, **9**
  limited Old World acceptance of, 3
  liquid (milk) from cut kernels, 6
  masa harina, 10
    see also tortilla(s)
  in Native American mythology, 32,
    33
  pellagra and, 24
  pork and, 4–5
    posole, New Mexican, **8**
  processing of
    alkaline, 10
    blue corn, 32
  syrup, 69
  varieties of, 32
  whiskey (bourbon), 35

corn, whiskey (bourbon) *(cont.)*
  balls, Christmas, **38**
  barbecue sauce, grilled chicken
    in, **35**
  eggnog, **36**
  history of, 36
cornmeal, 10
  blue, 32
    in Navajo triple corn muffins, **33**
    and pepper frittata, **31**
  ingredients added to, 4
  -maple coffee cake, **39**
  muffins, Navajo triple, **33**
  mush
    Balkan style with feta cheese and
      dill, **17**
    names for, 15
    with peanut sauce and greens,
      16
    pork scrapple, 20, 21
    technique for making, 16
    variables affecting texture of, 16
    vegetable scrapple, **20**
    see also polenta
Cortez, Hernando, 196
crab(meat)
  in Caribbean seafood pie in sweet
    potato crust, **67**
  and corn soup, Chinese, **7**
  and tomato soup, creamy, **111**
cranberry bean salad, fresh, with herb
    vinaigrette, **166**
cream
  tomato sauce, **129**
  whipped, white chocolate, **221**
cream cheese–toffee frosting, sweet
    potato cake with, **70**
crème brûlée au chocolat, **216**
Creole cuisine (Louisiana), 89
  red beans and rice, 148, **149**
  spaghetti sauce, **121**
  turkey gumbo, **183**
  vegetable gumbo, **79**

croquettes, spiced peanut, **242**
Cuban black beans and rice, **148**
culinary ashes, for processing corn, 10
cumin seeds, to toast, **118**
curry(-ied)
 lima bean chowder, **146**
 pastes, 89
 peanut coconut, chicken in, **238**
 turkey hash, **187**
custard
 corn, confetti, **25**
 history of, **224**

desserts
 chocolate chip cookie ice cream
  cake, **211**
 chocolate chunk bread pudding,
  210
 chocolate roll, black and white, **219**
 Christmas bourbon balls, **38**
 crème brûlée au chocolat, **216**
 fruitcake, New World golden, **271**
 fruit trifle, fresh, **224**
 mocha walnut torte, **206**
 peanut chip pie, frozen, **249**
 peanut shortbread cookies, **248**
 pears poached in spiced red wine,
  268
 pecan pie squares, **270**
 Pfeffernüsse, New World, **201**
 Praline brownies, **214**
 raspberry-chocolate truffle pie, **209**
 sauce, chile-ginger, **105**
 sweet potato pone, **69**
 tomato and apple pie, **137**
 vanilla pear and apple puree, **223**
 white chocolate ice cream, **221**
 white chocolate sauce, **221**
 white chocolate whipped cream, **221**
 see also cake
Diat, Louis, 45

dill(-)
 Balkan style cornmeal mush with
  feta cheese and, **17**
 pickled green beans, **157**
dim-sum stuffed peppers, **91**
dip, guacamole, **260**
dipping sauce
 cashew coconut, **262**
 spicy peanut, peanut beef kabobs
  with, **236**
 Thai style, **27**
Dorrance, John T., 112

egg(s)
 frittata, blue corn and pepper, **31**
 raw, health concerns and, 37
eggnog, bourbon, **36**
eggplant
 and pepper, and walnut caviar, **100**
 tomato and, 122
  casserole, spiced, **122**
English influences and dishes, 210
 turkey, 169
Escoffier, 43

Farmer, Fannie, 118
feta cheese: cornmeal mush, Balkan
  style, with dill and, **17**
filling, potato, **50**
fish
 fillets with chile, **97**
 salmon
  Provençal, braised, **130**
  smoked, and dried corn casserole,
   28
 tuna, tomato salad with chick-peas
  and, **133**
five pepper soup, **76**
focaccia, sweet pepper, **104**
French dressing, **118**

French-fried potatoes, 57

French influences and dishes, 88
    braised salmon Provençal with
        tomatoes, **130**
    potatoes, 43, 46, 57, 58
    turkey Provençal, braised, **179**

frittata, blue corn and pepper, **31**

fritters, corn and shrimp Thai style, **26**

frosting, toffee–cream cheese, sweet
    potato cake with, **70**

fruitcake, 271
    New World golden, **271**

fruited wild rice and sausage casserole,
    265

fruit trifle, fresh, **224**

fudge
    origin of the word, 213
    sauce, hot, **213**

garlic
    elephant, stir-fried string beans with,
        158
    to roast, 47
    roasted, and pepper puree, potato
        chowder with, **47**

gazpacho, **116**
    white, 116

ginger(ed)
    barley, bean, and bulgur pilaf, **150**
    -chile dessert sauce, **105**

gluten, 4

goulash, 77
    soup, **77**

Greek influences and dishes
    avocado, tomato, and cucumber salad
        with achiote dressing, **259**
    potato moussaka, **54**
    tomatoes, 108
        avgolemono, fresh, **112**
    turkey, *185*
        taverna, **184**

green beans, *see* string beans

green chile sauce, calves' liver with, **88**

greens
    cornmeal mush with, **16**
    peanut sauce with, **233**

grits, *see* hominy (grits)

guacamole, **260**

gumbo
    turkey, **183**
    vegetable, **79**

habanero chiles, 80, 89
    in Indian spiced lamb with peppers,
        86
    in island pepper pot, **80**

ham and peanut soup, country, **230**

harissa, 89

hash
    curried turkey, **187**
    pepper, **103**

herb(ed)
    tomato bread, **135**
    turkey breast with chestnut risotto
        stuffing, **176**
    vinaigrette, fresh cranberry bean
        salad with, **166**

Hershey, Milton, 212

Hershey Company, 212

Hershey's bar, 212

Hershey's Kisses, *213*

hickory grilled breast of turkey, **185**

hominy (grits), 10
    in American South, 14
    Milanese, **14**
    posole
        New Mexican, **8**
        vegetable, **9**

hot fudge sauce, **213**

Hungarian influences and dishes, 74–5
    chicken paprika, **92**
    goulash soup, **77**

Hungarian influences and dishes *(cont.)*
  mushrooms paprika, **93**
  paprika, 92
    lekvar, 95

ice cream
  cake, chocolate chip, **211**
  white chocolate, **221**
Indian influences and dishes, 73,
    89
  lamb with peppers, spiced, **86**
  peanut croquettes, spiced, **242**
  tomato chutney, **117**
  see also curry(-ied)
Indonesia, 89
Irish influences and dishes
  colcannon, **49**
  potatoes, 42, 46
island pepper pot, **80**
Italian influences and dishes
  blue corn and pepper frittata, **31**
  grits Milanese, **14**
  pasta fazool, **151**
  patate tricolore, **52**
  pesto, 161
  polenta stuffed beef rolls, **18**
  sweet pepper *focaccia*, **104**
  tomato(es), 108, 110, 133
    cream sauce, **129**
    marinara sauce, **127**
    pomodoro, origin of the word, 113
    sauce with peppers and
      mushrooms, **128**
    sun-dried tomato pesto, **134**
  tortellini salad with mixed peppers,
    101

Jamaican cuisine, 89
  grilled shrimp, **267**
Jerusalem artichokes, 264
  oven-roasted, **264**

Jewish influences and dishes, 62, 120
  mock chopped liver, **159**
  potato latkes, **63**
  vegetable cookery that mimics meat
    preparations, 159
Johnson, Colonel Robert, 120

karidopita, 39
ketchup, 109, 117
kidney beans
  red
    gingered pilaf of barley, bulgur,
      and, **150**
    and rice, Creole, **149**
  white (cannellini)
    pasta fazool, **151**
    pasta shells primavera stuffed
      with, **152**

lamb
  chili, Southwest, **83**
  with peppers, Indian spiced, **86**
latkes, potato, **63**
leek(s)
  in colcannon, **49**
  in potatoes vinaigrette, **64**
  potato soup, **44**
    vichyssoise, Thai-style, **45**
lima bean(s), 146
  chowder, curried, **146**
  in super succotash, **29**
  see also butter beans
Lindt, Rudolph, 197
Lisbon burgers, **124**
liver, calves', with green chile sauce, **88**
loaf, chicken pimiento, **96**
Louisiana cuisine, *see* Creole cuisine

Malaysian cuisine: chicken in peanut
    coconut curry, **238**

manioc (cassava), 253–4
maple
    -corn coffee cake, **39**
    mustard sauce, **266**
marinara, **127**
masa harina, 10
    tortilla(s)
        bread, yeast-raised, **11**
        process for making, 11, *12, 13*
        stuffing, roast chicken with, **12**
Mayan cuisine and influences, 74
    chile peppers, medicinal and other
        non-culinary uses of, 98, *99*
    chocolate (cacao), 195
    see also Mexican influences and
        dishes, pre-Columbian
meatballs
    sweet and pungent, with pineapple,
        256
    turkey (Cincinnati hot shots), **190**
Mediterranean influences and dishes,
    74
    tomatoes, 108–10, 133
    see also Italian influences and dishes;
        Spanish influences and dishes
Mexican influences and dishes, 5
    bean(s), 156
        -stuffed pasta shells primavera,
            152
    chile peppers, 74, 82, 89, 97
    chocolate, 195–6
        braised beef with spices and,
            200
        cheesecake, **203**
    peanut(s), 227
    posole, New Mexican, **8**
    pre-Columbian
        chocolate, 195–6
        corn, 5
        oregano, 135
        vanilla, 198
    pumpkin seed pesto, **161**
    seasoning pastes, 161

Mexican influences and dishes *(cont.)*
    tomato(es), 107–9, 110
        aspic, spicy, **131**
        Tarascan tomato soup, **114**
    turkey, 170–1
        mole (turkey in red chile sauce),
            181
        pibil, **192**
    see also Aztec cuisine and influences;
        Mayan cuisine and influences
Middle Eastern influences and dishes,
    75
    tomatoes, 133
Mississippi mud cake, **218**
mocha walnut torte, **206**
mole
    about, 170–1
    turkey (turkey in red chile sauce),
        181
Montezuma, 196
Moroccan cuisine, 108
moussaka, potato, **54**
mud cake, chocolate, **218**
muffins, corn, Navajo triple, **33**
mush, *see* cornmeal, mush; polenta
mushroom(s)
    paprika, **93**
    sauce
        double, turkey in, **188**
    tomato sauce with peppers and, **128**
mustard
    Dijon-onion puree, turkey cutlets
        with, **182**
    maple sauce, **266**

Native American influences and dishes
    corn
        and beans, 24
        on the cob, 34
        muffins, Navajo triple, **33**
        succotash, super, 29
    sunflower, 253

Native American influences and dishes
      (cont.)
   sweet potato pone, **69**
   see also specific cultures and tribes
Navajo triple corn muffins, **33**
New Mexican posole, **8**
New World Pfeffernüsse, **201**
nightshade family, 108
noodles, peanut sesame, **244**
North African cuisine, 89
   tomatoes in, 108
Northwestern cuisine: dried corn and
      smoked salmon casserole,
      28
nut(s)
   almonds
      to roast, 94
      in roast pepper Romesco sauce, 94
   Brazil, 252
      banana cake, **272**
   pecan(s), 252, 270
      in New World golden fruitcake,
         271
      pie squares, **270**
      polenta rounds, **22**
      in praline pound cake, **269**
   walnut(s)
      mocha torte, **206**
      and pepper, and eggplant caviar,
         100
      to toast, **159**
   see also peanut(s)

onion-Dijon puree, turkey cutlets with,
      182
orange: salad of tomato, avocado, and,
      with achiote dressing, **259**
oregano, 135
Oriental influences and dishes, 89
   corn and shrimp fritters Thai style,
      26

Oriental influences and dishes *(cont.)*
   marinated baby corn and peppers
      with black bean–garlic
      vinaigrette, **30**
   peanut(s), 228, 229
      sesame noodles, **244**
   See also Chinese influences and
      dishes; Indian influences and
      dishes; Malaysian cuisine;
      Southeast Asia cuisine; Thai
      cuisine; Vietnamese cuisine

pancakes, potato, *63*
paprika, 75
   chicken, **92**
   in Hungarian cuisine, 92
   lekvar, 95
   mushrooms, **93**
   origin of word, 78
Parmentier, 43, *44*
pasta
   fazool, **151**
   shells primavera, bean-stuffed, **152**
patate tricolore, **52**
patties, spicy turkey sausage, **180**
peanut(s), 16, 249
   apple bread, **246**
   beef kabobs with spicy peanut
      dipping sauce, **236**
   chicken wings, spicy, **240**
   chip pie, frozen, **249**
   coconut curry, chicken in, **238**
   croquettes, spiced, **242**
   "goober" as name for, *245*, 246
   history of, 227–9
   sauce
      with greens, **233**
      with greens, cornmeal mush with,
         16
      raisin, **232**
   sesame noodles, **244**

peanut(s) *(cont.)*
  shortbread cookies, **248**
  shrimp salad, **235**
  in slang expressions, 247
  slaw, **245**
  as snack, 234, *243*
  soup
    chicken, African, **231**
    country ham and, **230**
  vegetable harvest casserole, **241**
peanut butter, 229
pear(s)
  and apple puree, vanilla, **223**
  poached in spiced red wine, **268**
pecan(s), 252, 270
  in New World golden fruitcake, **271**
  pie squares, **270**
  polenta rounds, **22**
  in praline pound cake, **269**
pellagra, 24
Pennsylvania Dutch influences and
    dishes
  potato filling, **50**
  scrapple, 20, **21**
pepper, black *(Piper nigrum)*, 73
pepper(s), chile, 105
  capsaicin in, 98
  culinary possibilities of, 74
  fish fillets with, **97**
  -ginger dessert sauce, **105**
  in grilled shrimp Jamaican style,
    267
  history of, 73–4
  Indian spiced lamb with, **86**
  medicinal and other non-culinary
    uses, 98
  names of, 78
  potatoes with tomatoes and, **51**
  sauce(s)
    green, calves' liver with, **88**
    pastes and relishes based on, 89
  sexual associations of, 82

pepper(s), sweet bell
  and blue corn frittata, **31**
  and eggplant, and walnut caviar,
    100
  focaccia, **104**
  in goulash soup, **77**
  hash, **103**
  history of, 74–5
  in Indian spiced lamb with peppers,
    86
  marinated baby corn and, with black
    bean–garlic vinaigrette, **30**
  red
    in five pepper soup, **76**
    roasted, and roasted garlic puree,
      potato chowder, **47**
    roasted, Romesco sauce, **94**
  red, roasted (pimientos), 75, 78
    chicken loaf, **96**
    method of cooking, 95
    puree, 95
  sofrito, Puerto Rican, 99, **99**
  steak, **102**
  stuffed
    all-American, **90**
    dim-sum, **91**
  tomato sauce with mushrooms and,
    128
  tortellini salad with mixed, **101**
  see also paprika
pepper pot, island, **80**
Peruvian influences and dishes
  peanut(s), *237*
  potatoes, 41, 46, *50, 55*
    and tomatoes, 51
pesto
  pumpkin seed, **161**
  sun-dried tomato, **134**
Pfeffernüsse
  German, 201
  New World, **201**
pickled green beans, dill-, **157**

pie
    peanut chip, frozen, **249**
    raspberry-chocolate truffle, **209**
    seafood, Caribbean, in sweet potato
        crust, **67**
    tomato and apple, **137**
pilaf
    cashew, **261**
    gingered barley, bean, and bulgur, **150**
pimientos, 75, 78
pineapple
    and chicken soup, Vietnamese style,
        255
    history of, 251–2
    in New World golden fruitcake, **271**
    sweet and pungent meatballs with,
        256
piri-piri, 89
polenta, 15
    beef rolls stuffed with, **18**
    rounds, pecan, **22**
pone, sweet potato, **69**
pork
    barbecue, **119**
    corn and, 4–5
        posole, New Mexican, **8**
    scrapple, 20, 21
Portuguese influences and dishes, 73,
        86, 89
    Lisbon burgers, **124**
    potatoes with clams and tomatoes, **56**
    tomatada, 124
    tomatoes, 108, 109
posole
    New Mexican, **8**
    vegetable, **9**
potato(es), 41–71
    calories in, 60
    chuño, 41
    with clams and tomatoes, **56**
    colcannon, **49**
    filling, **50**

potato(es) *(cont.)*
    in France, 43
    French-fried, 57
    gratin of root vegetables and, **61**
    history of, 41–3
    in Ireland, 42
    latkes, **63**
    low-calorie methods of cooking, 60
    moussaka, **54**
    names and nicknames of, 46
    new, 68
    oven-fried, **57**
    patate tricolore, **52**
    roasted, **57**
    rolls, saffron, **62**
    salad, all-American, **66**
    scalloped, deluxe, **58**
    soup
        chowder with roasted garlic and
            pepper puree, **47**
        leek, **44**
        vichyssoise, history of, 45
        vichyssoise, Thai-style, **45**
    with tomatoes and chile, **51**
    varieties of, 68
    vinaigrette, **64**
    vodka, 48
    see also sweet potato(es)
pound cake, praline, **269**
praline, 269
    brownies, **214**
    pound cake, **269**
prawns, in Caribbean seafood pie in
        sweet potato crust, **67**
pudding, bread, chocolate chunk, **210**
Puerto Rican cuisine: sweet pepper
        sofrito, 99, **99**
pulses, 139
pumpkin, 141–2
    Halloween, 142
    seed pesto, **161**
    soup, West Indian, **147**

quiche, black bean, **156**

raisin peanut sauce, **232**
Raleigh, Sir Walter, 42
raspberry-chocolate truffle pie, **209**
red chile sauce, turkey in (turkey mole),
    181
red kidney beans
   gingered pilaf of barley, bulgur, and,
     150
   and rice, Creole, **149**
rice
   black beans and, Cuban, **148**
   pilaf, cashew, **261**
   red beans and, Creole, **149**
   tomato salad, **132**
risotto chestnut stuffing, herbed turkey
    breast with, **176**
Romesco sauce, 94
   roast pepper, **94**
root vegetables, gratin of potato and, **61**
Russian vodka, 48

saffron potato rolls, **62**
salad
   cranberry bean, fresh, with herb
    vinaigrette, **166**
   peanut shrimp, **235**
   peanut slaw, **245**
   potato, all-American, **66**
   tomato
    with chick-peas and tuna, **133**
    rice, **132**
   tortellini, with mixed peppers, **101**
   turkey, with chutney, **193**
salad dressing
   achiote: avocado, tomato, and orange
    salad with, **259**
   "French," 118
   vinaigrette, 64

salad dressing, vinaigrette *(cont.)*
   black bean–garlic, marinated
    baby corn and peppers with, **30**
   herb, fresh cranberry bean salad
    with, **166**
   potatoes, **64**
   tomato, spiced, **118**
salmon
   Provençal, braised, **130**
   smoked, and dried corn casserole, **28**
sandwiches, leftover turkey, 186
sauce
   bourbon barbecue, grilled chicken
    in, **35**
   dessert, chile-ginger, **105**
   dipping
    cashew coconut, **262**
    spicy peanut, peanut beef kabobs
     with, **236**
    Thai style, **27**
   green chile, calves' liver with, **88**
   hot fudge, **213**
   maple mustard, **266**
   mushroom, double, turkey in, **188**
   peanut
    with greens, **233**
    with greens, cornmeal mush with, **16**
    raisin, **232**
   red chile, turkey in (turkey mole), **181**
   Romesco, roast pepper, **94**
   spicy peanut, peanut beef kabobs
    with, **236**
   tomato
    Balkan style cornmeal mush with
     dill and, **17**
    cream, **129**
    Creole spaghetti, **121**
    double, chicken in, **125**
    to get rid of the seeds, 126
    marinara, **127**
    with peppers and mushrooms, **128**
   white chocolate, **221**

sausage
  beer-baked beans with apples and, **160**
  patties, spicy turkey, **180**
  and wild rice casserole, fruited, **265**
scallops, in Caribbean seafood pie in sweet potato crust, **67**
scrapple
  pork, 20, 21
  vegetable, **20**
seafood pie, Caribbean, in sweet potato crust, **67**
sesame peanut noodles, **244**
shortbread cookies, peanut, **248**
shrimp
  in Caribbean seafood pie in sweet potato crust, **67**
  and corn fritters Thai style, **26**
  in dim-sum stuffed peppers, **91**
  Jamaican style, grilled, **267**
  peanut salad, **235**
slaw, peanut, **245**
Smith, Betty, 46
smoky bean soup, **143**
sofrito, 75
  classical Spanish, 99
  sweet pepper, Puerto Rican, 99, **99**
soup
  bean
    chili, **145**
    smoky, **143**
  bloody Mary's consommé, **48**
  chicken
    pineapple and, Vietnamese style, **255**
  chowder
    chicken corn, **6**
    curried lima bean, **146**
    potato, with roasted garlic and pepper puree, **47**
  crab and corn, Chinese, **7**
  five pepper, **76**

soup *(cont.)*
  goulash, **77**
  peanut
    chicken, African, **231**
    country ham and, **230**
  pepper pot, island, **80**
  potato
    chowder with roasted garlic and pepper puree, **47**
    leek, **44**
    vichyssoise, history of, 45
    vichyssoise, Thai-style, **45**
  pumpkin, West Indian, **147**
  tomato
    avgolemono, fresh, **112**
    canned, 112
    crab and, creamy, **111**
    gazpacho, **116**
    Southern-style chicken, vegetable, and, **115**
    Tarascan, **114**
  turkey
    smoked, Vermont creamy cheddar and, **175**
    with wild rice and dried corn, **173**
  vegetable
    posole, **9**
    Southern-style chicken, tomato, and, **115**
Southeast Asia cuisine, 73, 89
  spicy peanut chicken wings, **240**
Southern United States influences and dishes
  chicken, tomato, and vegetable soup, **115**
  confetti corn custard, 25
  cornmeal, 23
    mush, 15
  country ham and peanut soup, **230**
  hominy grits, 14
  peanut(s), 228–9, *239*
  pecan pie squares, **270**
  see also Creole cuisine (Louisiana)

Southwestern and Tex-Mex dishes
  blue corn, 32
  chili, 78
    bean soup, **145**
    -cheese spoon bread, **23**
    chocolate, **199**
    lamb, Southwest, **83**
    powder, 78, 84
    sauce, commercial, 78
    Texas red, **84**
  tomatoes, 110
  vegetable casserole, Tex-Mex, **164**
soybean, 139
spaghetti sauce, Creole, **121**
Spanish influences and dishes, 251, 259
  capsicum peppers, 75, 78
  chile peppers, 73
  chocolate, 196–7
    braised beef with spices and,
      200
  five pepper soup, **76**
  peppers, 94
    roasted red, 95
  potatoes, 41
  roast pepper Romesco sauce, 94
  tomato(es), 107–10
    gazpacho, **116**
    rice salad, **132**
spinach, in patate tricolore, **52**
spoon bread
  about, 23
  chili-cheese, **23**
squash, 141–2
  green (zucchini)
    bread, **167**
    in summer garden sauté, **165**
  summer
    gratin of, **163**
    in summer garden sauté, **165**
  winter, 142
steak, pepper, **102**
stew
  posole, New Mexican, **8**

stew *(cont.)*
  turkey, taverna, **184**
  vegetable gumbo, **79**
stock, leftover turkey, **172**
string beans (green beans), 140
  dill-pickled, **157**
  mock chopped liver made with, **159**
  stir-fried, with elephant garlic, **158**
stuffing
  chestnut risotto, herbed turkey
    breast with, **176**
  tortilla, roast chicken with, **12**
succotash, 29
  super, **29**
summer garden sauté, **165**
summer squash
  gratin of, **163**
  in summer garden sauté, **165**
sunchokes, 264
sunflower, 253, 263
  -seed cocktail biscuits, **263**
sweet potato(es)
  cake with toffee–cream cheese
    frosting, **70**
  crust, Caribbean seafood pie in, **67**
  names for, 46
  pone, **69**

Tabasco, *81*, 89
Tarascan tomato soup, **114**
taverna turkey, **184**
tea, *207*
Texas red (chili), **84**
Thai cuisine
  cashew coconut dipping sauce,
    262
  Thai-style vichyssoise, **45**
Thanksgiving, 170, *177*
toffee–cream cheese frosting, sweet
    potato cake with, **70**
Toll House cookies, 211
tomatada, 124

tomato(es), 107–37
    and apple pie, **137**
    aspic, spicy, **131**
    in barbecue pork, **119**
    beefsteak, about, 120
    braised salmon Provençal with, **130**
    chutney, **117**
    eggplant casserole, spiced, **122**
    green (unripe), spiced fried, **136**
    herb bread, **135**
    history of, 107–10, 120
    jelly (inner part of the tomato), 126
    ketchup, 109, 117
    origin of the word, 113
    potatoes with chile and, **51**
    potatoes with clams and, **56**
    salad
        avocado, orange, and, with
            achiote dressing, **259**
        with chick-peas and tuna, **133**
        rice, **132**
    sauce
        Balkan style cornmeal mush with
            dill and, **17**
        cream, **129**
        Creole spaghetti, **121**
        double, chicken in, **125**
        to get rid of the seeds, 126
        marinara, **127**
        with peppers and mushrooms, **128**
        tomatada, 124
    soup
        avgolemono, fresh, **112**
        canned, 112
        crab and, creamy, **111**
        gazpacho, **116**
        Southern-style chicken,
            vegetable, and, **115**
        Tarascan, **114**
    sun-dried, 125
        double tomato sauce with,
            chicken in, **125**

tomato(es), sun-dried *(cont.)*
        pesto, **134**
    varieties of, 120
    vinaigrette, spiced, **118**
torte, mocha walnut, **206**
tortilla(s)
    bread, yeast-raised, **11**
    process for making, 11, *12, 13*
    stuffing, roast chicken with, **12**
Tree Grows in Brooklyn, A (Smith), 46
trifle, fresh fruit, **224**
triple chocolate bean cake, **204**
truffle, chocolate, and raspberry pie,
    209
tuna, tomato salad with chick-peas and,
    133
turkey, 169–93
    argot and slang expressions, 178
    braised, Provençal, **179**
    breast of
        hickory grilled, **185**
    cutlets with onion-Dijon puree, **182**
    European names for, 169
    ground
        bobotie, **189**
        Cincinnati hot shots, **190**
    gumbo, **183**
    health concerns concerning, 171
    leftover, 186
        in double mushroom sauce, **188**
        hash, curried, **187**
        stock, **172**
    Old World versus Aztec treatment of,
        170–1
    pibil, **192**
    in red chile sauce (turkey mole), **181**
    sausage patties, spicy, **180**
    smoked
        and Vermont creamy cheddar
            soup, **175**
        salad with chutney, **193**
        stock, **174**

turkey *(cont.)*
  soup
    smoked, Vermont creamy cheddar
      and, **175**
    with wild rice and dried corn, **173**
  stock
    leftover turkey, **172**
    smoked, **174**
  taverna, **184**
  versatility of, 171–2
  wild, 170, *191*
Turkish influences and dishes, 75
  tomatoes, 108

van Houten, Conrad, 197
vanilla, 198
  forms of, 222
  imitation, 222
  pear and apple puree, **223**
  sugar, **222**
vegetable(s)
  casserole, Tex-Mex, **164**
  gumbo, **79**
  peanut harvest casserole, **241**
  posole, **9**
  root, gratin of potato and, **61**
  sauté, summer garden, **165**
  scrapple, **20**
  soup
    posole, **9**
    Southern-style chicken, tomato,
      and, **115**
Vermont smoked turkey and creamy
    cheddar soup, **175**
vichyssoise
  history of, 45
  Thai-style, **45**

Vietnamese cuisine
  chicken and pineapple soup, **255**
  peanut beef kabobs with spicy
    peanut dipping sauce, **236**
vinaigrette, 64
  black bean–garlic, marinated baby
    corn and peppers with, **30**
  herb, fresh cranberry bean salad
    with, **166**
  potatoes, **64**
  tomato, spiced, **118**
vodka
  bloody Mary's consommé, **48**
  Russian, 48

walnut(s)
  mocha torte, **206**
  and pepper, and eggplant caviar, **100**
  to toast, **159**
West Indies cuisine
  achiote, 253
  pumpkin soup, **147**
wheat, 4
whiskey, corn, 36
white (kidney) beans (cannellini)
  pasta fazool, **151**
  pasta shells primavera stuffed with,
    152
wild rice, 253
  and sausage casserole, fruited, **265**
  turkey soup with dried corn and,
    173

zucchini
  bread, **167**
  in summer garden sauté, **165**

Photographic Acknowledgments

The photographs and illustrations reproduced in this book were provided with the permission and courtesy of the following:

The Bettmann Archive: 8, 19, 27 (left), 37, 44, 49, 61, 71, 93, 129, 177 (both), 185, 191, 202, 217 (top), 225, 232, 239, 243 (all), 247, 257, 260, 264, 266, 268

Bodleian Library, University of Oxford: 12, 99, 180

Culver Pictures: 13, 27 (right), 211

The Corn Palace, Mitchell, South Dakota: 21

The Potato Museum, World Food Collection: 30, 76, 136

Seth Rozin: 33 (all), 87, 100, 125, 133, 143, 160, 245

Nueva Corónica y Buen Gobierno, Felipe Guamán Poma de Ayala: 50

The Potato Museum: 53 (all), 59, 65 (both)

Museum of the University of Pennsylvania: 55, 150, 237

McIlhenny Company: 81

Jalapeño Festival, Inc., in conjunction with the Washington's Birthday Celebration Association: 85

Smithsonian Institution: 103, 134, 162

Maxwell Museum of Anthropology, University of New Mexico: 105

Campbell's Soup Co.: 112, 123

The Herball, J. Gerard: 117

H. J. Heinz Co.: 118

Norman Balch: 153

The Norman Rockwell Family Trust, copyright 1943. The Norman Rockwell Family Trust: 174

Chocolate Manufacturers Association: 199

Traitez Nouveaux et curieux du Café, du Thé et du Chocolat, Philippe Sylvestre Dufour: 207 (both)

Hershey Foods Corporation: 213

Look magazine: 217 (middle)

U.S. Camera: 217 (bottom)

Peanut Advisory Board: 231

Elisabeth Rozin grew up in Brooklyn, New York, and has a bachelor's degree from Hunter College and a master's degree from Brandeis University. Early travel and a love of eating led to her first work, *The Flavor Principle Cookbook*, that described the characteristic combinations of flavoring ingredients used by a variety of ethnic cuisines. Her second cookbook, *Ethnic Cuisine*, was an extension and elaboration of her work on ethnic flavoring traditions. She teaches and lectures widely on comparative and historic cuisine, contributes to both scholarly and popular journals, and is a consultant to the food and restaurant industry. Elisabeth Rozin lives in Havertown, Pennsylvania. She has four children and two well-fed dogs.

A NOTE ON THE TYPE

The text of this book was set in a typeface called Bodoni Book, named for Giambattista Bodoni, born at Saluzzo, Piedmont, in 1740. He was the son of a printer, and as a young man went to Rome, where he served as an apprentice at the press of the Propaganda Fide. In 1768 he was put in charge of the Stamperia Reale in Parma by Duke Ferdinand, a position he held until his death in 1813, in spite of many offers by royal patrons to tempt him elsewhere. His earliest types were those imported from the Paris foundry of Fournier, but gradually these were superseded by his own designs, which, in the many distinguished books he printed, became famous all over Europe. His later arrangements with the duke allowed him to print for anyone who would employ him, and commissions flowed in so that he was able to produce books in French, Russian, German, and English, as well as Italian, Greek, and Latin. His *Manuale Tipografico*, issued in 1818 by his widow, is one of the finest specimen books issued by a printer-type designer.

COMPOSED ON THE MACINTOSH BY DONNA DAVID
NEW YORK, NEW YORK

PRINTED AND BOUND BY COURIER BOOK COMPANIES
WESTFORD, MASSACHUSETTS

DESIGNED BY BARBARA BALCH

KNOPF COOKS AMERICAN

The series of cookbooks that celebrates the culinary heritage of America, telling different aspects of our story through recipes interspersed with historical lore, personal reflections, and the recollections of old-timers.

Already published:

Biscuits, Spoonbread, and Sweet Potato Pie by Bill Neal
Hot Links & Country Flavors by Bruce Aidells and Denis Kelly
Barbecued Ribs, Smoked Butts, and Other Great Feeds by Jeanne Voltz
We Called It Macaroni by Nancy Verde Barr
The West Coast Cook Book by Helen Evans Brown
Pleasures of the Good Earth by Edward Giobbi
The Brooklyn Cookbook by Lyn Stallworth and Rod Kennedy, Jr.
Dungeness Crabs and Blackberry Cobblers by Janie Hibler
Preserving Today by Jeanne Lesem

"Our food tells us where we came from and who we are…"